HOME WORKSHOP DIGEST

"How to make the things you need and want."

By Dean A. Grennell

DBI BOOKS INC., NORTHFIELD, ILLINOIS

ABOUT THE COVER

The number and variety of tools available to today's home craftsman is truly mind-boggling, therefore the existence of multi-purpose tools that can reduce one's investment is worthy of note. Pictured here is Dremel's new Disc-Belt Sander which can be used for sanding, shaping, polishing, cleaning and sharpening. Additionally, Dremel's Deluxe Moto-Shop combines a scroll saw, disc sander and a flexible shaft power take-off. Also shown is Dremel's new 4" table saw, a highly portable, high powered unit that can perform all of the functions of a full-sized table saw.

Publisher
SHELDON FACTOR

Production Director
SONYA KAISER

Art Director
TERI FIVECOAT

Art Assistant
DENISE HEGERT

Production Coordinator
BETTY BURRIS

Copy Editor
DORINE IMBACH

Photo Services
DANA SILZLE

Produced by

Charger Productions

ISBN 0-910676-14-3

Library of Congress Catalog Card Number 80-67742

CONTENTS

Acknowledgements

It has been observed that no man is an island and, less frequently, that the converse is equally true. A great many people contributed to the completion of this book, and helped to make it a vastly less dreadful affair than it might have been without their efforts and attentions. I will try to mention them here, with the clear and implicit stipulation that I'll probably miss some who deserve mentioning thoroughly.

I'm grateful for heredity and environment that gave me an intense zest and love for building things, as well as for a level of technology that offers tools and materials that can be afforded without undue trauma. Workshoppers of the latter Twentieth Century are the lucky heirs who enjoy the fruits of uncountable generations of progress, and I think we should show fitting and proper appreciation for the bounty available to us.

As for specific individuals, I'll start with Sheldon Factor, our publisher, who personally proofed and annotated all of the copy and layouts, as fast as we could mail them to him in Northfield, and demonstrated beyond a doubt that he knew the subject intimately and well. For his help, patience and understanding, he has my special thanks.

At right about the same level, Sonya Kaiser has more of the same, for her untiring and dedicated efforts in ramrodding the book through production, checking and re-checking; making requested changes in layout and making my end of the work much, much easier. A good production director is a pearl beyond price, and Sonya Kaiser is far and away the best of the many I've encountered.

Thanks, also, to Betty Burris, who set the type, and to Dorine Imbach, who proofed both the manuscript and type galleys; likewise to Dorine's husband Paul, who offered to let me photograph the clock he'd built, with the hands moving counterclockwise, for people who like to tell time by looking in a mirror.

More thanks, for sure, to Teri Fivecoat, Denise Hegert, and John Vitale of our art department for a fine job on the layout — sometimes under heavy difficulties — and for making needed changes with sunny good humor.

My grateful thanks, also, to a gentleman I've never met, named Robert Gunning, for writing a book entitled *The Technique of Clear Writing* (McGraw-Hill, 1949). I'd rate it as the one book and the only book about writing that really imparts helpful aid to the floundering would-be writer. Gunning said, for example, "Write like you talk," and "Write to express, not to impress," and "It is not enough to write so that you can be understood. You must write so that you cannot *possibly* be misunderstood!" In the pages that follow, you'll find places in which I bent or broke Gunning's guiding dicta, but I did it with full awareness, not unwittingly.

Thanks, also, to my wife Jean, for her help in collecting pertinent and helpful clippings and references from newspapers and magazines, for her suggestions, and for letting me have undistracted time at the typewriter or in the shop and darkroom, when there certainly must have been a lot of household chores that needed my attention. Thanks, too, to a long list of ancestors, relatives, descendants and friends — workshoppers all — who passed along bits of lore, helpful suggestions and tricks of the trade, many of which are mentioned in the pages that follow.

Last but not least, thanks to the workshoppers of the world — particularly to those who buy a copy of this — because the book would not and could not have been written or published without an audience.

INTRODUCTION.

WELCOME TO THE book at hand! It's called *Home Workshop Digest* and subtitled, "How to make the things you need and want." My credentials for its authorship are, quite simply, that I've been making the things I needed and/or wanted for the past several decades and, more pertinently, have noticed myself getting better at it by fits, starts and random lurches.

Sometimes you may feel a strong and urgent need for a given artifact that just simply is not offered in the marketplace. In such cases, the only solution that seems to work acceptably is to take the approach of making it yourself, inventing it along the way, if necessary, and designing it to taste. We will take up a few examples of such things, later on. They were things I needed and wanted badly and, in most cases, they were not to be had for any price or — in one example — something comparable was available for an outlay of several hundred dollars. In that instance, my substitute solution cost no more than a few pleasantly absorbing weekend afternoons, hardly as much as ten bucks for materials and — frosting on the cake! — it serves my needs considerably better than its multi-C-note counterpart.

I can confide that the personal satisfaction deriving from the successful solution of such a problem borders upon the downright sinful. Better yet, they've not yet worked out a technique for taxing such intangibles as satisfaction, so it's clear profit and even more glorious as a direct result.

In taking up this book, I hope to be able to help the reader toward a realization that using modest manual skills and comparatively simple and inexpensive tools can result in useful artifacts, backed by smug self-satisfaction and undiluted pride. It really isn't all that difficult and unattainable, given the appropriately hard-nosed approach and *modus operandi*. As you slog your way doggedly on through the chapters that follow, you'll encounter clear proof that my approach tends to be rather starkly functional. Some of the construction projects illustrated do not have inlays of lapis lazuli — practically none do, in fact — and some even went into use as bare wood, not even painted or varnished.

Let it be frankly conceded, right about now, that some of the items discussed here which I wanted or needed, are not apt to be the things for which you feel an equally desperate longing. I'm sure you'll find some things here for which you'll feel the same urgent need that an earthworm has for a parachute; so it goes. The point, however, is that if you can manage to stick it out to the end of the book, it's hoped that you may be infected with the basic attitude and philosophy of the whole thing; with the ability to generate the cerebral sparks that are the seeds from which unique and useful pieces of work grow.

In preparing to write this book, I've bought several other books more or less concerned with the same subject, and have looked at a lot of others. In the latter category, one work touched upon the intricacies of making dovetail joints and I turned to that page with considerable interest because, candidly, I've yet to make my first dovetail joint. It led off the discourse with something to the gist of, "The dovetail joint is a sign of superior craftspersonship..." At

The front end of Grennell's elderly IBM Executive typewriter has been propped up here to show the pair of masonite anchor plates fastened to the top of the desk with a pair of flat head wood screws apiece. The two front feet of the machine rest in the two-inch holes in the plates, keeping the IBM from performing a partial pirouette each time the carriage zips to the right.

which point, I returned the book to the display rack and walked away, fastidiously wiping my fingertips on the seat of my pants. Anybody who'd go *that* far, I figured, wouldn't stop there...

I object to a word such as the sesquipedalian atrocity just quoted on grounds that — as the Lady Alisande so memorably phrased it in Twain's *Connecticut Yankee* — "It falleth not trippingly from the tongue." Actually, of course, that's a paraphrase. not a direct quote, and I'd be the first to admit that I've done some shameful things with the English language (and a few others), and even hope to do so again, perhaps before we get to the last page of the book. My sole reason — an explanation, not an excuse! — has always been to keep the copy pleasantly readable.

I'm well aware that many members of what I think of as the delightfully opposite sex engage in woodworking and, if they prefer to think of themselves as craftswomen, it's entirely their prerogative, so far as I'm concerned. But if we have to bloat every single word until it's absolutely all-inclusive, ponder if you will the absurd suggestion that, since termites work in wood, too, it might be better to think in terms of "craftsperson/termiteship." May we please table the rest of that argument and perhaps hide it

with a...uhh...personhole cover?

If I have a prejudice about writing, and I'm sure I do, it's that I think the reader's eye should skim along the printed lines as easily as a fingertip passed over a smooth, taut length of wire. If the moving fingertip encounters a barb, it is a sign that the writer has done something incorrectly. Writing should be easy to read, fun to read, and informative, as well. If writing is hard to read, if you have to keep stopping and backing up in efforts to make sense of it, you're apt to think of something else you'd rather do and the book languishes unread; a depressing waste of time, money and pulpwood timber.

I suspect you've been wondering exactly what I mean by references to the functional-first approach, and we need look no further than the table that supports the venerable IBM on which I'm typing this. Its top is a hunk of solid wood door-core, about 41x26 inches and the upper surface is precisely 25½ inches above the floor because that puts the keyboard close to the same altitude as my elbows when I'm seated before it, with fingertips on the keyboard.

A peculiar characteristic of the IBM Executive typewriter dictated the inclusion of a further feature not found on most typing tables. Every time you hit the carriage return button, the massive platen zips to the right like a berserk battering ram and twists the entire machine slightly clockwise from its previous location. Thus, every few lines, you have to stop and wrench it around to its original position; a distracting nuisance.

My solution to that particular dilemma was to attach two 3½x3½-inch plates of quarter-inch tempered masonite to the top, near the front edge, with a two-inch round hole in each piece, positioned so as to accept the two rubber feet on the front of the typewriter. It has kept the old IBM from wandering about the desk for the past eight years now and, if I needed another typing table, I'd want one exactly like this one. To my mind, that's the final proof of a satisfactory design.

As noted in the text, it's better not to purchase equipment until and unless you're certain it's going to get sufficient use to justify the cost. The drill grinding attachment, removed from its box for the first time to serve as an illustration of this point, was purchased several years ago at $15.99 because it seemed like it might be a handy item to have. To the present, however, none of Grennell's drill bits have shown a need for being resharpened. Remember: It's wiser to save your money!

The coffee table and matching stool were built about 1955, using surplus pieces of solid core door stock. Tops and upper edges were covered with tan Formica attached with contact cement and the exposed edges of the legs were covered with oak veneer to match the rest of the wood. Two No. 14x4½ flat head wood screws reinforce the glue that holds each table leg to the table top. Lower photo shows how the stool was dimensioned to nest beneath the table when not being employed.

We will be discussing a broad variety of tools and equipment in the pages ahead, and it's far from my intention to seem to be beguiling you into laying out the cost of one each of everything. Quite the contrary, I'm a firm believer in not buying anything unless you really, *really* need it. If I could reclaim the original retail cost of all the tools in my shop that I've used but rarely, if ever, it would be a substantial sum and the heck of it is, I'd probably spend the whole wad for something else that I wouldn't use much!

For just one example, I once bought a gadget for resharpening drill bits, just because it sounded like a handy thing to have on hand in case of need. That was two or three years ago and I've yet to even take it out of the box, because all of my drill bits are still sharp.

We will be dealing, mostly, in terms of working with wood and woodlike materials, but I propose to crank in some discussion of certain aspects of metalworking that can

A further accessory for the ensemble was this removable chess board that was built up from pieces of common ¾-inch plywood with a convenient sunken flange to hold captured chess pieces or similar items. The squares are made of Formica used on the table and stool tops, with the darker squares in gray Formica that matched the tan material in appearance. It was planned that the entire board would be covered with more Formica, but time for that has not been available, so far...

enhance your capabilities to a most worthwhile extent; things such as drilling, tapping and threading, for purposes of producing useful fastening systems that cannot be procured off the shelf at your local store. Taps and dies remain relatively inexpensive, even in these inflated days, and the ability to fashion your own fasteners is much too valuable to overlook.

As we proceed through the chapters, discussing the various tools, their use and misuse, I propose to drop in various workshop projects, by way of varying the fare and, likewise, to offer suggestions as to things you can do with your gadgets and newly whetted expertise. There are few spectacles so pitiful and depressing as a workshop buff, surrounded by shiny new tools and a supply of materials,

automatically disqualified for hobby status. In the fine, original semantic context, *amateur* meant someone who does what they do for the sheer love of it; stemming from the Latin *amor,* to love. Sadly, popular usage has shifted the word around to mean something done at levels well below professional skill.

Nevertheless, there are many good things to be said for the things that are done because one wants to, rather than because they have to be done. Not to get too deeply philosophical about it, but I think that those whose fulltime work produce little by way of tangible artifacts — salespeople, accountants, bank tellers, as examples — have a better than average chance of extracting exceptional satisfaction and pleasure from making things that are

who can't think of a single thing to *do* with them.

Among the many satisfying aspects of workshopping is the ability to dream up and turn out gifts to get you off the hook for birthdays, Mother's Day, Father's Day, Christmas, Hannukah, Ramadan or whatever. A gift seems to take on a special, personal quality if it's handmade by the giver and, while it might seem ill-bred to bring up the further consideration, it usually costs less. Accordingly, we'll try to include suggestions of easily-made gifts to delight the hearts of children of all ages.

I think — and many others seem to agree — that having a hobby is beneficial to the soul and general outlook. As a rough observation, if you do it for a living, it's

useful, or beautiful, or — better yet — both, in the home workshop.

We've made several references to the satisfaction that can be found in workshopping, but there's another face to that coin and I guess you'd spell it as "atifa¢tion," referring to the by-means-uncommon situations in which your facilities and skills can save you useful chunks of tax-paid income, for ultimate diversion to riotous living, or suchever channel that turns you on. It is a sad but inescapable fact of life that the cherished and expensive gewgaws of our modern civilization are much prone to break down, usually at the most inconvenient moment possible.

I'd have to advise that it's highly unlikely that anything discussed in this book will enable you to escape a $78 repair bill for having your color television set fixed professionally. But there are routine emergencies of lesser technical complexity, many of which prove vulnerable to a reasonably equipped and resourceful workshopper.

As just one example, the side rail on my side of our bed fractured like a brittle twig, some fifteen or twenty years ago. Faced with the prospect of purchasing an entire new bed, at a time when all my assets were tied up in accounts-payable, I improvised a rather Spartan repair job

attaining that status, and then some. The repair job, I should note, has stood up staunchly to the present.

Another rewarding channel for your shoply skills is the construction of furniture and allied needfuls for use about the home. As the designer/contractor, you can engineer such things to just about any level of durability for which you see a clear need. A quarter-century or so ago, we didn't have a coffee table, and felt the need of one, so I geared up and built one, with a matching foot stool that nests cleverly beneath the table, if desired.

Seven boisterous young Grennells have grown to

Factory furniture isn't always as sturdy as one might wish and occasional hasty repair jobs, such as this one, can save a night's sleep and the cost of replacement. If the wood hadn't fractured at bedtime, the repair might have displayed a flossier level of elegance. The emergency surgery has withstood the better part of two decades, during which Grennell has been meaning to paint it, or at least put the jam-locked nuts on the inside, where they won't show; some time, soon now...

with two strips of 1/8x¾-inch aluminum band stock and two ¼-20x1½-inch stove bolts. The repair job took less than half an hour of labor and well under fifty cents in materials, meanwhile conserving $150 or so that simply wasn't available at the time. On such occasions, being a passably competent workshopper is worth all that you put into

adulthood — well, the youngest is coming up 14, but the rest are 23 and older, now — around that coffee table and stool, but it still looks very much as it did the day I finished it and I'd bet you could pacify a herd of rampaging elephants with either one and the furniture would remain as solid and free from wobbles as they are today. I have strong doubts that coffee tables and matching foot stools, with that exceptional degree of durability, were available on the retail market in 1955, or at any time since. The cash outlay may have been as much as $18 or $20 — dollars were bigger in those days, you may recall — and that amortizes the long-term cost down to well under a buck a year, to the present.

Early in 1966, we emigrated from Wisconsin to California and the high cost of moving — nearly seventeen cents a pound, net — dictated the abandoning of several of my more massive craft projects at that time. One that I

without straining or tiring a single muscle.

In recent times, I made another attempt to re-create that old typing chair, but it didn't come off too well. The basic approach is simple enough: Just lie on your side atop some large pieces of paper, on the sidewalk or a similar flat surface, and have a helpful associate trace the outlines of your back, thigh, shin and feet onto the paper. You use the resulting dimensions to establish the profile of the chair.

The second attempt fit as well as could be expected, but it lacked the total comfort of the first one and, worse, it was heavy and it took up too much space. So I went back to the standard dining room chair that I'm still using, albeit

The original stool had screws reinforcing the glued joints and the covering plug of one is visible here. Stool at right is of contemporary vintage and was made of leftover pieces of wood, assembled entirely with glue and formed to taste with a belt sander. With the glues available today, one can get away with that, if the item isn't subject to high-stress usage.

continue to miss, right keenly, was a custom-tailored typing chair to match my typing table of that era. The chair, in appearance, had about the same amount of innate aesthetic charm as a mud puppy with psoriasis, but it was just superbly, sensuously, sinfully comfortable and I could sit in it and maul the IBM keyboard for hours on end

with undertones of the chronic discontent that serves as the real mother of invention at least as frequently as does necessity.

Perhaps, later in the book, we'll take another shot at that project. Speaking of the book, let's get on with it, without further ado, shall we?

A PLACE TO WORK

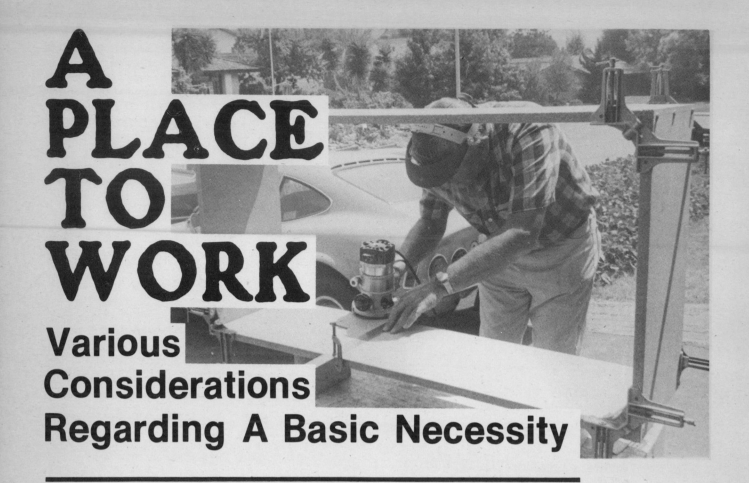

Various Considerations Regarding A Basic Necessity

BEFORE YOU CAN BEGIN to accomplish anything useful, you need some manner of workbench, table or similar solid and steady surface on which the different operations can be performed easily and efficiently. Over the years and many moves, I've built, used and abandoned more such facilities than I really care to recall.

Some were veritable masterpieces, massive and sturdy; a few were even painted. Most of them — in the course of extensive use — proved to have certain design flaws that I took pains to avoid when making up later efforts.

One of the worst fiascos had the fatal flaw of boasting much too much area; a full thirty-two square feet of surface. I had built the supporting framework from 2x4s, with sections of 4x4 for the legs. The top was a full 4x8-foot sheet of ¾-inch plywood, topped by a sheet of tempered masonite the same size. I ran metal moulding all around the edges and felt well pleased with the result — until I began to use it...

The problem — my problem, at least — is that flat, horizontal surfaces seem to attract what I call *glotsch*. I'll define that as random, miscellaneous material of little value which, somehow, I can't quite bear to discard. It builds up and accumulates and, I'll swear, breeds in the dark. The broad surface of that hapless work table would, in just a few days, grow a solid layer of glotsch up to two feet in depth. What that meant was that, if you wished to get access to all the clear surface available, you had to relocate something like seven cubic yards of debris and bric-a-brac. I never made that mistake again.

Black & Decker makes a likely looking device they call the Workmate, a sort of super sawhorse with capabilities as a vise and the whole affair folds compactly for storage when not in use. I've never used the Workmate, but I bought one of the smaller versions, called a Benchmate, built a sturdy little stand upon which to mount it and find it extremely handy for all sorts of operations.

One of the Benchmate's more useful capabilities is that

Chapter 1

it will hold boards and the like, up to twelve inches or so in width, with rock-like solidity. I cut some pieces of ¾-inch particle board to the size of one or two sheets of sandpaper and affixed sheets to both sides in various grades, using pressurized spray disc adhesive. This affords a remarkably fast and convenient method for truing-up workpieces to dead-flat planes, removing small irregularities and so on. Benchmate accessories include a remarkably useful mounting bracket for a router.

The workbench that gets the most use at present is a simple and unimpressive affair, its form dictated by my current needs and work habits. I've fallen into the custom of doing most of the assembling operations on my driveway, which slopes fairly steeply down to the street. As I don't appreciate sloping work surfaces, I built the little bench with three legs, because a basic law of geometry is that three-footed things don't wobble. The long side with two legs is uphill, away from the street. The third leg is in

Swiss-made Zyliss vise can be attached to the edge of a bench, either in conventional mode, as in the lower photo, or inverted as in the upper view for use of remote clamp that enables it to hold workpieces of any length.

the center of the opposite long side, and it has a telescoping foot at the bottom, with a provision to loosen the foot or lock it in place.

The bench is stored elsewhere when not in use, being quite light and easy to carry about. When setting it up, I just place a small level on the uphill side and fidget it about a bit until it's level, right-to-left. Then it's a simple matter to turn the level ninety degrees to check the front-to-back slope, reaching down to loosen the clamp and tilt the affair until it's level on that axis, as well.

The three-legged approach has one obvious drawback, of which I've been reminded on countless occasions: Any moderate weight applied to either front corner will tip it in a most distracting manner. Apart from that, it has worked out to be an absolute jewel. The bench was put together quite casually, with a 24x36-inch piece of common ¾-inch plywood for the top. Two short lengths of 2x4 were glued to the lower surface of the top to serve as anchor points, using the yellow grade of Elmer's glue; a twenty-eight-inch piece on the side with two legs and a twenty-four-inch piece for the one-leg side. Four-inch strips of one-inch board (actual thickness, ¾-inch) formed the legs, which were clamped and glued to the vertical width of the 2x4 strips. Scrap pieces were used to secure the angle braces shown in the accompanying photos so that, for all its lightness and hasty construction, it is remarkably steady. The design is built around triangles and triangles are incompressible for all practical purposes.

Given a surface that is level and flat, you can use it as the base for assembling all manner of projects. With a

The Black & Decker Benchmate is an exceptionally flexible and versatile system for holding workpieces or tools. Below, it's used to hold two sheets of sandpaper that have been fastened to a piece of particle board with contact cement. A small wooden box is being worked across the paper to true up its exposed edges.

Photo below gives a better view of the Benchmate stand, still with the board holding two sheets of sandpaper. Two more sheets of different grit size are cemented to the opposite side of the board and similar boards are stored on the lower shelf of the stand, which is fairly heavy.

protective layer of waxed paper between the workpieces and the bench surface, C-clamps and pipe clamps can be used to "make big ones out of little ones" such as making up edge-glued assemblies from strips of 2x4 or other appropriate sizes. Since it only has six square feet of flat surface, clearing it off is never a lengthy chore. The rear edge, from which I usually work, is thirty-two inches from the ground to the top surface and this seems a convenient height for typical operations performed on it.

My more-or-less permanent workbench in the shop was crafted out of a good-sized solid-core door that I discovered in a dumpster on a memorable occasion. Like the feckless work table of long ago, it suffers from a tendency to accumulate glotsch, and from a strategic error uniquely its own, as well. By intent trial-and-error research, I've arrived at the belief that such a bench, for maximum comfort and efficiency, should have its upper surface about even with the upper edge of one's belt. On my frame, that works out to roughly forty-one inches. So I built the supporting framework for the bench top out of pieces of 2x4, anchoring the far ends to the vertical studs of the shop wall and using other pieces of 2x4 for the legs in front...and made the upper edges of the crosspieces just forty-one

inches in height. It wasn't until I had it all together that I realized, in gloomy rue, that I'd neglected to allow for the thickness of the top, itself, making it precisely 1¾ inches too high!

Win some, lose some. To compensate, I've made a small section of duckboard from wooden strips, 1¾ inches in thickness, so that I can stand on that to nullify the oversight and it's easier on the feet than the bare concrete.

My eight-inch table saw — friend and companion since 1962, and fondly known as Euripides — gets picked up from the shop and carried out onto the driveway for such sessions. Once, with dogged patience, I shifted it about until I found the magic site where all four of its feet were in firm and solid contact with the surface of the drive. At that point, I took a can of pressurized spray paint and branded the driveway inconspicuously at all four corners so as to be able to relocate the position quickly and easily in the future. It seems to work just fine.

Since table saws generate quantities of sawdust, most if not all of that residue winds up on the driveway and, at the conclusion of the session, it's a simple matter to put everything away and break out the garden hose to flush the sawdust down into the gutter and out of my life forever.

Photos show the B&D Benchmate extended and empty. Workpieces can be held between the two aluminum-covered jaws in the center, or between the movable plastic stops that can be re-positioned into any of the holes visible here.

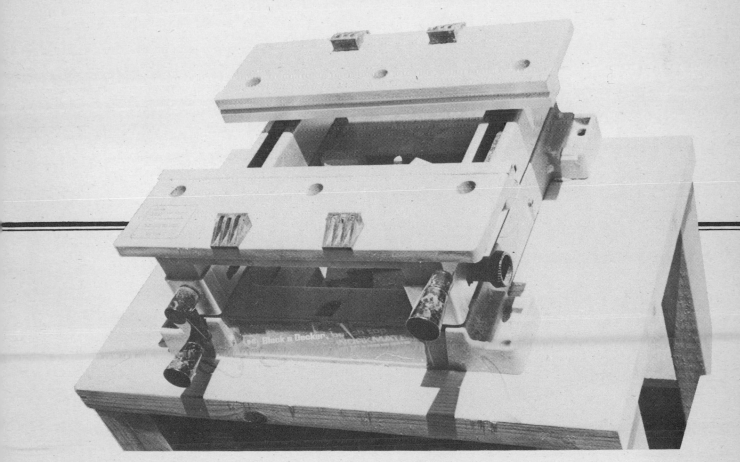

Working in the driveway, I've found, offers a lot of solid advantages, especially if the house is situated so the driveway is on a southern exposure. In my Southern California habitat, it's usable for most of the year, barring rainy days. If the ambient temperature is below 65 degrees Fahrenheit — the critical temperature, below which aliphatic resin glues, such as yellow Elmer's, do not set up well — smaller assemblies can be put in the family automobile to cure. The car has black upholstery and it functions as an efficient, solar-powered drying oven, usually holding temperatures twenty to forty degrees higher than the outdoor reading.

The foregoing discussion describes an admittedly specialized application, with no more than limited application for a reader in — for example — Anoka, Minnesota. For many, indoor facilities will be the practical way to go. Fortunately, most of the dwellings in less temperate areas feature basements or cellars, in which the central heating system usually is located, so that the resident has a capacious work area of reasonable comfort when the North Wind howls and rages across the land.

Few indeed are the houses in Southern California with basements. The excuse they use is that the possibility of earthquakes makes them a hazard to the heath, and it could well be that they have a point there.

A general-purpose, all-around workbench, for use on a reasonably flat and level floor, is not too difficult to fashion. Keep in mind the inherent problem that may lurk in extravagant amounts of surface — unless, of course, you're one of those compulsively tidy souls who needn't worry about such matters — and keep it to handy dimensions. At an early opportunity, acquire a bench vise of moderate size and anchor it solidly to the left-front corner, or the right-front if you happen to be left-handed. The bench itself needs to be sufficiently solid so that work performed on pieces in the vise won't set up vibrations that will shake everything off the bench onto the floor. That can happen on an extended session with a hacksaw or file.

There is a natural tendency to set up a workbench against a wall, or in a corner, so that only one or two edges are accessible. Give some thought to a free-standing design with its entire periphery available for use, so as to double or

Grennell's most-used workbench was casually assembled from scrap lumber and glue, with details here and on following pages. Designed for use on a sloping driveway, its single downhill leg is adjustable and lockable in length, permitting it to be leveled front-to-back, as at left. Top of opposite page shows same level being used to adjust it from right to left. Details of the triangular leg braces can be seen in the lower photos. The top is a piece of ¾-inch common plywood.

Two strips of 2x4 were glued to the lower side of the plywood top to serve as anchoring points for the legs. Details of the front leg adjustment are below and top of facing page, using the anchored bolt discussed elsewhere here.

Scraps of wood were glued to the legs and braces, using yellow Elmer's glue and C-clamps. On rare occasions, a joint may come loose, but it's quick and easy to fix, with more glue, a C-clamp and a bit of curing time. The important thing to keep in mind about a bench with three legs is not to put a lot of weight on either of the two front corners, which would cause it to tip over.

quadruple the working area. One or more storage shelves can be provided below the primary working surface and various hefty materials can be stored upon the shelves to help in anchoring the entire bench to the floor. Alternatively, if you have solid beams and joists overhead, you can plant a small jack in the center of the bench and use a piece of 4x4 to impose stress against an overhead construction member to create a bench with a ton or so of unyielding rigidity; it's well worth serious consideration.

If you're operating a woodworking shop in a confined environment, such as a basement, be mindful of the problems and hazards posed by the resulting fallout. Sawdust and — much more pertinently — sanding dust floats in the air and slowly settles upon every available surface. At best, it's a nuisance. At worst, it's a latent disaster. Fine particles of wood, suspended in midair, constitute a potential explosive that can be set off by the pilot flame of a water heater, a central heating system or cigarette lighter. In general, this applies only if you've been using power-sanding equipment so industriously that the dust is a visible haze in the air; unlikely, but it bears keeping in mind. At such times, either improve the ventilation or wear a gauze mask over your nose and mouth to keep from getting your lungs filled with cellulose particles.

There are few things more distracting and downright annoying than a four-legged workbench that teeters and jitters from this leg to the opposite one as you try to work on it. By the time you get the bench built and set up, it's usually too late to take small amounts of material off the lower surface of a too-long leg. The easiest and simplest approach is to shore up one of the opposing short legs with a thin wooden wedge, tapped smartly into position. If you know the floor is uneven, you can leave one of the legs a bit short and incorporate a telescoping foot, similar to the one on the three-legged bench illustrated here. At any rate, there is absolutely no acceptable substitute for a solid and unyielding work surface.

In addition to a workbench of some sort, suitably tailored to your personal requirements, your shop will need storage facilities for tools and materials. The lower portion of the workbench often can be used to good effect as a part of the storage space. Heavier materials, stored in that area, serve as helpful ballast to keep the bench from moving about under working stresses.

If your shop is in a partially finished area, such as a basement or garage, you may be able to attach hanging racks to the overhead construction as a storage space for lumber, dowels, rods and similar raw materials.

There is also the matter of providing conveniently accessible storage space for items such as screws, bolts and nuts, nails, washers, and the other varieties of small

The advantage of a three-legged bench is that, while it may tip if weight is imposed injudiciously, it will never teeter and jiggle under ordinary use, as four-legged benches are inclined to do, unless carefully propped.

fastening devices. Here, the ruling consideration is that you should be able to find and get at them, when the need arises. If they're purchased in typical hardware store bubble-packs, it works reasonably well to drive small brads or finishing nails into nearby woodwork so as to hang the packs in much the same manner as they were displayed in the store.

If you stock certain items in such quantities that makes the nail hangers impractical, try to get a few cardboard boxes with removable lids in which to segregate the various items. Use some of the self-adhesive labels on the exposed ends of the boxes to identify the contents.

You may prefer to obtain one or more of the ready-made storage cabinets that come with a quantity of small plastic drawers. These seem to work out better for some people than for others. I've never had a lot of luck with them, personally. I don't seem to get around to affixing labels as to the contents of each tiny drawer, relying upon the ability to squint through the front panel at the contents, which may — or may not — be identifiable.

fluorescent light fixture at a comfortable height above the bench. The diffused light goes far to eliminate distracting shadowed areas and it avoids the harsh glare of undiffused light bulbs. If you need light concentrated upon a particular area, one of the small study lamps may prove quite helpful. For example, I have one of those that can be turned on to illuminate the working area of my drill press and it's invaluable for accurate alignment of the drill bit tip in the punch-marked spot.

For certain fine and finicky operations, you may wish to consider a design adapted from the traditional cobbler's bench, with a central post that comes up between your knees to hold a work surface of suitable size and height. Be sure to make it somewhat narrower toward the end you face. I built an affair such as that once, leaving it the same width throughout, only to discover that an extended session with the knees well apart caused marked stiffness in the hip joints on arising.

Summing up a few general observations: Try to avoid the pitfall of building a bench much larger than you're apt to need. Give some thought to the probable cycle of yearly

A handy way to retain control of felt-tipped markers around the shop is to drill holes in a small piece of scrap wood of a size to give a snug grip on the caps. Thus, you have an assortment of colors, always handy.

We've spoken mostly of stand-up workbenches because they seem better suited to most types of shop activities. For certain operations, it's highly practical to provide a work space designed for use while seated. That assumes you'll be engaged at the given operation(s) for a reasonable period of time, rather than getting to your feet frequently. As a general rule, height of the work surface should be about the distance from your elbows to the floor when you're seated with your forearms held horizontally. Any surface much lower than that can be regarded as guaranteed cricks in the neck.

Proper illumination for the working area is quite important. A favored approach is to suspend a four-foot

temperature fluctuations so you don't end up either frozen or roasted out of business for months on end. Provide facilities for periodic removal of the sawdust, drill chips and general debris of shop activities to keep operations from foundering in a welter of byproducts, meanwhile making certain that the probable fallout won't create problems in other nearby areas. Maintain a degree of flexibility and adaptability so that, if it doesn't work out to your liking, you can build another bench or whatever, improved with the accumulations of your experience with the first or earlier examples. An associate of mine is fond of observing that it doesn't take any training to be miserable. That seems to hold water.

—TOOLS—

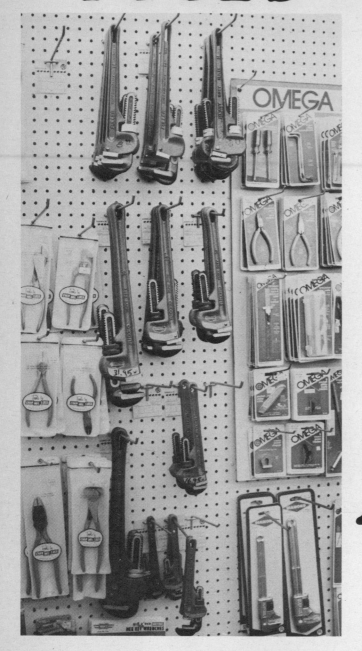

—OF THE TRADE—

Chapter 2

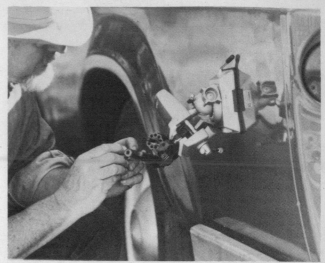

Above, this vacuum-base Pana Vise attaches securely to any smooth, reasonably flat surface, with full swiveling in any direction for ultimate convenience anywhere. Left, a display of wrenches and pliers (courtesy of Nail Apron, Mission Viejo, California). Pipewrenches are designed so that their grip tightens as turning pressure is applied.

Manual Hand Tools

A SHOP without tools hardly merits the designation. A shop is a place where tools are used, the type and nature depending upon the principal activity of the shop. Entire books can be — and have been — written on tools alone. Let us touch briefly upon several tools, most of them more or less basic to the workshopper's needs. Several of the tools we'll be mentioning will be given more extensive coverage elsewhere in the book, but we'll try to give them at least a passing mention here, and I've a horrid premonition that I'll realize I neglected something really crucial, about the time all this comes roaring off the presses.

Hammers and Mallets: We might term these percussion tools, as they gain their effect by storing kinetic energy during the swing, to deliver it all in one abrupt lump. There are countless specialized designs, such as a mineralogist's rock hammer, or a cobbler's tack hammer, but the claw hammer favored by carpenters is the version most commonly encountered, with its two curved claws that enable it to pull nails as well as drive them. Another common type is the ball-peen hammer, with a rounded knob at the end of the head opposite the flat face, for peening metal to shape. The peening end may take various other shapes, such as the cross-peen head illustrated here.

Mallets are hammers with heads made of something other than metal, and hammers may have heads of brass, plastic, lead or similar non-ferrous metals, to avoid damage

Above, from left, a small hammer
with a brass head to prevent damage to
to steel workpieces; the familiar
carpenter's claw hammer; a small
ball-peen hammer, with flat face
and rounded knob for peening metal.

Center above, a cross-peen hammer made in England
and distributed in the U.S. by Brownell's of Montezuma,
Iowa. The flattened end is used for peening — sometimes
spelled peining — which is shaping metals by hammering.

To the right, from left, an extremely handy and useful mallet with its head
made of incredibly tough polyurethane plastic — not generally available on
the market, unfortunately; a handmade mallet, turned out on a wood lathe;
a large mallet with a rubber head, found alongside a freeway, many years ago.

to the object being struck. Mallets have heads of wood — lignum vitae is a great favorite — rubber, plastic, coiled rawhide. Several years ago, a friend then engaged in the plastics industry made me a few mallets with heads of polyurethane that somewhat resembles an art gum eraser. It's incredibly tough, to the point where you can drive tiny finishing nails into hard wood with hardly a visible mark left on the face of the mallet. The pity is that no one seems to offer these commercially. I would not take any sane price for the two I have left, and mention it here in case you gain access to some of that type of plastic and feel inclined to try making a mallet of it.

For most hammering needs, I favor several dainty taps, rather than a few vicious clouts, and the hammers I use the most are the small ball-peen types, such as the one crafted from the head of a ¾-inch bolt by hacksawing off the last 1¾ inches, truing up the cut end and rounding off the flats in the little Unimat; a patience-taxing project, in itself. A hole was drilled with the No. 7 bit and tapped ¼-20. A four-inch length of ¼-inch cold-rolled steel rod was cut and threaded to match at one end, then turned into the head with a drop of Loctite to hold it forever and the other end

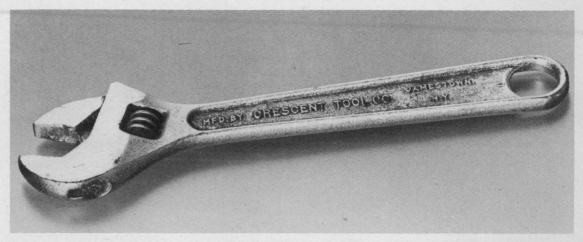

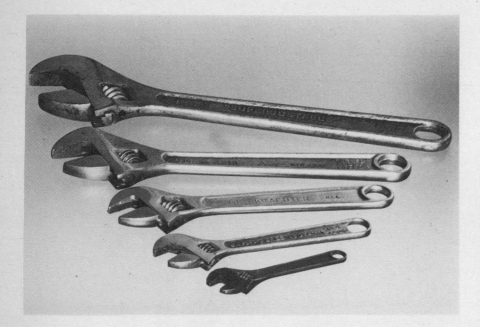

Above, a genuine Crescent wrench, made by the Crescent Tool Company of Jamestown, New York. Many people refer to all adjustable wrenches by that term, regardless of make. Left, adjustable wrenches ranging in size from four through twelve inches. Below, another Nail April display of the many types of wrenches and pliers available to handle various needs.

was driven into a metal-ferruled file handle. The resulting hammer weighs but a few ounces, but it has proven addictively handy.

Wrenches and Pliers: We could call these torque tools, since their chief use is in tightening or removing bolts and nuts, with their built-in leverage amplifying the user's strength considerably. Wrenches are either fixed in size, or adjustable. The fixed type include types such as open-end, box-end and sockets. There are wrenches with an open-end and box-end at opposite ends, or with two sizes of the same type at either end. Socket wrenches usually are used with a ratchet handle, variable by means of a selector to apply torque in either direction. It's generally more economical to buy socket wrenches as a set, although the sockets are available individually. There are sockets in metric series, as well as in fractional-inch series, and you'll need the metric sort to cope with foreign-made vehicles and such uses. The square opening at the top may be ¼, 3/8, ½-inch, or even larger, to fit the lugs on the ratchet handles and there are adapters from one socket to the other, as well as universal joints to enable you to work around corners,

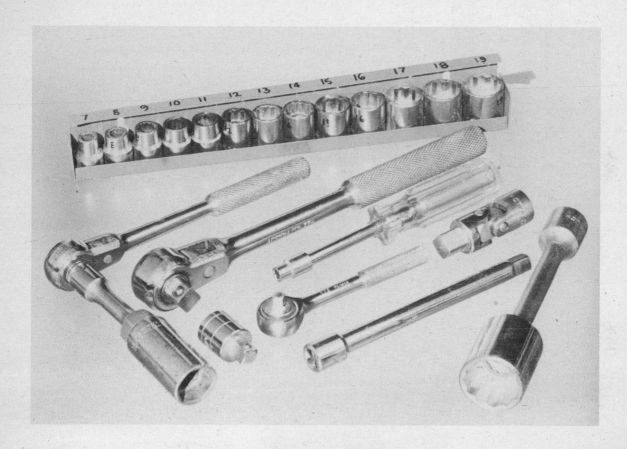

Socket wrench sets, as above, can handle a great variety of operations that would be all but impossible for any other tool. The square lugs are available in ¼, 3/8 and ½-inch sizes, with step-down adapting connectors, as above, with swivels, extensions and sockets of all sizes, including the metric set at the top. Right, Nail Apron display of sets of open-end, open/box-end and metric wrenches show the variety to be had.

and so on.

Adjustable wrenches deftly evade the problem of inch versus metric, within their given operating ranges, and are extremely handy, although not the best choice for really high-torque applications. Since they only are in contact with two of the six faces of the bolt head or nut, heavy strain will round off corners of the hexagon and you can end up nursing a set of bloody knuckles and contemplating a hex that may no longer accept a perfectly fitted box-end, unless restored to shape by patient filing. The popular term for a familiar pattern of adjustable wrench is Crescent wrench, from the Crescent Tool Company of Jamestown, New York, and a set in two-inch increments from four to at least twelve inches is extremely handy about the shop.

Pliers, in their many forms, are another basic tool without which it would be trying to attempt shopwork. Like the adjustable wrenches, they're a dubious choice for

Open/box-end wrenches, above, are available to handle any hexagonal nut or bolt head, in inch or metric sizes. Right, a folding pocket hex-driver to handle seven of the common sizes of Allen-head fasteners. Below, a simple wooden block, with holes drilled in the top in several sizes as an effort to keep track of the different hex wrenches.

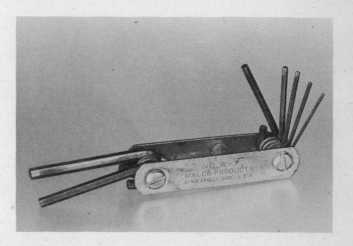

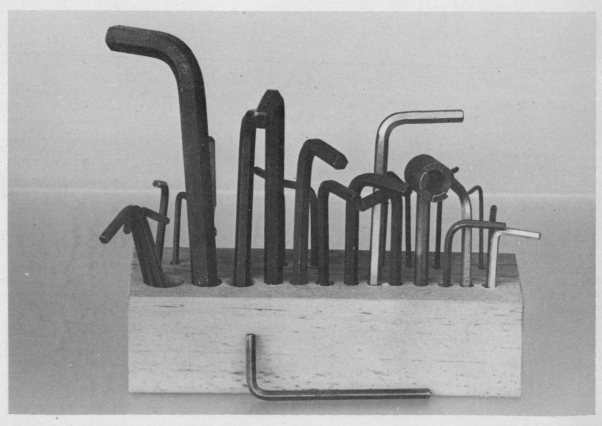

high-stress applications because they're apt to damage the item being gripped, but pliers are extremely handy for their suitable uses. There are combination pliers that adjust to two jaw spacings, and Channel-Lock pliers with several spacings available and the quite indispensible Vise-Grips that offer compound leverage and a really ferocious amount of force, if needed. Some patterns of Vise-Grips have a small additional lever to aid in breaking them loose, once tightly applied, and specialized patterns have broad jaws suited for bending small pieces of sheet metal, or a tong arrangement for use as a welding clamp, and so on.

Needle-nose pliers are good to have, as are the side-cutting pliers and the specialized pliers available from electronics suppliers for stripping insulation from various sizes of wire. In the same general category, a few pairs of tweezers can prove most useful for a lot of the chores that come along.

The familiar double-set pliers must be among the most common of all tools. It's hard to imagine that there is a household or shop in the land without at least one example of this truly indispensible tool! It adjusts to provide a tight grip on flat or rounded workpieces of many sizes and also has wire-cutting jaws.

From left below, channel-lock pliers, adjustable to keep the jaws reasonably parallel across a wide range of sizes; the extremely useful Vise-Grip pliers; battery pliers; double-set pliers; side-cutting pliers; needle-nosed pliers with an integral set of wire-cutting jaws; and a small pair of tweezers to hold small items.

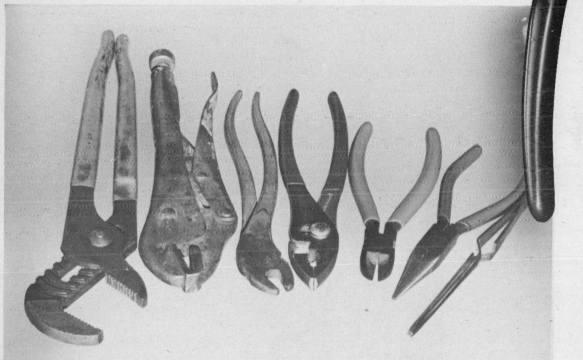

A closer look at the pair of shop tweezers: The tips are held shut under spring tension and pressing the broad center area opens them.

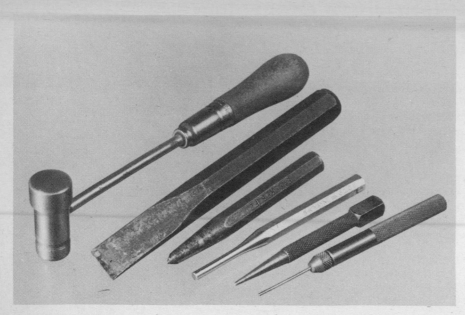

At left is the small, handmade hammer discussed on page 26. With it, a cold chisel, a center punch, a 3/16" pin punch, a nail-set punch, and a small pin punch with replaceable tip from Brownell's. Punches and chisels fill many uses in the workshop.

Punches and Chisels: These are, primarily, extensions of the impact tools such as hammers, to direct and apply the percussion in the desired manner. A pointed center-punch is used to make a small hole in metal to serve as the aligning guide for drilling a hole at that precise location. Nail-set punches are used to drive the heads of finishing nails or brads beneath the surface so that the hole can be filled with putty and covered with paint. Pin punches, in an assortment of diameters, are used for driving out or seating friction-held pin fasteners. Cold chisels are used for cutting off bolts or nuts that have rusted into immovability, or for peening a mark into a seated nut and exposed thread to assure it won't move.

Vises and Clamps: The vise on my bench has seen upward of a half-century's use and it's bearing up staunchly. It has a stub of anvil at the far end that has provided all the anvil I've needed to date, and it swivels and locks over an arc of about 180 degrees. Its jaws are 3½

inches wide, and it opens to about four inches. Its primary purpose is for holding workpieces during assorted operations, but I find I use it frequently as a sort of horizontal arbor press for assembling press-fitted components, and sometimes as a clamp for holding objects together while the glue sets.

If I ever feel the time has come to replace or supplement my heirloom vise, I have my eye on the Pana Vise, from Pana Vise Products, 2850 29th Street, Long Beach, California 90806; descriptive literature free on request. I'd term the Pana Vise a state-of-the-art approach for holding and positioning an endless variety of workpieces. By selecting one of the three base designs plus one or more of the clamping assemblies, the Pana Vise can be adapted for maximum convenience and efficiency in such diverse activities as fly-tying, working on circuit boards, assembling small and intricate devices and so on and on.

Pipe clamps and C-clamps appear so frequently through these pages that any discussion would be sheer redundancy,

These adjustable clamps, with hardwood jaws, open and close by turning two handles that rotate the right and left-hand threads so that the jaws clamp across a broad range of different angles. Yes, it is interesting to speculate upon how you'd go about making such a thing. It must be possible, because there they are. Perplexing, isn't it?

All of the store displays appearing in this chapter were photographed with the courteous permission of Nail Apron, by way of giving you an idea as to the bewildering variety of tools in brand-new condition rather than showing the ravages of many years of strenuous use. At left is part of their display of vises in different sizes, designs and special types.

Here are two more examples of Pana Vise — maker's address appears on the opposite page — at left with the highly versatile vacuum base that was shown on page 24, and below with a base that attaches to the bench by means of three screws or bolts, adjustable to nearly any position.

beyond noting that they come in a broad range of sizes and specialized designs, such as the edge-gluing clamp, with its second screw at right angles to the primary one. That, by the way, is another example of a tool that looked handy, so I bought it, but can't recall that I've ever used it. As noted, I usually employ the pipe clamps, with scraps of wood to protect the workpiece from damage by their jaws.

The Black & Decker Bench Top Workmate appears frequently here, also. For some reason, I came to think of it as a BenchMate, and suspect I've referred to it thus in places.

Spring clamps are likewise handy things to have on tap for low-stress positioning, light gluing operations and the like. I have four pairs, couldn't get along without them, and often wish I had more. As with the C-clamps, I hold the conviction that there's no such thing as too many!

Shopsmith Maxi-Clamp — One of the newest items available to the workshopper as the book at hand approaches completion, is the Shopsmith Maxi-Clamp. In the briefest description, it might be termed a state-of-the-art C-clamp, but it's actually much more than that. I'd call it a shop aid whose outer limits of versatility and useful application are so far-flung as to defy realistic assignments of boundaries, at this early stage of its career.

You see, the Maxi-Clamp is not only a C-clamp, but we might also think of it as an I-clamp, a U-clamp, an O-clamp, an L-clamp, and quite possibly other letters of the alphabet, as well.

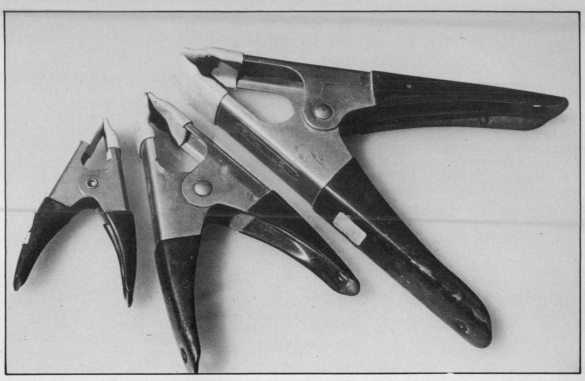

Another tool without which it would be hard to get along is the spring clamp, here in three sizes from Stanley. They are used to hold workpieces under pressure when gluing wood together, as well as for many operations where you need extra hands.

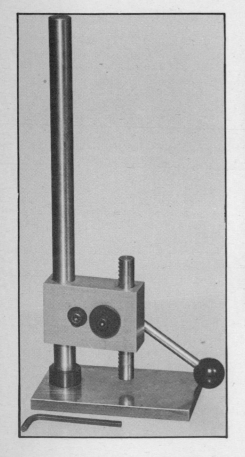

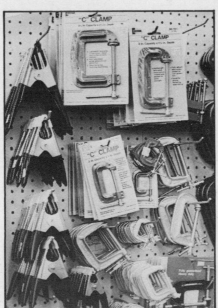

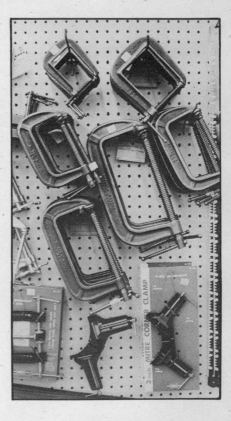

Above and right, another tool that fills many valuable needs is the C-clamp in its many sizes and shapes. The main trouble with C-clamps is that you never seem to have quite enough of them — or the biggest one you have isn't quite as big as you need. At lower right above are two of the miter corner clamps; another tool of incomparable usefulness for aligning and holding. At left is a small arbor press from B-Square, adjustable for applying moderate downward pressure against workpieces across a considerable range of heights by turning hex-head holding bolt.

The Maxi-Clamp is based around 3/8-16 threaded rod and nuts of the same thread, with multi-directional fixtures intended to harness tractor/pressor forces generated by threaded components of the kit. To me, the great virtue of the system is that it can be augmented, as the need is seen, from your neighborhood hardware store, by purchase of additional lengths of threaded rod, hex nuts, couplings, wing nuts, washers and other fixtures for that common and popular thread size.

Included in the Maxi-Clamp set are four quick-acting knobs that are, as the well-prepared instruction manual puts it, purposely double-bored. By holding the knob at a slight angle, it can be slid into place quickly, then straightened and tightened by means of engaging its partial threads with those of the threaded rod.

The instruction manual suggests a number of useful applications for the Maxi-Clamp, including use for gluing picture frames easily by maintaining equal pressure on all four corners at the same time — an O-clamp, as termed above. I suspect that the world's workshoppers are going to figure out a lot of uses for the system that the Shopsmith folks never dreamed of, since it appears to be almost infinitely flexible and adaptable.

Drill Braces and Bits: Next to knives, axes and hammers, this must be one of the race's oldest tools. I have one, use it frequently, but couldn't guess how many years it's been since the last time I drilled a hole with it. Its chuck holds a sturdy screwdriver bit with a blade 3/8-inch wide and a tapering, four-sided shank that fits the chuck of the brace. There is a knurled collar that provides a ratchet in either direction or locks rotation both ways in its center position,

so that you can operate in partial arcs when space is restricted. In its current configuration, as a sort of super-screwdriver, it's superb for dealing with long screws of the No. 14 size or so; operations that would wear out your wrist if handled with a common screwdriver.

As noted in the chapter on Rigging SLR View Cameras, my first choice for making large holes in wood and the like, out to around six inches in diameter, is the Pawood hole-cutter, used in the drill press. I have, however, a few adjustable drill bits for wood, one with the four-sided shank for use in the brace and another with a three-sided shank to fit the drill press chuck. The latter, for some curious reason, has a threaded tang, the same as for bits used in the brace. After buying it, I used it — just once! — in the drill press and, even set for the lowest rotating speed, the wooden workpiece came leaping off the table at me. I used an abrasive head in the Dremel Moto-Tool to grind enough of the threads off the tip to cure it of that objectionable trait and now it works quite well, when fed at the operator's selected pace, rather than by the threaded tip. Even if you clamped the workpiece to the drill press bed, the threaded

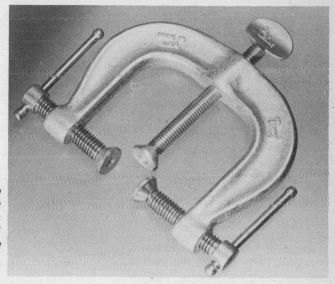

The three-jawed edge-gluing clamp, at right, is an example that looks handy, but does not seem to see extensive use; at least, this one hasn't. The idea is that you fasten the opposed jaws to a shelf or whatever and apply pressure with the third jaw against the piece being glued to form a separate edge. Below, the Shopsmith Maxi-Clamp has double-bored thumb nuts.

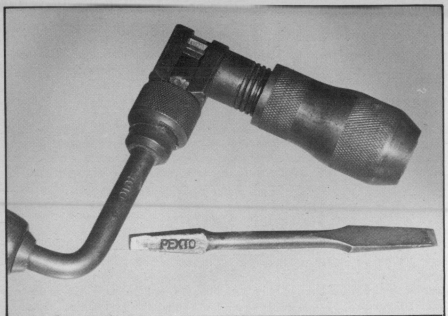

The business end of a carpenter's drill brace, with the screwdriver blade that is so handy for setting large and stubborn screws. Below, one of the brad-point drill bits that require a high speed of rotation to function well. The strip of tape serves as a guide for depth when drilling 3/8" dowel holes.

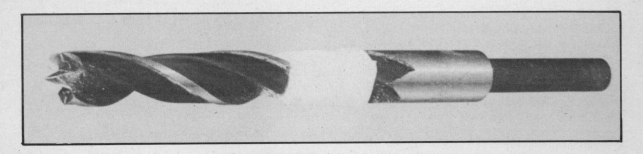

As discussed on page 33, this drill bit has a three-sided shank for use in a drill press, but it also had a threaded feed tip that made it feed much too fast for drill press use. The threads were ground off to correct that problem and it now performs quite nicely in the press.

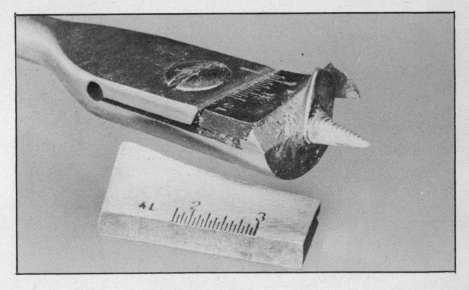

tip fed it so rapidly that it stalled the driving motor. This would be a handy item if they'd supply it with a tapered, unthreaded point; perhaps a three-sided point, such as the admirable Stanley auger bits for use in power drills have.

You can, of course, employ conventional, spiral-fluted metal drills for making holes in wood, though the walls of the resulting hole are rather rough. Similar drills are offered, with a small central point and sharp cutting points at the outside edges, such as the one shown, which came with a little doweling kit for use with 3/8-inch dowels. Such drills look as if they'd work just great, but unless used at a high number of revolutions per minute (RPM), they are apt to prove quite disappointing in most woods.

The Stanley auger bits, discussed here and elsewhere, are matchless performers, especially if you fiddle with them to get them boring holes actually of the stated diameter. The trouble is, they're rather expensive — around $3.50 to $6 each, depending upon diameter — and, worse, they are

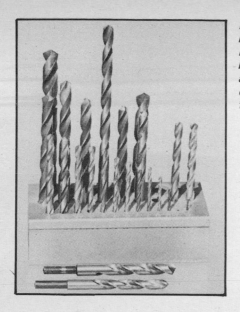

Left, part of the accumulation of metal drill bits of the fractional inch series, with a handy stand to hold and organize them. The two at the bottom are 5/16 and 3/8" carrying ¼" shanks, enabling them to be used in ¼" chucks.

Right, an Irwin drill bit to handle an infinite range of sizes between 7/8 and 3" diameters. Its shank is four-sided, for use in a drill brace, but the shank could be cut off and the feed tip de-threaded to adapt it for use in a drill press.

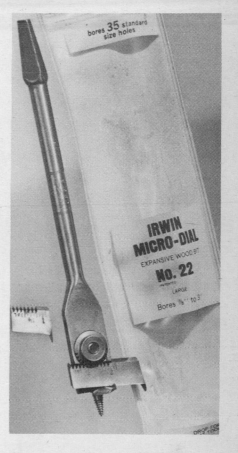

Here's a homemade holding block for the set of Irwin Speed-Bor spade bits as well as for the handy Stanley PowerBore wood bits, with a ½" chamfering bit, as well. Such holders also serve to prevent damage to the cutting edge of bits.

encountered in stores hardly more frequently than Brazilian banghoos. The local K-Mart was the only place I've seen such bits and the last time I stopped there, they were closing them out; a pity, I think.

The spade bits, such as the Irwin Speed-Bor, are extremely handy and rapid in operation, especially if kept properly sharpened. They're available in diameters from ¼ to 1½ inches and a small holding block, such as the one shown, save a lot of time and broken fingernails over tossing them all together in a box. The shanks of such drill bits, usually, are ground with three flats, to fit three-jaw chucks, and the flats should be aligned with the chuck jaws to prevent slippage, since the torque between the bit and chuck is quite considerable in the larger diameters. Tighten the chuck securely with the chuck wrench to prevent damage to the shank of the bit.

Similar small drill bits — some fixed and others adjustable — are available for making holes to fit various

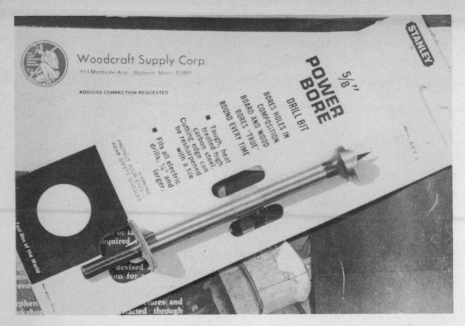

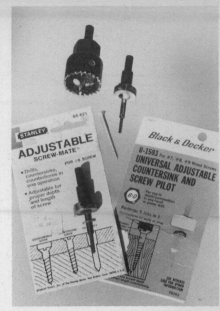

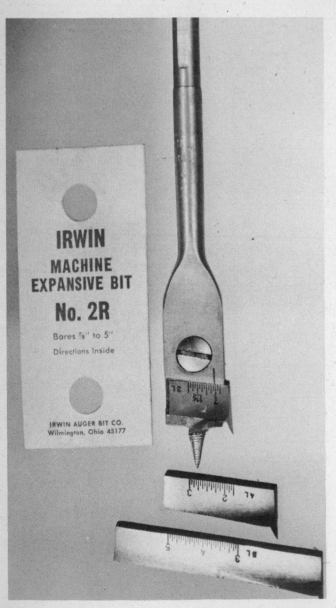

Woodcraft Supply Corp., 313 Montvale Avenue, Woburn, MA 01801, still lists the Stanley Power Bore bits in their catalog. Properly sharpened and used, such bits make holes in wood that are glass-smooth. Above, adjustable bits to drill fitted holes for wood screws, with a Black & Decker hole-saw bit using interchangeable cutter cups. Left is an overall view of the Irwin No. 2R expansive machine bit that was modified as discussed here earlier.

wood screws precisely and they are well worth buying and using if you employ wood screws in substantial quantity. As noted elsewhere, I've come to favor sheet metal screws, particularly for attaching metal to wood, since they've a rapid thread that seats quickly, with rather rough areas between threads that serve to prevent them from turning loose in use. The flat-headed wood screw is a good choice for wood-to-wood use, as in reinforcing a glued joint, and it can be seated flush with the surface by means of a properly adjusted screw hole drill, or countersunk so that the hole can be filled in with wood putty and sanded, or covered with a short length of dowel glued into place and sanded flush.

Planes, Wood Chisels, Gouges, Rasps and Files: I have a small block plane and an even tinier plane that accepts disposable razor blades, but find I use them on no more than the rarest occasions. I'm sure other workshoppers make vastly more extensive use of such tools. It's just that I tend to prefer using the table saw for most such applications, together with sandpaper, employed in the several manners discussed elsewhere. Much the same applies to wood chisels and gouges. I still have the monster gouge that came with the keenly-mourned Delta wood lathe, long ago. I hung onto it when the moment of sad parting came, convinced that it'd be terribly hard to find another like it. Chisels are needed for joints incorporating a mortise and tenon, and for similar applications. An explanation, not an excuse: I have rarely if ever encountered a need for more

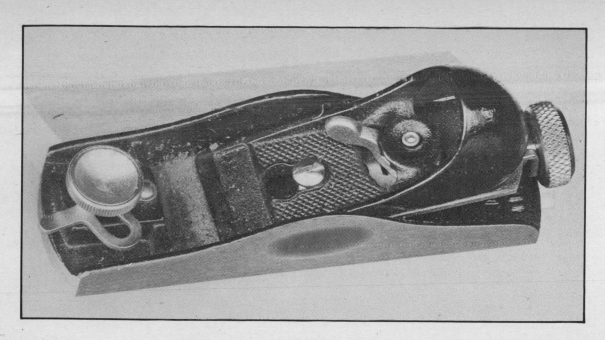

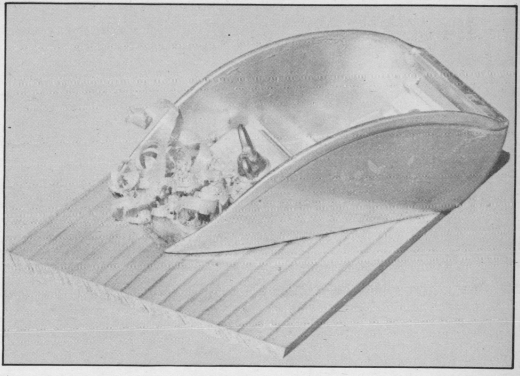

strength at a joint than modern glues provide, when properly employed. One of the rare exceptions is the internally-doweled joint used for attaching the legs to the table top in the chapter on Building a Table. As also noted, in the chapter on Building Bookcases, I favor externally-applied dowels to reinforce the butt-glued joints with particle board, and sometimes add a few screws to other glued joints; more for peace of mind than for clear and urgent need. As far as I've been concerned, the advent of the first Elmer's Glue, back in the early Fifties, with the improved versions such as the yellow aliphatic resin versions since then can be thought of as the arrival of the...uhh...gluebird of happiness. A joint using the hide glues of the earlier era, I found, was rather prone to come apart if you thoughtlessly sneezed in the same room with it.

Two small planes, the one immediately above designed to use safety razor blades. These are another example of the sort of tool that seems as if it should be quite handy but, somehow, seldom sees much use. Perhaps it is that most of the chores for which a plane might be used are handled via the table saw, belt sander or some other sanding device.

With such feeble adhesives, I'll concede a clear need for mortises, tenons, and the like. It's my current — admittedly callous — assessment that it's a question of whether you're making an item to fulfill its intended purpose, or making it primarily to impress other workshoppers with your expertise. That assumes, of course, that the envisioned stress will not be of an extreme nature.

Thus it is that my chisels and gouges see little use, and stay sharp for long intervals. The rasps and wood files, such as the Stanley Surform, see quite a bit more use and, as noted here and there, I see no sin in occasional uses of a metal file for fine shaping of wood.

Armand Swenson of Fallbrook, California — generally conceded to be the top custom pistolsmith around — is fond of referring to a file as a "Swedish milling machine." In his skilled hand, it entirely deserves the term. With any steel that a file will touch, I've seen Swenson sculpture it with exquisite delicacy, almost molecule by molecule, it seemed.

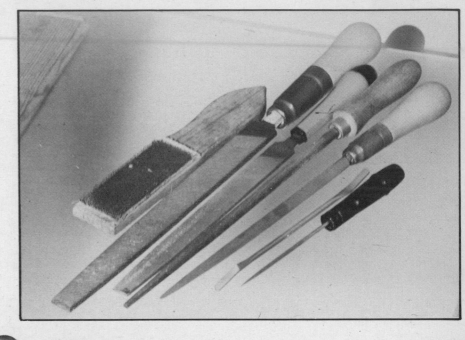

Given enough skill and patience, files can accomplish practically anything, as noted here. At right are a few examples of the many sizes and designs, with a file card for cleaning the teeth. Chalk, put on the teeth before use, will help to prevent clogging the teeth with filings. Below is one of the many sizes and shapes of the Stanley Surform, suited for rapid removal of wood with its sharp-edged holes.

The "monster-gouge" that came with the old Delta wood lathe has been retained, still sees occasional use, even in lack of a wood lathe. With it are a small gouge and a ¾" flat wood chisel for size comparison.

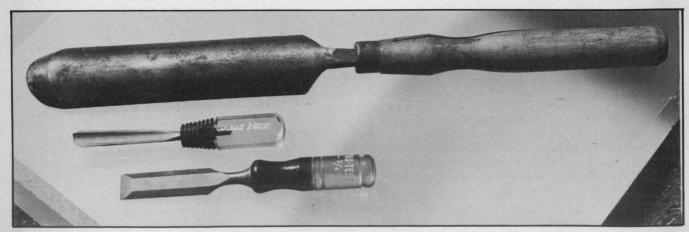

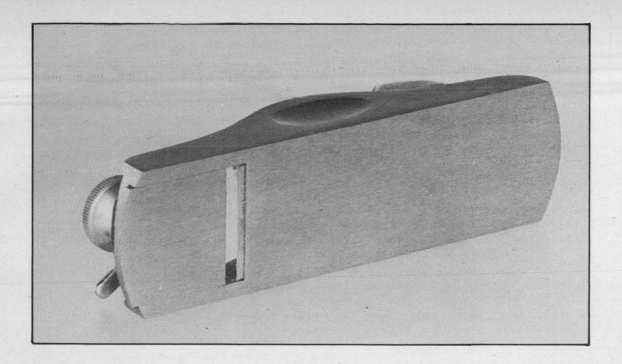

Files come in a vast variety of sizes, forms and types. There are single-cut, double-cut, three-cornered, rattail, slotting, checkering, oval, flat/convex, half-round, square, diamond, knife-edge, concave and gosh only knows how many other variants. In the Wisconsin days, I'd often stop at the Four Wheel Drive plant, up at Clintonville, to scout for possibly handy items available at steeply reduced prices from their sales and salvage office, out behind the main plant. I carried away files by the metric dozen, and still have most of them in case of possible need. One with a diamond-shaped (lozenge) cross-section was used for a while as a file and then I ground off the teeth (nearly all of them, at least) and sharpened the edges to make up a small double-edged knife. My brother Ralph added the handle composed of leather washers, an aluminum cap and brass retaining screw. I doubt if it's caused a sleepless night among the custom cutlers of the world, several of which are friends of mine.

The small plane, appearing above and below, has an adjustment to vary the width of the opening through which the edge of the blade projects. By moving the blade up and down, slightly, and changing the width of the opening, the depth of the cut can be regulated for the best effect when planing woods of various sizes and characteristics.

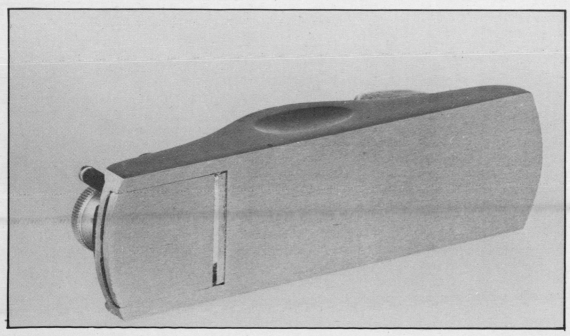

The hacksaw at right has seen some forty-odd years of frequent use and it's bearing up nobly, having repaid its purchase cost countless times over. Several fresher versions of the same invaluable tool appear below. The primary use of the hacksaw is for cutting metals and by using the carbide blades on the opposite page, they'll carve up glass, files, or nearly anything.

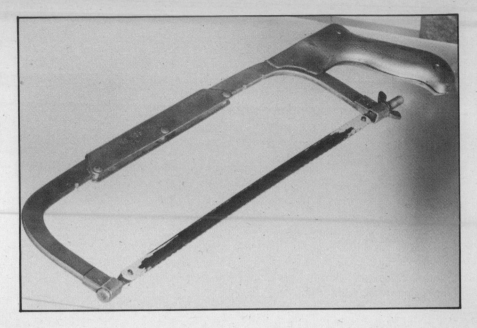

Saws: A hacksaw hangs from a nail, just above the vise on my workbench, and I use it quite frequently for cutting off pieces of cold-rolled rod, drill rod, flat stock, extruded angles, and the like. It's fitted with a 32-tooth blade, which I find best for just about any application. When cutting any metal except aluminum, a small amount of Rapid Tap cutting fluid speeds and eases the job quite usefully. I've kept one of the Remington Grit Edge hacksaw blades, with tungsten carbide particles embedded in its edge, on hand for quite some while now. I've not used it to date, but I'm sure that the time will come when it will be indispensible; probably at a time and hour when all the hardware stores

The traditional hand saw, here in the respected Disston make, usually is employed in the 8-point tooth pattern for ripping — cutting with the grain of the wood — and in 10-point for cutting across the grain with best efficiency.

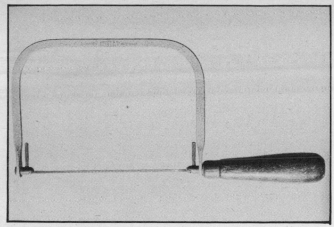

The tool above is variously known as a scroll/coping/jig saw. It's used for fine, intricate cuts and, by using a starting hole, it can be used to cut from the interior of the workpiece. At right are several examples of the backsaw in 13-point pitch for fine, precision cutting.

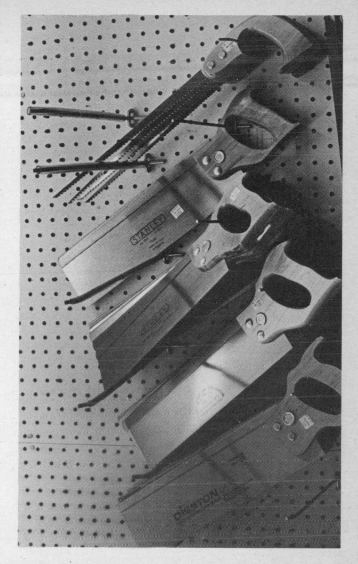

are closed. Remington also makes a carbide-embedded wire hacksaw blade for intricate cuts in extremely hard materials.

I've a small, fine-toothed backsaw, a tiny jeweler's saw, and a jigsaw or coping saw — to give the last both of its common terms. There is also a grundgy old handsaw that came with several blades at a low price, used perhaps once a year for a cut where the various power saws won't reach. As discussed in the chapter on Sharpening Edged Tools, I haven't felt the need for other saws and, for once, haven't bought them.

Remington's Grit Edge hacksaw and rod saw blades have a cutting edge of tungsten carbide particles, second only to the diamond in hardness, to cut difficult materials.

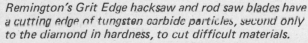

Shears and Snips: Now and again, a need comes up to cut sheet metal, leather, canvas, or comparable fairly tough materials. Though I sold hundreds of pairs of Wiss' superb tin snips in the old days, in their numerous sizes and patterns, my only pair of shears is some manner of dubious cheapie brand, but entirely adequate for my rare needs of such a tool to the present. I also have a little pair of straight jeweler's snips — J. Wiss & Sons' Model J-7 — and a pair of Wiss right-hand compound snips, commonly known in the sheet metal trade as aviation snips. In addition, the darkroom has two paper cutters, an eight- and twelve-inch cut, and I use both of those fairly frequently on materials for which they're suitable. I just went out and checked the cheapie snips and found that the sole designation is "10-inch," no maker's name, nor clue as to origin.

Torches: There is a fairly frequent need to apply moderate amounts of heat, as in soldering, or setting up installations sealed with a few drops of Loctite. I have a Weller Model D550 electric solder gun that I usually use for soldering electrical connections and, for most other soldering operations, I've come to use one of the small hand torches fed from a steel bottle that constitutes its handle. A decade or two ago, there was a specialized need for fine wire solder and a spool of 50/50 — half tin, half lead — was obtained in .040-inch diameter. I've used it for all my soldering, ever since, and more than half the spool remains. With bar solder currently selling at around $12 a pound, I'm glad I have it.

Detailed coverage on the tools used for measuring, marking and layout appears in a chapter under that heading. There are other small hand tools I may have forgotten to mention in passing, but the foregoing comprises the bulk, I'm fairly certain. There are a few pairs of safety glasses, a plastic face shield on adjustable headband, and an old pair of welder's gloves, all of which I'd rate as vital on frequent occasions for protection. A gauze filtered face mask would be a handy item, I've often thought, recalling the time I formed up a choice hunk of rosewood on a sanding disc in the drill press and sneezed purple for the greater part of the following week. The airborne sanding dust from cocobolo wood, incidentally, produces an allergic rash on many people, quite comparable to poison oak or poison ivy. That lowers the popularity of the otherwise handsome and durable material.

There are, of course, any number of other small, manual-powered, hand tools, such as spokeshaves, drawshaves, miter boxes, rotary hand drills operated by a geared crank like an old-fashioned eggbeater, trowels, bolt cutters, pipe wrenches, broken screw extractors, flexible snakes for clearing stopped-up drains, as well as the force cup or plumber's friend and the sometimes-handy little gizmo called a Drain King. The last screws onto the end of a garden hose and, when the water is turned on, a spring-loaded valve causes it to expand and seal the pipe before water goes out the end in hopeful attempts to clear a blocked drain under pressure of the water main. In theory, it sounds good. In practice, it may prove disappointing.

Your own routine or anticipated activities will and should govern the tools you need to buy. In writing this, I've leaned toward covering the tools I have and use with enough frequency to justify having paid for them. I don't own a miter box and, to be candid, wouldn't give one shop

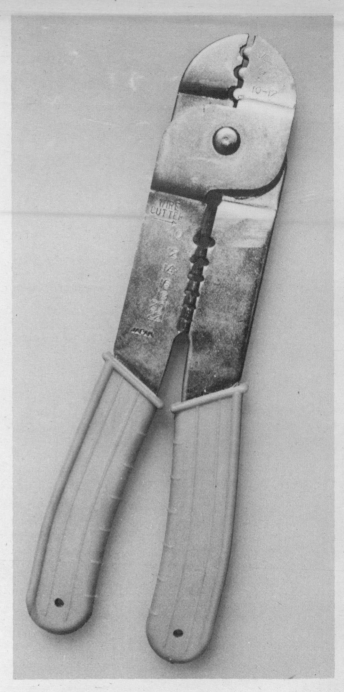

A remarkably handy tool for cutting and stripping the insulation from electrical wires, as well as crimping connectors into place is the tool, above.

Left, an assortment of metal shears, in several sizes and patterns, including the compound-leverage pattern often termed aviation snips, with a few sets of tongs.

Below, from top, the small jeweler's saw is quite handy for fine cutting of wood, plastic and the softer metals; diagonal side-cutting pliers are for close-in trimming of wire and similar materials. The small backsaw at the bottom makes smooth precision cuts in any wood.

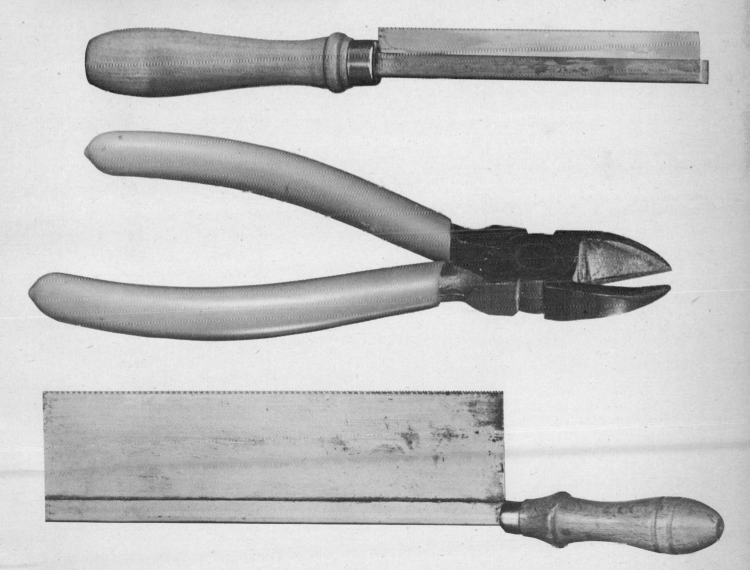

space. If I hadn't been using table saws since the latter Fifties, I'm sure I'd feel differently about them. The thing is, I've found it a long, tough grapple to coax accurate 45-degree cuts out of a table saw and shudder to contemplate trying to do it with a miter box.

In the same vein, I don't own a pipe wrench at present, and haven't needed one since moving away from the house that had a swimming pool. A pipe wrench came with that house and I think I left it there. Once freed of pool maintenance, which can be a real blast, I've had no need for a pipe wrench, and I feel grateful for that.

One last pass through the shop, peering intently for things I forget to mention, turned up just a few items. There were a pair of putty knives, quite handy for spreading, scraping and general cleanup. There was a draftsman's brush, often used for getting rid of coatings of sawdust, sanding dust and the like, plus a pushbroom, a

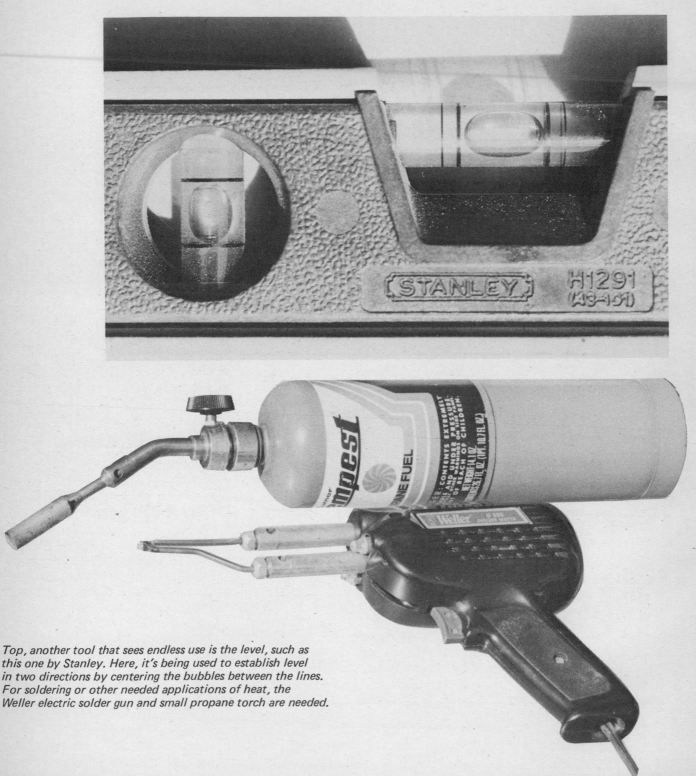

Top, another tool that sees endless use is the level, such as this one by Stanley. Here, it's being used to establish level in two directions by centering the bubbles between the lines. For soldering or other needed applications of heat, the Weller electric solder gun and small propane torch are needed.

whiskbroom and a small scrub brush. There was a glass cutter, which I've rarely been able to use with the sort of results I had in mind, and a scribing marker with a pointed tip of tungsten carbide, reversible to protect the point from unwary drops to the concrete.

There was also a pair of two-ton capacity, hydraulic bottle jacks, purchased for a specific lifting operation, which I'm planning to re-employ, with a suitable framework, to make up a laminating press that should prove useful, and a 3/8-inch drill bit with a tungsten carbide tip for making holes in masonry. The masonry bit has not been used often enough to pay for its room and board.

The point of all this gets back to the admonition in the introduction about restricting your purchases to tools you'll use often enough to justify the cost. If you wish to collect tools as a hobby, feel free to do so, and try to pardon my pragmatism.

A pressure air hose would be handy, but the Dust-Off can, available from photo stores, can be used for removing dust, chips and the like. Two-ton hydraulic bottle jacks were used in raising and installing the 580-pound metal lathe and are invaluable when LOTS of muscle is needed. At bottom, an overall view of the same Stanley level.

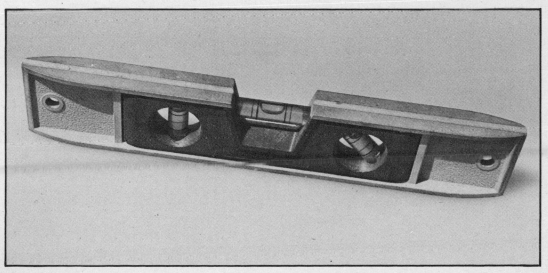

POWER HAND TOOLS

Inexpensive mounting stands, such as the one above, can convert small and equally inexpensive electric hand drills into remarkably useful drill presses, with the drill press's useful ability to drill holes that are absolutely perpendicular.

Up to this point, we've dealt with those tools that depend primarily upon the muscles of the operator for their useful effects, although many use leverage or stored inertia to amplify the available muscle-power.

In this section, we'll take up those hand-held tools incorporating electric motors to aid in performing their useful works. In most instances, the electricity is obtained by plugging a cord into a nearby wall socket, so that their application is limited somewhat by the distance from a socket and the length of the available extension cords. In a few examples, power is provided by self-contained batteries, often of the rechargeable variety.

Electric Drills: These are shop tools so extremely useful and moderate in cost that there is justification in terming

them indispensible. The primary use is in drilling holes, but various accessories are available to broaden their capabilities quite impressively. To cite just a few examples, you can use the electric hand drill to power wire brushes, disc sanders, drum sanders, rotary files, paint mixers and so on.

The most common and popular size of electric hand drill has a three-jawed chuck that accepts tool shanks up to ¼-inch in diameter. Some offer a variable speed feature, so that rotating speed is controlled by pressure upon the trigger switch.

The 3/8-inch electric hand drill is the next larger size and it may feature a reversing switch, as well as variable speed and a lockable trigger switch to permit operation without

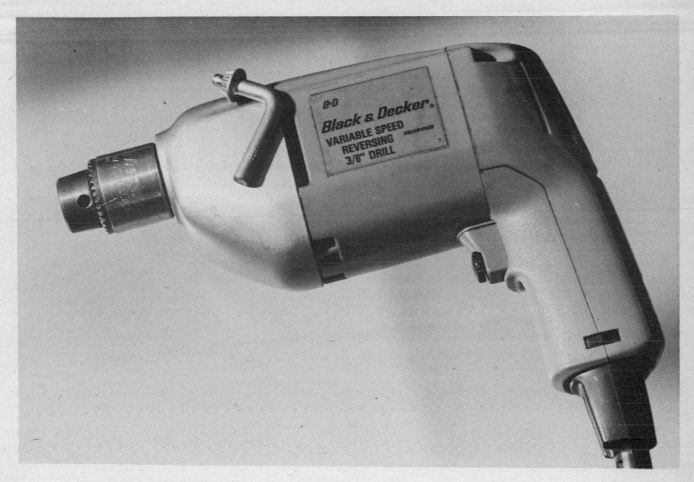

Electric hand drills, such as this Black & Decker variable speed, reversing 3/8" model, are extremely versatile, due to the large number of accessories and attachments that are available for use with them. This one is double-insulated, for added operator safety. A holder for the small geared chuck key can be fashioned from a heavy rubber band to secure it to a handy place on the power cord as an aid to keeping track of its whereabouts.

holding the switch down. Such drills can be used, with a screwdriver bit in the chuck, to drive or remove screws in a quick and convenient manner.

Inexpensive stands are available to convert several of the small electric hand drills into drill presses and accessories are offered to guide or convert electric hand drills into portable drill presses for jobs where a conventional drill press would be impossible or impractical to use.

Drill bits are available with ¼-inch shanks in the larger diameters, permitting the drilling of up to ½-inch holes with a ¼-inch electric hand drill, provided its available torque is powerful enough to cope with the material being drilled at that diameter.

The Dremel Moto-Tool: This is a small motor with a chuck that accepts shanks up to 1/8-inch in diameter, with graduated collets to handle smaller sizes. The version usually encountered has a dial switch to regulate rotating speeds to the desired number of revolutions per minute (rpm), and the peak speed is quite high. A large assortment of bits are available for the Moto-Tool, enabling it to be used for drilling, grinding and shaping nearly any material.

Several accessories are offered for use with the Moto-Tool, such as a clamp to hold it motionless so that the workpiece can be grasped and maneuvered with both hands. A routing guide enables it to be used as a hand-held router and another accessory stand converts it into a small drill press suitable for fine precision work.

Now that's a Drill Team! In one convenient box, you have the fractional-inch series from 1/16 through ½" in 1/64" increments, plus all of the numbered series from 1 through 60, plus the lettered set from A through Z, each drill bit neatly nestled in its own fitted hole in one of the hinged holding racks. This one came from Manhattan Supply Co.

Stanley Power Bore bits have three-sided shanks and a three-sided, unthreaded guiding tip for use in power drills, drill presses and the like. When properly sharpened, they produce superbly smooth-walled holes in nearly any wood, even when run at low rpms. The so-called brad-point wood drills do not compare with the Power Bore for smooth cutting and ease of use, merchandiser's claims to the contrary, unless they are run at higher speed than most electric drills offer.

Electric Hand Saws: These are offered in two basic types: rotary and oscillating. The rotary — often termed a SkilSaw, from a well-known brand of the tool — has a pistol grip and trigger switch, with a spring-actuated guard that covers the exposed edge of the circular blade when it is not actually cutting. Such saws can be used to remarkably good effect in lieu of a table saw and holding accessories are available to enable them to perform many operations normally handled by a table saw or radial arm saw.

The rotary electric hand saw often proves uniquely suited for jobs that would be difficult or impossible with other tools. As but one example, plywood and similar materials often are supplied in 4x8-foot sheets that are cumbersome and unwieldy to maneuver through a table saw, but the sheet can be placed on a workbench and cut to any desired size with the rotary hand saw. If a straight and

The Dremel Moto-Tool, here in the Model 370, with variable speed control, is another highly versatile tool for countless small grinding and shaping operations about the shop. At left, it's installed in the Model 210 drill press stand to create a small precision drill press, with table movable and the drill stationary.

accurate cut is desired, a straightedge can be clamped to the workpiece to serve as a guide for the saw. Take appropriate precautions to avoid scarring the top of the workbench, such as placing the workpiece atop a pair of boards to provide clearance beneath the cut, and adjust the cutting depth of the saw accordingly.

The oscillating electric hand saw — often termed a saber saw — accepts a variety of different blades for use on woods or metals, with narrower blades for intricate scrollwork and wider blades for straight cuts. Like the rotary type, it often proves capable of making cuts that would be difficult for other tools, due to the nature of the workpiece. As an example, I've sometimes used my rotary hand saw for trimming small branches from trees, with the aid of one or more extension cords, and the electric jigsaw has sometimes been employed for similar purposes.

Electric Sanders: Sandpapering the workpiece for final forming and finishing is an operation that can soak up a vast amount of elbow-grease if handled manually. Powered sanding tools save a lot of time, as well as effort. The Stanley Swirlaway sanding head, installed in an electric hand drill, can be set up so that its shaft is either flexible or in rigid alignment to the disc holder. It accepts five-inch discs of sandpaper, readily available in an assortment of grit sizes and, as you'll note here and there in this book, I use it frequently.

I also have two of the oscillating electric sanders, one of which is convertible to straight-line push/pull operation by moving a lever. Although sandpaper is more or less available in ready-cut sheets to fit such tools, I usually cut my own strips from the standard 9x11-inch sheets of sandpaper by scribing a mark on the back side with the carbide-pointed scratch awl, folding the paper at the line and then tearing it.

The oscillating sanders get their most frequent use in final finishing, for purposes such as easing sharp edges and corners and smoothing away remaining tool marks. If an extremely smooth final finish is the object, it's usually accomplished by hand, using a full sheet of sandpaper folded in thirds and worked with the grain of the wood. Oscillating sanders tend to leave a distinctive swirly pattern of tiny scratches in the surface, even when used with the finest grades of sandpaper.

If any substantial amount of stock removal is necessary, the electric belt sander is by far the best tool for the purpose, fitted with a suitable grade of belt. My belt sander is a comparatively recent addition to the shop and I find myself wondering why I waited so long, since I use it frequently to remarkably good effect. As noted here and there through the book, I sometimes clamp it into the Black & Decker Bench Top Workmate, with its belt uppermost, and lock the trigger switch on so that I can hold the workpiece against the belt with both hands. This seems to be an effective approach, provided you don't let an unwary knuckle come into contact with the moving belt.

It's a project I've not tackled as yet, but I believe it would not be unduly difficult to construct a small stand that would hold the belt sander with the belt surface vertical, so that an adjustable working surface could be used to position the workpiece at any desired angle. Such a rig should prove extremely useful for forming and finishing operations.

The Router: This tool, with a suitable assortment of bits, can handle so many workshop chores that it certainly approaches indispensibility, in my opinion. When I first bought mine, several years ago, I made the minor error of purchasing several interesting-looking bits for it in high-speed steel, only to discover that the abrasive ingredients in particle boards would ruin them in dismayingly short order. By that time, I had noted which bit designs I used a lot and which ones I used but rarely, if ever. I replaced the often-used bits with the somewhat costlier versions having cutting edges of tungsten carbide, and those have seen a lot of use, showing no detectable signs of wear to the present.

My router is a Black & Decker Model 7620, which they designate as commercial heavy duty, and its no-load operating speed is rated at 22,000 rpm. The bits are secured in a chuck with the aid of a pair of small open-end

1 *Accessory routing guide turns the Moto-Tool into a small precision router.*

2 *Bits are installed in the Moto-Tool by depressing the lock button and turning the hex nut that locks the chuck.*

3 *Here are a few — by no means all! — of the bits, cutoff stones and rotary file accessories for use in the Moto-Tool.*

4 *A representative sampling of the broad variety of bits for ¼" shank routers to extend flexibility of such useful tools.*

5 *Operating speed of the Dremel Moto-Tool is continuously variable across a wide range by the rotary switch, here.*

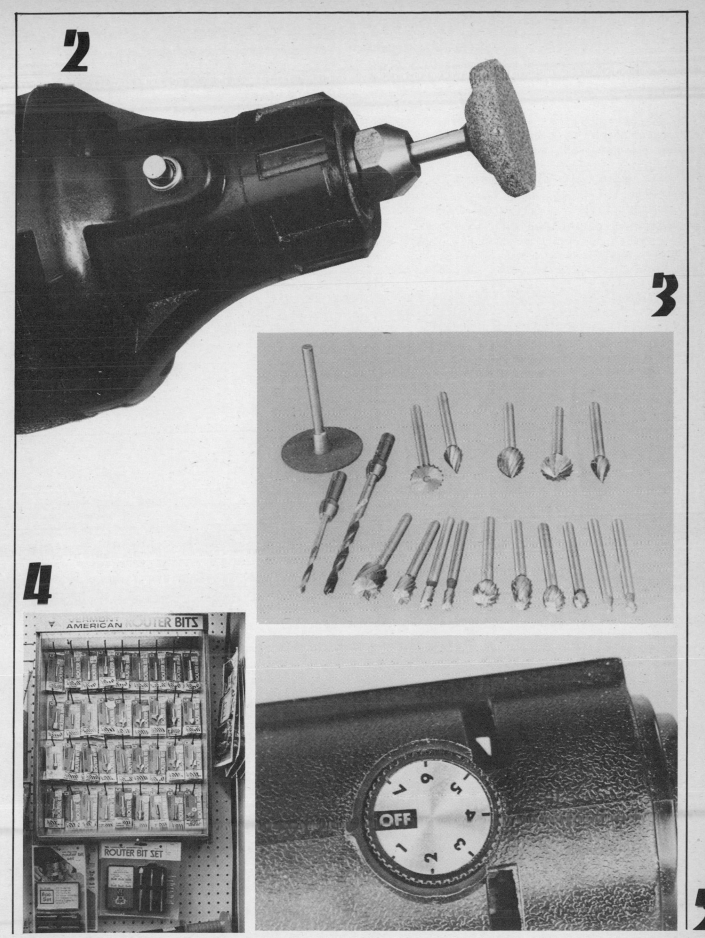

2

3

4

5

wrenches that came with it. The router bit shanks are nominally ¼-inch and, checking the collection with the mike, I find the diameters vary from about .2490 through .2496-inch.

The straight bits are the ones that have seen far and away the most use, along with the edge-trimming bit with its carbide blades and guide roller. I have carbide straight bits in 3/16, ¼, 3/8, ½, 5/8 and ¾-inch diameters, as well as a HS steel bit in 1/8-inch. The ¼-inch is the one I usually use for circle cutting, in conjunction with the guide for that purpose. The ¾-inch carbide straight bit has seen more use than all the rest put together, much of it in tough and raspy particle board, and it remains as razor-sharp as the day I bought it, for twenty-odd dollars, if memory serves.

I bought an inexpensive metal tool box to hold all of my router accessories, and I recommend that as a most helpful approach to keeping track of all the handy little gizmos. The router itself reposes on a shelf above the bench, with its three-pronged cord neatly coiled about its motor, and the tape-labeled tool box of accessories is stored beneath the bench. I drilled a number of ¼-inch holes in a piece of scrap wood to hold the assortment of bits for quick and convenient access to the given one needed.

I've fallen into the habit of using the drafting T-square as the guiding straightedge for the router, held in place by C-clamps, and a few times along the way, the whirring bit went right on through to make shallow cuts in the aluminum crosspiece of the T-square, cutting the metal as if it were warm Velveeta (carbide bits, of course). It was no catastrophe. As a matter of fact, the grooves serve quite helpfully for aligning the T-square to the lines ruled for making the routed channel.

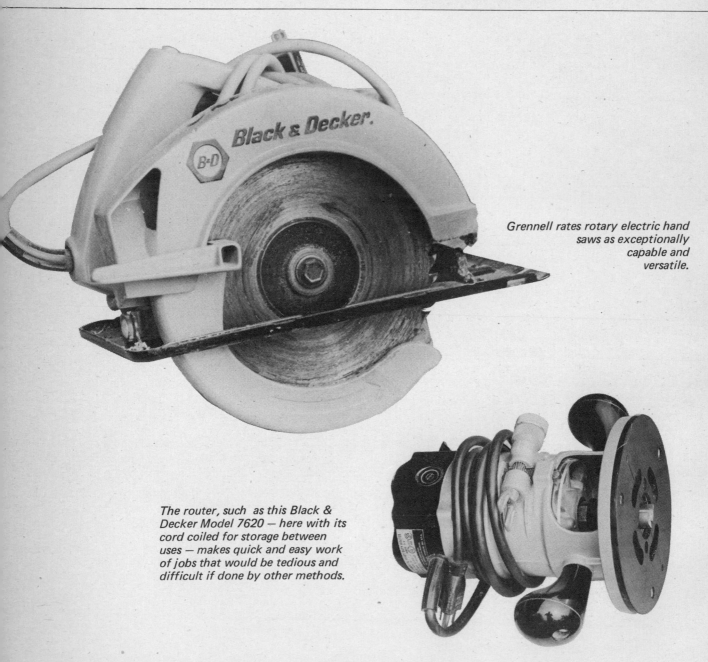

Grennell rates rotary electric hand saws as exceptionally capable and versatile.

The router, such as this Black & Decker Model 7620 — here with its cord coiled for storage between uses — makes quick and easy work of jobs that would be tedious and difficult if done by other methods.

Curious as to the working speed of the cutting edges of the router, I worked it out for the ¾-inch bit diameter and got a thin scantling over 49 miles per hour, at 22,000 rpm, or just under 4320 feet per minute/72 feet per second. Quite early in getting acquainted with routers, you tend to learn that this is one tool with which eye protection is mandatory, particularly when routing particle board. The hurtling fragments are like facing up to a sand-blaster.

It seems pertinent to note that I do not recommend routing in aluminum, despite the ease of routing a shallow groove in the T-square crosspiece. Tungsten carbide, for all its hardness — second only to the diamond — is a brittle material, and easily broken, as I discovered when a carbide scriber slipped from my fingers to the concrete floor, never to be the same again. I would not care to be in the near vicinity if a carbide blade came unfastened from the bit while rounding a 3/8-inch corner at nearly 50 mph!

Cautionary comments notwithstanding, the router is certainly one of the most flexible and useful power tools available to the home workshop. The price tag survives on mine and I note that I paid $64.99 plus sales tax for it, a bit over six years ago, which brings its current cost down to about a buck a month. If I could rent so handy a tool for that figure, I'd regard it as a great bargain, despite the fact that I've invested half-again the cost of the original router in bits to use in it. It's true that a few of the chores the router handles so well could be done with a dado blade on the table saw, but if you worked much particle board, you'd be buying a new set of dado blades about every Saturday. Saturday.

If the faithful router ever wears out — heaven forbid! — all I want is another one, exactly like this one.

The oscillating electric hand saw, or saber/sabre saw, such as this Rockwell Model 4300, enable the user to perform cuts in woods, plastics, sheet metals, tubing and similar materials, all with handheld convenience.

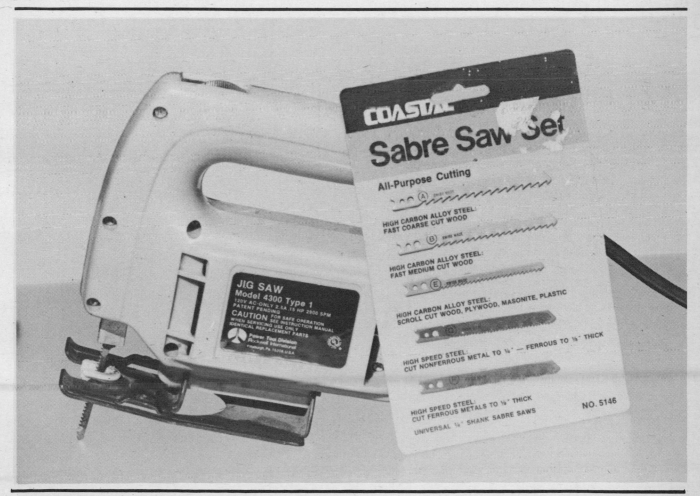

In trying to separate the discussion into appropriate categories, I've reserved this section for those useful devices that repose upon the floor or bench when used, rather than being held and maneuvered in the hands.

Table Saws: I would incline to rate this as one of the most basic and indispensible tools in the shop, since it is capable of doing so many operations quickly and easily that would be extremely arduous or challenging to do with a hand saw.

My first table saw was a home-rigged affair, built around a small arbor I managed to scrounge up to fit the headstock of the old Delta wood lathe. I made a platform that bolted to the lathe bed, using lengths of one-inch wooden dowel at each corner to position the saw bed in relation to the circular blade in the arbor. As I recall, the blade was rather small, about four or five inches in diameter, but it operated with a degree of exquisite precision unmatched by any readymade table saw I've owned or operated in the years since. There have been many times since those days when I'd've given an eyetooth or two to have the use of it again for a little while.

The obvious disadvantage of the lathe/saw conversion was that it tied up the lathe for its accustomed use, and had to be removed for a return to turning operations. That consideration prompted the purchase of an eight-inch table saw and a drill press, both by Atlas, which were on sale at a local lumber yard at prices I was incapable of ignoring. Both have performed heroic yeoman service in the years since their acquisition in 1962 and I consider the modest investment returned countless times over.

A small but plaguing problem with the table saw is that its blade has gotten out of parallel alignment with its bed in fairly recent times. The blade mount is held to the bed through elongated bolt holes and, in theory, one should be able to loosen and realign the blade and bed to a fitting and proper relationship. In practice, the presumably simple step has defied my most valiant efforts to the present. I've lost count of the number of times I've gritted my teeth, rolled up my figurative sleeves and tackled the rectification of the annoying status quo. On each humiliating occasion, the blade seems to end up right back where it started: detectably slaunchwise to the bed. That necessitates warping the rip fence more or less into alignment with the blade and crafty manipulation of the miter guide to achieve a cut of the angle I had in mind.*

The Atlas saw has a two-pronged plug at the end of its cord, with no provision for a third grounding wire. I had noticed, various times, that I could get a thoroughly detectable electrical shock upon touching any part of the saw, depending somewhat upon the insulating nature of my footgear. One day, without thinking much about it, I set the router down on top of the saw for a moment and there was a crackling spark that activated the circuit-breaker in the multi-socket outlet on the workbench, into which both tools were plugged. The router has a three-pronged, grounded cord plug. I was extremely glad I hadn't discovered the problem by simultaneously touching both the saw and some metal portion of the router!

A friend, Becky Cartwright, who understands electronic affairs, informed me that the problem could be solved by plugging in the saw properly and, through trial and cautious

POWER SHOP TOOLS

*As it turned out later, this particular problem managed to flounder through to a solution, as discussed in Chapter 13.

A pivoting blade guard of transparent orange plastic covers the edge of the Dremel saw, here with the fine-toothed 4" Sears crosscut blade in place. Such safety devices should be left in place and used, whenever possible, due to the length of time required to grow replacement fingers!

Dremel's Model 580 4" table saw runs at 10,000 rpm and comes with a rip fence and adjustable miter guide. Its switch can be padlocked to prevent use by unsupervised children or others.

error, I established that the prong of the plug connected to the white cord should be inserted into the right-hand slot of the socket, as viewed from the ground-wire hole at the bottom. Since that time, I've taken considerable pains to plug the Atlas saw in properly and have had no further troubles, even if I set the router down on the saw bed. I note this by way of acquainting you with the possibility of hazards when using older shop equipment that is not grounded. Many modern electrical tools are double-insulated, and labeled accordingly, so as to avoid such problems, regardless of which plug prong is inserted into which socket slot. If a doubt exists in your mind on that particular score, I suggest that you consult an electrician and consider having the motor rewired. Raw wattage from an electrical outlet can be fatally hazardous to the health!

For those workshoppers who need to saw comparatively small pieces of wood — such as in the construction of models — perhaps with severe limitations as to working and storage space, Dremel makes a compact little table saw — called the Model 580 — that handles blades of four-inch

diameter. Its maximum cut is about 1-1/8 inches and the cut is adjustable from that depth to any desired shallower one. The blade can be tilted through angles from a bit over 90 to a trifle less than 45 degrees in relation to the saw bed for cutting compound miters and similar applications. It is a handy little item, within its cutting capacity. It comes with an adjustable rip fence and miter guide, as well as a circular ripsaw blade having thirty teeth.

Several of the outlets that handle Dremel shop tools such as the table saw have few suitable accessories for them available as separate items. The four-inch saw blades are a bit hard to find, but I found and bought a finer-toothed crosscut blade in that diameter at the local Sears-Roebuck store. It produces a usefully smoother cut than the ripsaw blade that came with the Dremel table saw.

A good feature of the Dremel Model 580 is the inclusion of a switch that can be padlocked in the off position, to prevent its use by unattended children. It operates at a no-load speed of 10,000 rpm, and it would be extremely hazardous to tiny, inquisitive fingers!

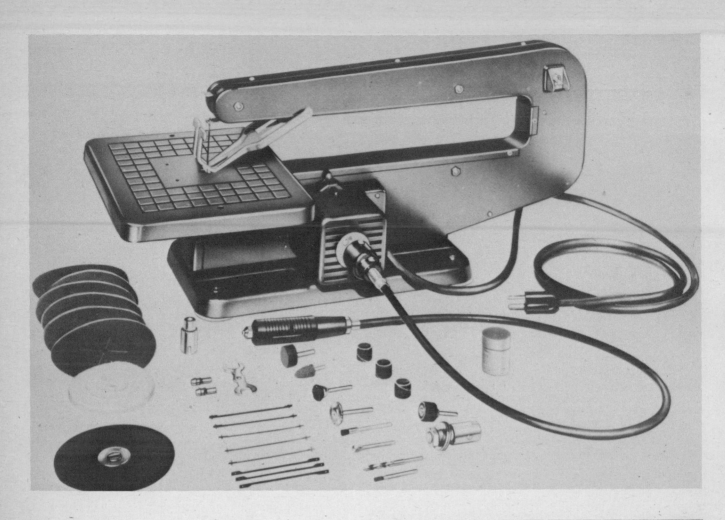

Dremel's Moto-Shop is a 15″ power scroll saw with a driven
coupling to which a sanding disc or flexible shaft can be
connected. Some of the accessories usable with it are
shown in the manufacturer's photo, above. Right, although
the resulting cut is impressively fine and smooth, you can
use a small sanding head in the flexible shaft to smooth or
re-shape the cut area after sawing, if desired.

The Dremel Moto-Lathe is a 1½x6" wood lathe driven directly by its integral motor to a no-load speed of 3450 rpm.

Dremel Moto-Lathe: This is a compact tool, directly driven by an integral electric motor at a no-load speed of 3450 rpm. It will accommodate workpieces up to six inches in length and 1½ inches in diameter. Its headstock spindle carries a 5/16-24 male RH thread, and it is supplied with a spur center and live center tailstock. This is a remarkably handy little lathe to use and it should prove ideally suited for projects such as making model aircraft in applications such as turning engine cowlings, making wheels to scale, or small sets of chessmen, and so on. A well-prepared and comprehensive instruction manual comes with the Moto-Lathe, clearly showing and telling how to use it for the different operations and placing appropriate emphasis upon safety precautions to be observed.

Dremel Moto-Shop: This is a fifteen-inch power scroll saw, with a driven coupling to which you can attach a sanding disc or a flexible shaft and accessories such as those used with the Dremel Moto-Tool. As a scroll saw, it is rated to handle soft wood to 1¾ inches in thickness and hardwood up to ½-inch, aluminum to ¼-inch and copper to 18 gauge. By making a 5/32-inch starting hole and threading one end of the blade through it, inside cuts can be made. The table can be adjusted in angle for making bevel cuts, and it can be raised or lowered when the working teeth become dull, so as to bring a fresh set of teeth into use. Replacement blades are available in two grades: fine (No. 8029) and coarse (8030).

One of the few mail order sources for all of the Dremel equipment described here, as well as the necessary supplies and accessories, is Woodcraft Supply Corporation, 313 Montvale Avenue, Woburn, Massachusetts 01888. Their catalog is listed at fifty cents per copy, postpaid, for the Spring-Summer 1980 edition, and it lists Dremel's Moto-Lathe accessory kit that includes four lathe tools — one each: round nose, 60-degree skew chisel, 30-degree skew chisel and parting tool — plus a 1-3/8-inch faceplate, wood screw drive center, honing stone and twelve assorted sizes of dowels for turning.

Dremel's Model 730 disc-belt sander uses a 1x30" sanding belt or replaceable
5" sandpaper discs for shaping, polishing, cleaning, chamfering, deburring or
beveling metals, woods and certain plastics. The no-load operating speed of
the disc is 4400 rpm and that of the sanding belt is about 2600 fpm; nearly 30 mph.

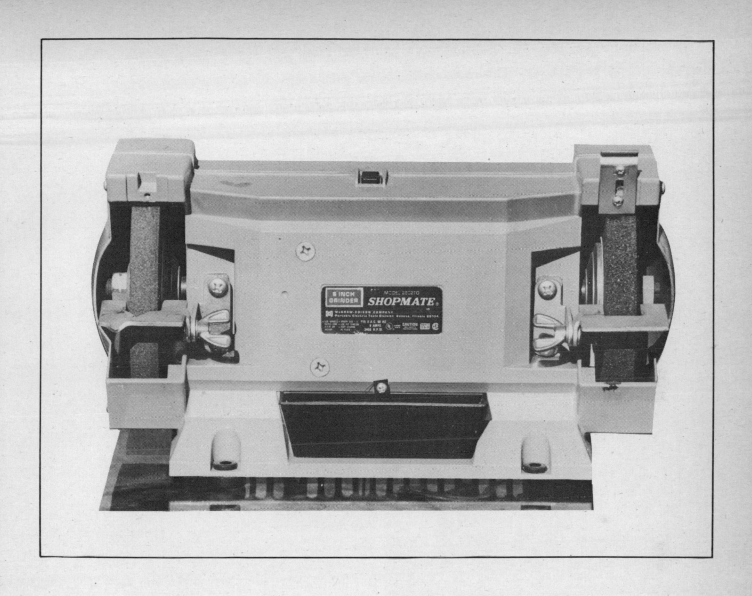

A bench grinder, such as this 6″ model from McGraw-Edison, is useful for the heavier sharpening and grinding operations. Various grit grades of stones are to be had, as well as buffing wheels for use in polishing metals. Operating speed of this one is 3450 rpm. That's 18.85 inches per revolution, 65,031 inches per minute, or 61.6 mph.

Dremel Disc-Belt Sander: This is a lightweight and portable combination sander for shaping, polishing, cleaning and deburring metal, wood and certain plastics. It uses a 1x30-inch-long sanding belt and two belts are supplied with the machine, one each in 80 and 120 grit, plus one 80 grit, five-inch, self-adhesive disc. The table for the disc sander features an adjustable table and miter gauge for accurate sanding of most angles. The disc operates at a no-load speed of 4400 rpm, while the sanding belt travels at 2600 feet per minute (fpm).

Bench Grinders: The customary design of such tools positions the electric motor in the center, with a shaft at each end to carry grindstones of different grit specifications, or cloth buffing discs and similar accessories. It is extremely important to shield the eyes from flying bits of metal and/or abrasive particles by means of safety glasses, a face shield or a plastic shield attached to the grinder. When doing extensive grinding on a single piece of metal, you'll want a container of water nearby for cooling the metal. Friction of grinding produces considerable amounts of heat. If the metal is overheated, it can lose the temper and/or burn your fingers.

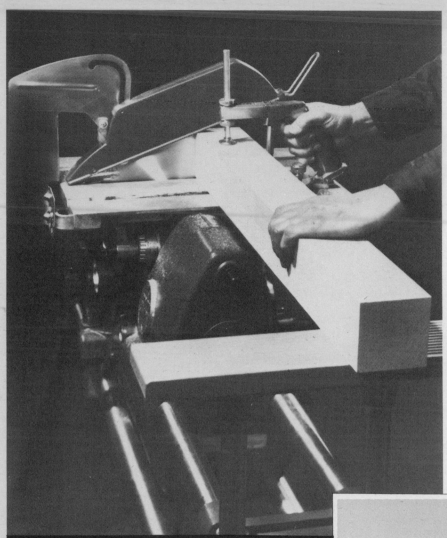

The Shopsmith Mark V system offers extreme versatility in power shop tools, since it converts quickly into your choice of a table saw, a 34" wood lathe, a drill press, a horizontal boring machine, or a 12" disc sander. Many other accessories are available for its use as a jointer/planer, belt sander and nearly every woodworking operation short of making toothpicks.

The Shopsmith Mark V: First of all, this is an elegant and capable thirty-four-inch wood lathe, but it's a lot of other things, as well. By quick and simple shifting of its basic components, it converts into a 16½-inch vertical drill press; a horizontal boring machine; a ten-inch table saw; and a twelve-inch disc sander. That's just the basic Shopsmith Mark V, as supplied. Additional accessories are available, powered off the motor that drives the Mark V, including an eleven-inch bandsaw; a four-inch jointer/planer; a six-inch belt sander; an eighteen-inch jigsaw; plus other attachments for shaping, routing and drum sanding.

The suggested retail price is about $1000 for the Shopsmith Mark V and standard accessories and they will provide a home-study course in woodworking and a power woodworking text for another $67 — prices are subject to change, of course.

From there, it ranges upward through seven plateaus of luxury to what they term The Ultimate Shop, currently quoted at $3264. For that figure, you fairly well get one each of everything, and your sole remaining problem would be to find room for it and keep track of it all. Descriptive literature is free on request from Shopsmith, Inc., 750 Center Drive, Vandalia, Ohio 45377.

Since the accompanying text was written, "Operation Up-Chuck" was brought to a successful conclusion, with the 580-pound 10x24" Jet metal lathe from Corbin hoisted onto the massive handmade bench — the top is solid wood, 4" thick! — secured, leveled and wired. The pair of hydraulic bottle jacks were used, with much careful planning and worry lest an earthquake should come along. Never put a penny in Dr. Richter's scale with a lathe up on blocks!

Metal Lathes: If a wood lathe is handy about the shop — as indeed they are! — a metal lathe is considerably more so. It is more or less possible to work metal on a wood lathe, given sufficient skill and patience, but it takes a lot of time and it is a freehand operation, as opposed to the admirable precision of regular metal lathes.

My small Edelstaal Unimat metal lathe is mentioned several times in other chapters, and it has seen extensive use. The Unimat, such as mine, is no longer available in the U.S.A. — it was made in Austria — and I have written to the current maker of the small lathe that is more or less the Unimat's replacement, called a Machinex, requesting a photograph of the new version for inclusion here. Unfortunately, after several months, I've had no response from the makers of the Machinex and, for reasons I'm about to discuss, I'm not inclined to buy a Machinex solely to photograph.

As the book at hand nears completion, I've added a 10x24-inch metal lathe to the shop equipment, as sold by Corbin Manufacturing & Supply, Box 758, Phoenix, Oregon 97535. Corbin offers a wide assortment of lathes, milling/drilling machines, power hacksaws, and similar shop equipment at remarkably favorable prices. Their price on the 10x24 inch lathe, for example, is something like $200 below the suggested retail price from the manufacturer. Their complete catalog of machine tools can be ordered at $1, postpaid, from the address given.

A rather frustrating state of affairs, just now, is that I'm so overly occupied in pushing this book to the last page and off to the roaring presses that I've had to sidetrack the lathe-raising project — officially designated as Operation Up-Chuck — until the book is done. When/if a second edition of *Home Workshop Digest* appears, as we hope it will, there should be some discussion therein on the coarse and fine points of metal lathe operation. At the moment of writing, I still feel a serious lack of expertise in the matter myself and, in poring over the various books available on lathe operations, I note a need for discussions that cover the anxious moments when the utter neophyte strives to cope effectively with the new tool. With any decent sort of luck, HWD-II will include something along such lines. I look forward to that, and I'm hoping you're the same!

SHARPENING EDGED TOOLS

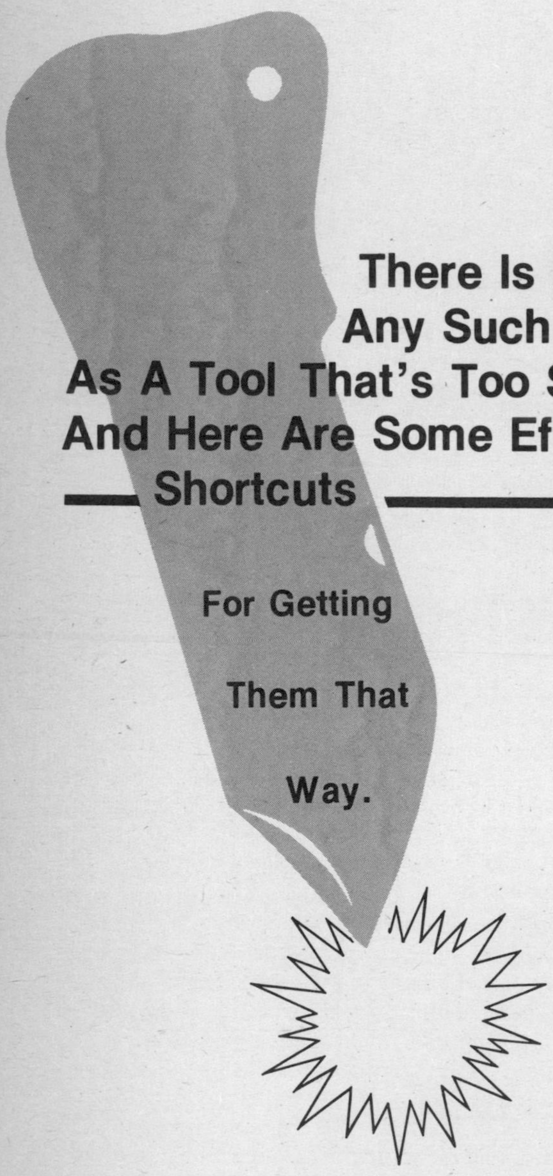

**There Is Hardly
Any Such Thing
As A Tool That's Too Sharp,
And Here Are Some Efficient
—— Shortcuts ——**

For Getting

Them That

Way.

Chapter 3

KNIVES, PLANES, chisels, and similar workshopper's tools work best when their edge is razor-keen. Once the edge is lost, restoring it to like-new condition, or perhaps even better, can present quite a formidable challenge. Sometimes, it seems, the harder you work to sharpen the blade, the duller it gets; which can be downright disconsolating.

There are several avenues and approaches that I've found helpful and the best choice may depend, to some extent, upon the nature and composition of the item you are sharpening.

Hardness, in steels, is rated on the Rockwell C-scale; with 58-62 RC considered about as hard as is practical for most purposes. Many steel tools, particularly the less expensive ones, are considerably softer; perhaps down in the 40-44 RC levels. The softer alloys tend to seem marvelously quick and easy to sharpen. The problem lies in the fact that they get dull again, at least as quickly and easily.

There are a great many sharpening aids and devices on the market, several of which are illustrated and described here. There are whetstones, India stones, Arkansas stones, Washita stones, grindstones, emery stones and similar terms too numerous to list. They vary considerably as to the roughness or smoothness of their surface. In theory, one uses a coarse stone to obtain the start of an edge, switching to a finer stone to complete it. In practice, this does not always work impressively well. Any edge that is not too hopelessly lost can be restored in a short time, using the finest (smoothest) stones available; that's provided the stone is used properly.

The key secret lies in the use of honing oil. At first glance, you'd think it silly to put oil on a sharpening stone, because you want to remove metal and oil would just reduce the friction, right? Wrong. Honing oil has little or no lubricating properties; its sole function is to keep the metal particles from filling the spaces between the working surface of the stone.

If you try to sharpen with the stone alone, even the best stone you can get, the pores of the stone fill with tiny metal particles quite quickly and it loses its bite against the blade. From that point on, the only thing you'll get out of further efforts at sharpening is exercise.

Put a few drops of honing oil on a small piece of rag and rub the surface of the stone with it briskly to loosen and remove the clogging particles. As you return to the project, your fingertips will telegraph an entirely different sensation as you feel the stone unmistakably biting into the edge. After a few strokes, check the edge with a cautious fingertip and the improvement should be clearly obvious.

Stroke first one side of the edge, then the other, bringing the stone surface against the edge, as if you were trying to peel thin slices off the stone. Start at the base of the blade, next to the handle, working out to the end or point with each stroke, in a wiping motion, as illustrated here. Continue with this approach until you can discern no further gain in sharpness, then move on to the strop, if it's indicated.

The strop in the accompanying photo is well over twenty years old, and it's worked hard, all the way. I'd be the last to term it a thing of beauty, but it works just great. It's an old scrap of thin, pliable scrap leather, salvaged from

Three typical small sharpening stones, with an Al Mar knife called "The Falcon," a can of honing oil and two small India stones, half-round and triangular in shape.

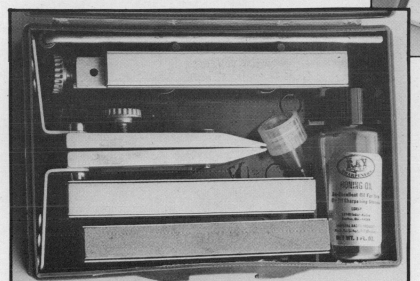

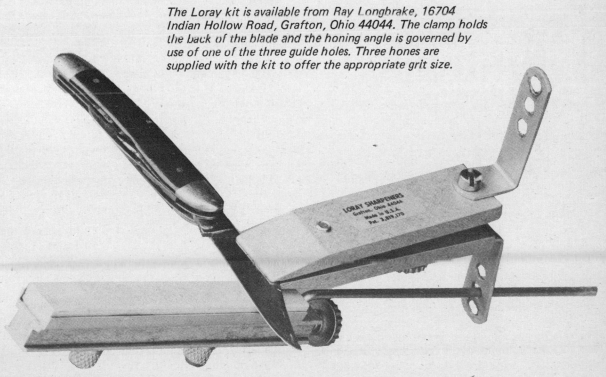

The Loray sharpening kit comes in this compact plastic carrying case. It's shown in use, below.

The Loray kit is available from Ray Longbrake, 16704 Indian Hollow Road, Grafton, Ohio 44044. The clamp holds the back of the blade and the honing angle is governed by use of one of the three guide holes. Three hones are supplied with the kit to offer the appropriate grit size.

the leftovers of a project my two older sons engaged in for Cub Scouts, 'way back when. I just attached it to an old scrap of board, rough side uppermost, rubbed some fine jeweler's rouge into the rough surface, and have been using it ever since, with great satisfaction.

In use, one end of the board is secured in the bench vise and the two sides of the edge are stroked along the rouge-impregnated leather, alternately. In this case, you pull the edge, rather than push it, as indicated by the arrows in the photos. If you've ever seen a barber stropping an old-fashioned straight razor, the procedure is much the same, and so are the results. In hardly over a minute, nearly any knife can be brought to the point where it will shave the hair off your arm, dry. Use extreme caution when doing

Jeweler's rouge was rubbed into the rough side of this piece of soft scrap leather and two C-clamps hold it to a piece of board. In use, the board is held in the bench vise by one end and blades are stropped in both directions.

Honing oil is not a lubricant, nor a preservative, but it is essential for successful sharpening since it keeps metal particles from clogging the pores of the sharpening stone.

this, however! As a better test, and a safer one, you can take a scrap of thin paper and try slicing it edgewise, as illustrated.

Cutting paper, by the way, is one of the quickest and surest ways to blunt an edge, even on the harder blades. On the other hand, some workers prefer to do their final stropping on a few thicknesses of mimeograph paper for the ultimate scalpel keeness.

When sharpening a blade, it is helpful — and sometimes quite important — to sharpen at the exact angle of the existing edge. This is especially true in such examples as plane blades or chisels. If you succumb to the temptation to increase the angle, so as to get the job done more quickly, you form a new edge, at a more obtuse angle, and it will not work as it did before unless you get it back to the original angle. Planes and chisels usually have a one-sided edge, with all the angle on one face and the opposite one dead-flat. To sharpen such an edge successfully, the flat side must not be compromised by taking a few angled strokes for the sake of getting done quickly. Doing so will greatly impair the tool's performance, even if you manage to get a truly ferocious edge on it. The shavings would just jam against the changed edge, instead of lifting smoothly in the intended manner.

My favorite sharpening instrument for knives and similar tools is the Case Moon Stick, so called because its slender rod is composed of a manmade substance that was developed as a highly heat-resistant coating for space capsules, to cope with the hellish temperatures encountered when entering atmosphere at trans-planetary velocities.

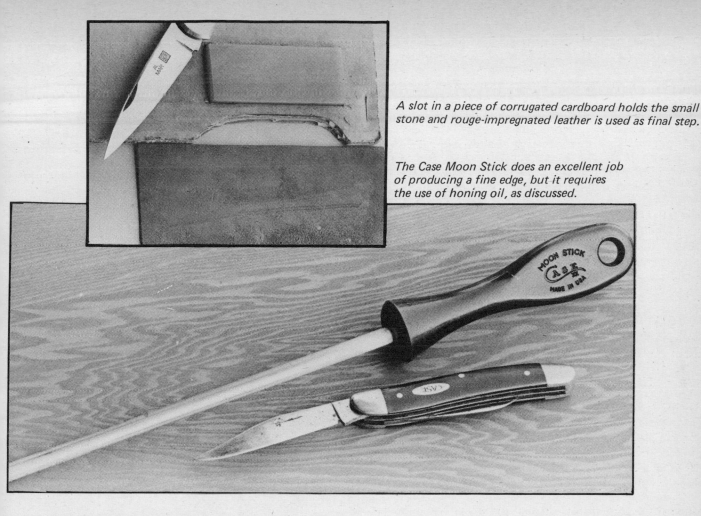

A slot in a piece of corrugated cardboard holds the small stone and rouge-impregnated leather is used as final step.

The Case Moon Stick does an excellent job of producing a fine edge, but it requires the use of honing oil, as discussed.

Much the same hard, white ceramic material is used in several similar sharpening systems such as the Crock Stick, also illustrated. They all work extremely well, but they must be used with honing oil for any pretense of efficiency.

You can make up a simple but effective hone by attaching suitable types of abrasive paper to a piece of wood or particle board, using contact cement and, when fastened down immovably, perhaps in two or three graduated coarse-medium-fine surfaces, such things can make quick, easy work of even such formidable tasks as sharpening an ax.

A piece of fine 3M WetOrDry paper, 400 or 600 grit, can be installed on an electric sander — oscillating or reciprocating — and the sander can be held in something such as the Black & Decker Workmate, with its working surface uppermost. By applying some honing oil to the paper and developing a judicious touch, at the proper angle, you may be able to establish at least a preliminary edge rather quickly on many different things that require sharpening.

A few years ago, I built the rotary stropping disc shown in the accompanying photos. An inexpensive arbor kit was purchased at the hardware store and a disc was cut from nominal one-inch white pine lumber, using the circle guide in the router. With the arbor installed in the wooden disc, slightly countersunk below the surface of the disc, I hit upon a quick and easy method to true it up perfectly flat and perpendicular to the axis of the arbor shaft. I just chucked it in the drill press and held a sheet of coarse sandpaper on the press bed, gently lowering the spinning disc down into contact with the sandpaper, switching to a finer grade of sandpaper after examination showed that the entire lower surface of the disc was uniformly ground flat.

A piece of scrap leather was fastened to the face of the disc with contact cement and trimmed flush with the edge. Once it was rotating, the exposed rough surface was impregnated by holding a piece of jeweler's rouge against it, alternating direction of rotation. I had mounted the disc in a 3/8-inch reversible Black & Decker electric drill and rigged the setup illustrated here to enable it to operate with the disc surface in a horizontal plane. As the Black & Decker drill is variable in speed, as well as reversible, it was simple to lock the trigger in operation and adjust the speed as desired.

As projects go, I carried the entire affair off in quite a satisfactory manner but, as sometimes seems to happen, after a short time I found myself going back to the familiar old piece of scrap leather on a hunk of board, without bothering to set up the fancy new rotary affair. When sharpening is done properly, as with the Case Moon Stick and a few drops of honing oil, I find I can get the edge within just a few whiskers of the desired sharpness and then it requires no more than a dozen strokes in each direction on the old strop.

A minor drawback of the rotary hone lies in its differential effect, if that's the proper term. Since the circumference of a circle on its outer surface is considerably larger than one farther in, there is a variation in speed and net distance traveled. As a result, it works on the edge unevenly; more on the outside and less on the inside. I discovered that after I'd gotten it all built but, by noting it here, perhaps I can save you all that bother.

Naturally, the edge is dragged rather than pushed across the spinning leather. If you were to hold the edge the wrong way, there's a considerable risk you might discover you'd invented and built a power knife-thrower; or perhaps a finger pruner. When using the rotary hone, I made it a firm habit to touch the surface of the leather with a fingertip to verify direction of rotation before bringing the tool edge cautiously into contact with it.

Tools such as hoes, shovels, scythes or grass-whips tend to get extremely dull, indeed, in normal use. There is a strong temptation to clamp such an item firmly in the vise and attack its edge with a flat file. I would have to counsel against this approach or at least urge great diffidence and caution in employing it. I have carried a prominent scar on my left hand, at the base of the index finger, since the summer of 1936, when I acquired it while trying to sharpen a hoe held in the vise, using a flat file. The file slipped and the luckless knuckle skidded along the edge which, by then, was quite sharp enough to grate against the bone. Take my word: It's an experience well worth going to great pains to avoid!

The better approach — at least for preliminary sharpening of such things, including the cutter blade from a rotary lawnmower — is to put on the face shield or safety glasses and use a power grinder. Either the conventional bench grinder, with two stones of different coarseness or a single grinding wheel in the chuck of the drill press works reasonably well. Most such edges need not be razor sharp and it would serve little purpose to try for that, since they'd only be blunted back in the first minute or so of further use.

To this point, we've said nothing about resharpening saws, either the straight, push-pull type or the circular variety. It can be done, I've seen it done, but have never tackled it, myself. Instead, I've adopted the approach of just buying a new circular blade of the same type and size when an old favorite becomes too obviously use-worn. Not the way to go? I couldn't agree more completely. Perhaps, one day, I'll undertake the resharpening of circular saw blades. When/if I do, I've got three or four dozen old, dull blades upon which to practice.

My need for sharpening straight hand saws is minimal, indeed, since I use such things only on the rarest of occasions. I have a small backsaw and a much tinier jeweler's saw and a rusty old saw that came with interchangeable blades off a bargain counter for perhaps $1.98, decades ago. Once, when setting up housekeeping in the latter Forties, I bought a good hand saw, made by Disston, and kept it around for several years. Once, while trying to cut a piece of wood, precariously clamped between my left knee and a stair bannister, I managed to earn another impressive scar on my left hand with it; near the base of the thumb, this time. When my oldest son, Chuck, was in the process of setting up housekeeping, he voiced a wistful longing for the old Disston and I bequeathed it to him on the spot.

On a recent encounter, Chuck noted that he'd taken the Disston in to be sharpened and the craftsman viewed it with open-mouthed reverence and asked where he'd gotten it. "You just can't get one like that, anymore," he assured

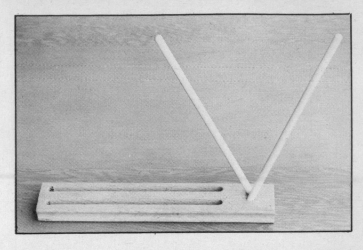

Crock-Stick sharpener positions two honing rods at an angle for sharpening alternate sides of the edge.

Wooden disc was fitted with an arbor having a ¼" shank and a circular piece of rouge-impregnated leather. It's held in a Black & Decker 3/8" drill that is variable and reversible.

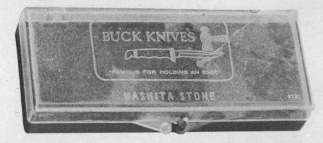

This is the plastic case for the Buck Washita stone that appears at the bottom of the opposite page, Despite their trademark, Buck doesn't recommend cutting bolts this way!

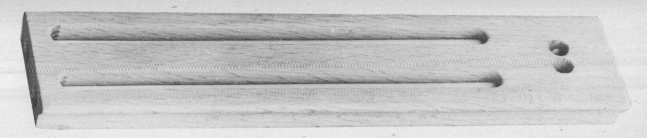

Crock-Stick on the opposite page takes down and stores in this manner, with a hole on the back to hang it from a nail.

Chuck, and he may be entirely correct, but it's been out of the shop for the better part of a decade now and I've yet to miss it in the slightest.

It was noted elsewhere that I bought a sharpening jig for drill bits several years ago and have yet to use it. That does not imply that I never sharpen a drill bit, for I do so fairly frequently; the bits designed for use on wood, that is. I sometimes use a drill bit intended for metal when drilling wood, if there is no other way to get a hole just that size, but I blush faintly when doing so.

I have at least one each of all the available sizes of the nice little wood bits made by Stanley, ranging by eighths from 3/8 through 1-inch and, in some sizes, I have more than one. These are eminently admirable, a bit expensive and, in the local area, they seem to be stocked only in the K-Mart stores, of all unlikely outlets. In some diameters, I have more than one for the simple reason that, as received, they seem to drill holes slightly larger than the nominal diameter. For example, a ¾-inch dowel is a sloppy fit in a hole made with the ¾-inch Stanley bit, despite the fact that the dowel mikes .750-inch, dead on the nose (You're right: That's unusual in itself!). So I chucked one ¾-inch bit in the little Unimat lathe and worked it down, painstakingly, resharpening its delicate edge after reduction of the major diameter, using a half-round India stone, honing oil and a lot of patient, dainty strokes, pausing every little while to try a test hole in pieces of scrap wood, until a piece of dowel, inserted and pulled out smartly, gave an audible pop of displaced air.

Properly finished and sharpened, the set of Stanley auger bits produce holes that are a joy and wonder to behold, with sides that are simply glassy-smooth. Once you coax and cajole them into boring holes the same diameter as stamped on the shanks, they're even greater.

Here, C-clamps and an angle bracket are used to position the power-stropping disc horizontally. In use, it's turned on, adjusted for speed and reversed for use on other side.

Buck Washita stone is a natural mineral, cut and finished to shape.

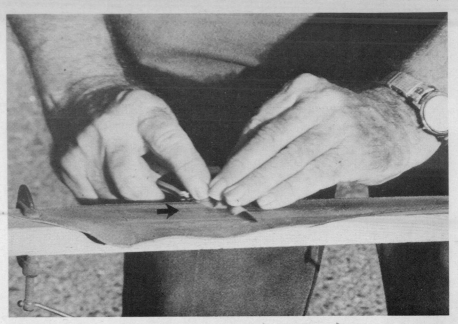

In stropping, the edge is "dragged" rather than using the pushing or slicing approach customarily with stones.

When the rotary strop is turning, it's best to touch it lightly with a fingertip to verify direction of its rotation before holding the blade to it, to prevent digging in the edge and possibly injuring yourself.

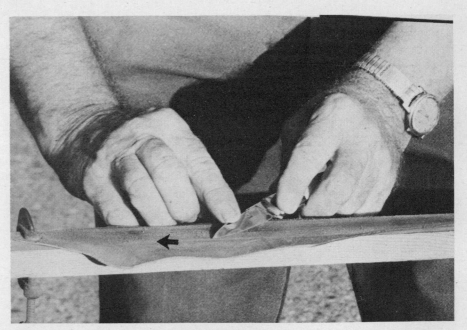

Here and in the photo immediately above, arrows show the direction in which the knife is moved when stropping.

Pencil point indicates the cutting shoulder on the Stanley Power Bore drill bit that benefits from careful honing and shaping to size.

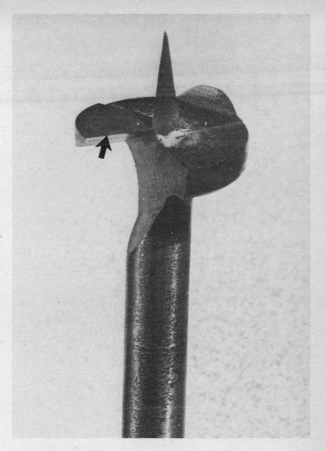

Arrow points to the second edge of the Stanley Power Bore bit. This removes wood freed by the outer edge and likewise needs sharpening.

Long since, I've built up a collection of the Irwin spade-type bits, in every available diameter from ¼-inch through 1½ inches and, again, the set is something I simply could not do without. They do get dull after prolonged use, however, particularly when employed on tough materials such as particle board, and they benefit from sharpening. As was discussed regarding blades of planes and chisels, this is another angled-to-straight edge and it's fatal to good performance if you turn the vertical face of the edge in, even ever so slightly. Work on the angle, matching it as closely as you can, using the flat face of the half-round India stone and some honing oil, reapplied as needed. Take care not to grind one side lower than the other, of course.

Lathe cutter bits usually carry an extremely obtuse edge — that is, comprising a rather large angle, though by no means greater than ninety degrees! — but they need to be sharp, for all that. When a lathe bit shows signs of having gone dull, I take it over to the bench vise and use an extremely fine-grained little white stone and plenty of honing oil and a lot of patient elbow-grease, with occasional squints at the progress through a jeweler's loupe (surely one of the most indispensible wee gadgets around the shop), until it looks sharp again. Maintaining the proper angle is crucially important in this instance.

It goes without saying that, once you've acquired the fine knack of sharpening shop tools, you can use the same basic techniques to put a shaving edge on the kitchen cutlery for the lady of the household. Don't do so without duly advising her, however. As an example of the bad things that could happen, she might attack a tomato, onion or cucumber, never suspecting the knife edge now rivals a surgeon's pet scalpel, and you might end up having to do the dishes for the next couple of weeks while the wound heals. The probable dialogue resulting from such an occurrence would be well worth avoiding, too...

Honing oil and the well-worn India stone in half-round pattern work well for restoring the superb cutting ability of the Stanley Power Bore bits.

MEASURING,

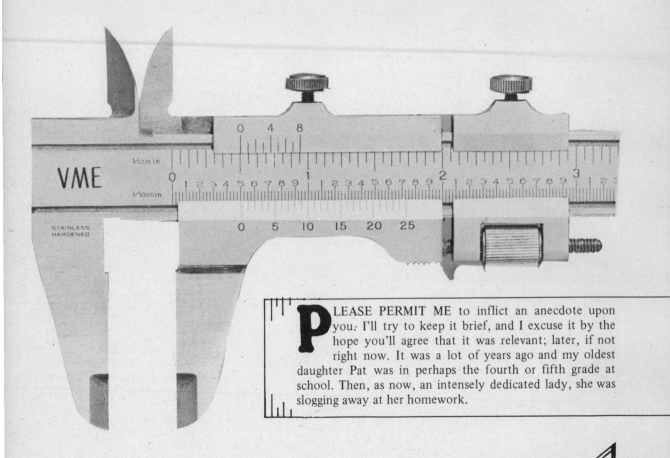

PLEASE PERMIT ME to inflict an anecdote upon you. I'll try to keep it brief, and I excuse it by the hope you'll agree that it was relevant; later, if not right now. It was a lot of years ago and my oldest daughter Pat was in perhaps the fourth or fifth grade at school. Then, as now, an intensely dedicated lady, she was slogging away at her homework.

MARKING

AND LAYOUT

The Highest Possible Degree Of Precision In This Critical Phase Can Make A Lot Of Difference In The Excellence Of The Final Product

Chapter 4

Opposite page, the business end of Grennell's favorite vernier caliper, capable of measuring to the nearest .001" for slightly over five inches, inside, outside, steps and depth, as needed.

Above, an inexpensive steel rule, graduated in several different scales, including centimeters and millimeters.

"Are measurements always exact and precise, or only approximate?" she wanted to know.

My visceral response was direct and effortless, but I got up and went over and peered intently at the question as it appeared on the work sheet. She had quoted it flawlessly.

One of my basic mottoes is, "Never trust a suspicious person." I scented entrapment and responded accordingly.

First off, I assured her that any and all measurements are precise only to some given degree or extent.

I explained about the manufacturing tolerances usually set forth on blueprints, where a machinist might be able to turn out a shaft that was up to .001-inch oversize, or .0015-inch undersize, and it would still be passed by the inspector as acceptable.

The Mayes "Squangle," an adjustable square and/or triangle capable of several jobs, per instructions.

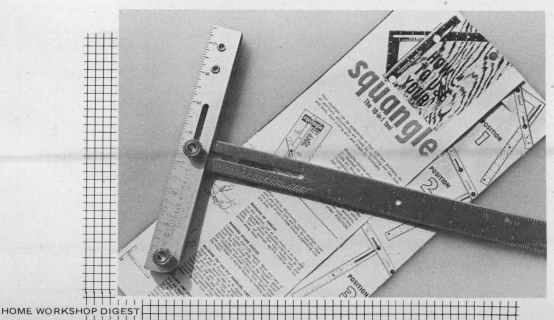

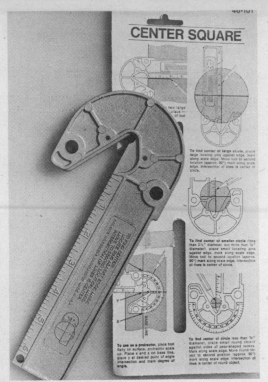
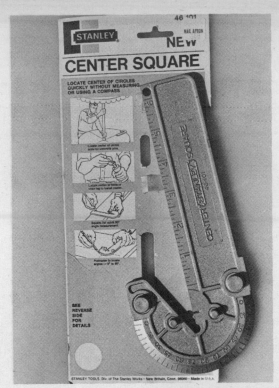

Front and back views of the Stanley No. 46-101 center square, with the packing card that carries suggestions and instructions for its use. It can be used as a conventional square, or for finding the centers of circles, as a protractor, and similar uses.

I dug out my micrometer and showed her how easy it is to split inches into thousandths, or even ten-thousandths. We used the micrometer to measure the thickness of a hair, a sheet of paper, and a few things like that. I pointed out that even here we were only measuring the approximate average thickness across the quarter-inch circle spanned by the jaws of the mike, and were not able to allow for the compression effect of the micrometer jaws upon the slightly yielding medium being measured.

I then showed her how things get bigger as they grow warmer and smaller as they cool, pointing out that no matter how insanely accurately you measured something, it would get longer, shorter, thinner, thicker, wider, narrower, whatever, just as soon as its temperature changed by even so much as a fraction of a degree.

Measuring weight proved even more formidable. I tore off a small piece of paper and we dropped it onto the bathroom scale; not even the faintest quiver. I put it on the pan of a sensitive scale that had been balanced before and it tilted the beam impressively. Re-balancing the beam, I had her write her name on the paper with a soft lead pencil, put it back on the pan and we were able to weigh her signature in tenths of a grain (equal to 1/70,000 of a pound).

I went into it more thoroughly, but I promised to spare

Those who reload cartridge cases need and use scales of exceptional precision and sensitivity for weighing powder and such operations. This Model 5-0-5 scale, from RCBS, weighs to 505 grains in tenth-grain increments. A grain is 1/7000-pound.

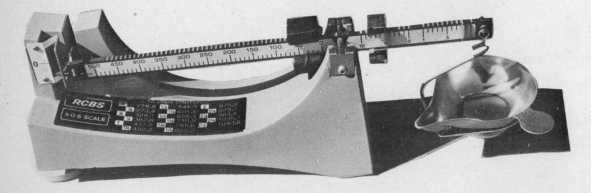

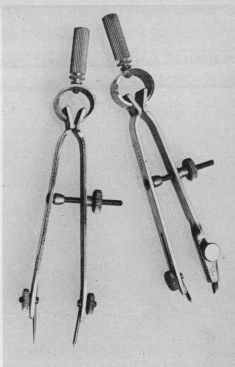

If you wish to lay out non-circular curves, as for cutting with a scroll saw, the inexpensive draftsman's French curves, such as those above, can prove a handy way to do it smoothly.

Draftsman's dividers and lead-point compass are useful for picking up or laying out dimensions, finding centers as detailed four pages later and for many other employments.

you the nittier details. Suffice to say, she wrote down, "Only approximate," which I considered a pretty concise summation of my lecture.

Next evening, she came home considerably perturbed. "Miss Bray marked that wrong," she revealed, "You know what she said?"

I told her I'd be interested to hear.

"She said measurements were always exact and precise, otherwise how could they build houses. I was the only kid in class who had it wrong, and everybody laughed at me."

A couple of decades later, the recollection still makes me

want to grit my teeth and kick inoffensive things. Where I erred, of course, was that I hewed to the answer I thought – knew! – was right and ignored the practical step of considering what was the most likely answer that the questioner had in mind. All measurements in building houses are exact and precise? Balderdash and birdlime! Stucco and plaster cloak a multitude of slovenly measuring. Check your own house, any house at all, and see if you don't come around to agreement with that.

One is tempted to issue the flat statement that there is no such thing as too much precision, and striving for the ultimate obtainable is the only way to go. With idealism a

A dial caliper, such as this one from Brownell's of Montezuma, Iowa, uses a pointer to indicate the finer increments, sparing the operator the slightly eye-straining chore of squinting to see which pair of vernier lines match on the scale.

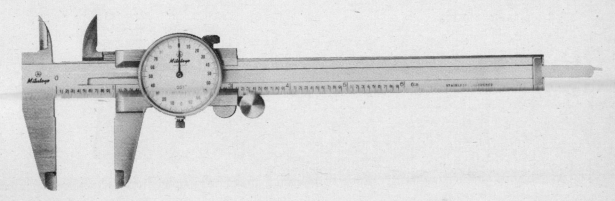

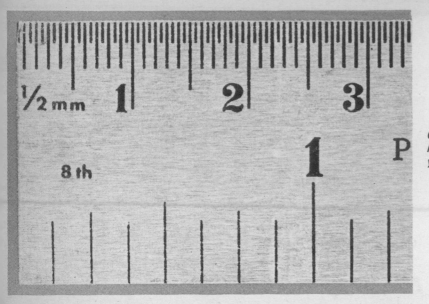

Close looks at various scales on the Pioneer No. 3200 steel rule. Would you say that first ½mm was shy?

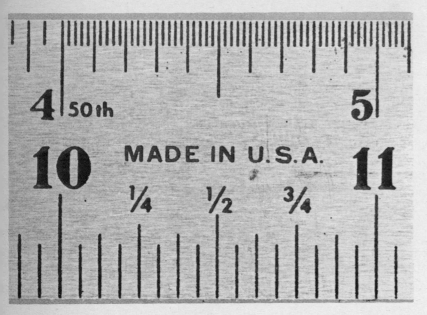

A few inches are ruled in tenths and fiftieths; a fairly handy system.

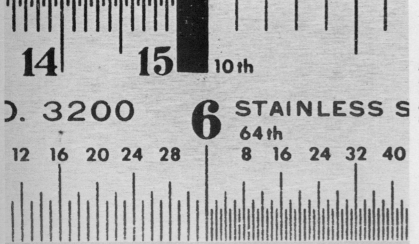

Breaking inches into 1/32s and 1/64s is a rather tedious and precarious way of handling dimensions. See how quickly you can find 29/64 as an example of the twisty complications.

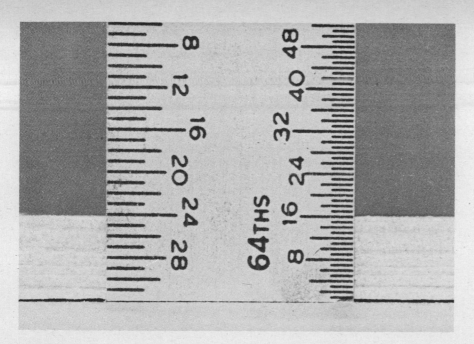

Here, and in later photos, we'll be measuring the thickness of the same little strip or planklet, made up on the table saw. Note the slight variation when using two different scales on opposite ends of the same small steel rule. It's obviously fairly close to ¼-inch, or 2/8, 4/16, 8/32, 16/64, and so on, but is the measurement "exact and precise?"

bit less fanatical, however, it soon becomes apparent that, for any given project, there is a level of precision that is practical and necessary. Further precision beyond that is a waste of time, effort and attention.

Consider: If you are trimming the bark off a length of tree trunk, bent upon making a fencepost of it, there is no urgent need for the resulting post to be dead cylindrical to .0001-inch or less. Irregularities of an inch or more would be entirely acceptable in such an application.

If you're grinding an objective lens for a telescope, or fashioning a replacement balance wheel for a lady's wristwatch, tolerances become a great deal more critical. It's largely a question of sensible and realistic proportion. As a rough rule of thumb, we can say if it fits and works, it's okay and if it looks good, that's even better.

At one or more other places in this book, I make faintly caustic comments about carpenter's steel squares, noting that I have seldom if ever encountered one that was an actual, honest ninety degrees between one leg and the other. It is a simple thing to verify. Take two, put both shorter sides on a flat surface and bring the two long sides together. If both are a true ninety degrees, the long vertical edges will fit each other perfectly, top to bottom. If they're both 89 degrees, the edges will be farther apart at the top and if they're both 91 degrees, the gap will be at the bottom. Needless to say, if you happen to grab one 89 and one 91, they'll appear to match perfectly.

With nothing but a straightedge, scribe or pencil, and a set of dividers or a compass, it's possible to construct an accurate line at right angles to another line from a given point. Step one: draw a circle with the selected point as its center. The circle can be of any convenient diameter, as can the remaining arcs drawn in the remaining steps of the basic geometrical operation.

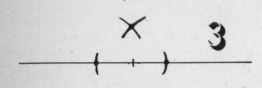

In step two, intersections of the circle give us two points on the line, equidistant from the selected point. Placing the point of the compass precisely on each in turn, we scribe a pair of short arcs so as to intersect above the selected point, step three.

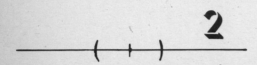

So there's a second acid test for detecting not-quite-right angles. For this, you need a straightedge equal to at least twice the length of the short side, and a flat surface as long as the long side, perhaps with a piece of paper. Put the short edge of the square to the straightedge and scribe a fairly fine line down along the long edge. Now flop the square over, with the other side down, and re-position the shorter arm to the straightedge and bring the long arm back to rule another line down the long arm, as closely as possible to the first line.

If the two lines are — or appear to be — exactly parallel throughout their length, you have encountered that unlikely rarity, a really square square, and I suggest that you buy it.

In step four, a line is ruled through the initial starting point and the intersection of the constructed arcs. In theory, this creates a perfect ninety-degree angle. In actual practice, the accuracy of the angle depends upon the precision of the lines.

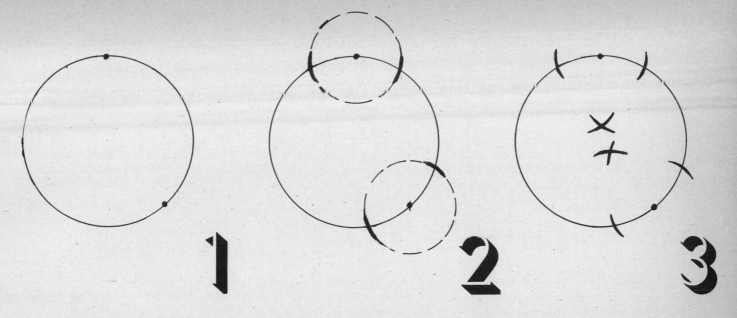

Finding the center of a circle is done in much the same manner. Step one: select two points, a convenient distance apart. Step two: draw circles from those points to form arcs with circle circumference. Step three: position compass point at each intersection in turn to scribe intersecting arcs, as illustrated.

The same flop-and-try procedure makes short work of establishing the bona fides of most similar instruments. In my own experience, a good draftsman's T-square, or draftsman's triangles at price levels somewhat above the cheapest, tend to be as close to the prescribed angles as I usually need, so I lean to using them, rather than the bargain-counter carpenter's squares from the local hardware store.

Let me hasten to add that a good carpenter's square (preferably one at a true ninety degrees, which may be far from cheap) can do a lot more than scribe right angles, in skilled hands, I have watched in humble awe as skilled sheet metal workers performed arcane miracles of layout with nothing but a steel square, a set of trammel points, a scratch awl and perhaps a cud of Plowboy, laying out complex compound curves that, when bent up, form segments of a round elbow or similar topological feats of magic.

I am not about to turn all this into a treatise on elementary geometry, but I will try to crank in a few illustrations showing how a straightedge and a compass or even a pair of dividers can be used to construct an accurate right angle, or to find the center of a circle of any diameter. Such things are handy to have in reserve.

For measuring, transferring or laying out given dimensions, several devices are available and more or less suited to a number of purposes. Let's discuss a few of these, along with the virtues and shortcomings of each.

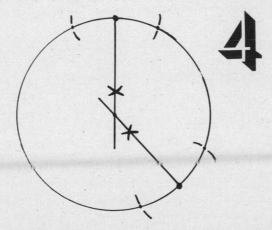

STEP 4

Step four: scribe lines between the starting points and intersections of the two sets of constructed arcs. Lines cross at the center of the circle. If you're curious to test your accuracy, make a third set and see if its line intersects the first two.

Ward & Harrington

NAIL APRON

Three sets of scales, as discussed in the text. Reading from the top down, Grennell's pocket tape in both inches and centimeters, the lumberyard meterstick, and a fairly typical wooden yardstick. All are useful, depending on the need for precision and the degree required. There are 25.4mm to the inch, or you could call 1mm 1/25.4-inch, if you wish.

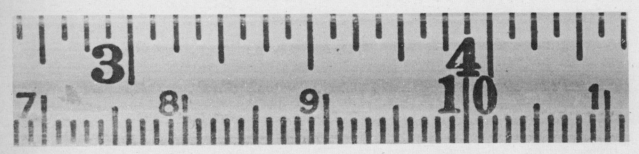

Here's a closer look at the double-gaited scale, at about 3.75 diameters magnification. It offers a quick and quite effortless means of comparing and converting the two systems, with acceptable precision. 100mm=3-15/16 inches, right?

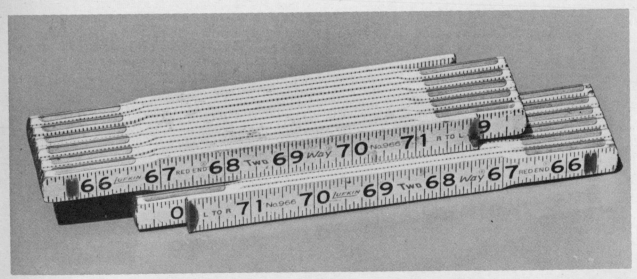

Above and on the facing page are views of the Lufkin No. 966 Red End folding rules, which are of the inside-reading design. These rules are quite decently accurate down to 1/16-inch, and finer fractions can be interpolated fairly well.

No, that's not one folding rule reflected in a mirror! Depending upon the side you start from, you've a choice of having the numbers read from right to left, or vice versa. You'll find many applications where this proves a great convenience.

At the bottom, in terms of sophistication and out-of-pocket cost, we have the lumberyard yardstick, usually offered as an advertising premium at no cost, with the firm's name in big letters. Usually, these are graduated to 1/8-inch, and most of them are fairly close to the money, especially in view of their cost.

A few years ago, a local lumber yard was passing out metersticks, graduated in millimeters and centimeters on one side and the usual inches by 1/8-inch increments on the other. The firm has changed hands and the new owners discontinued the practice, making me wish I'd collected a few more when they were available.

In general, I view the metric system with considerable askance, but I've become rather addicted to the speed, precision and convenience of using those metersticks. When using inches, as you get down into the thirty-seconds and sixty-fourths and beyond, keeping track can become pretty doggoned eye-crossing and, what's worse, you can miscount and be off by a few notches.

The same old patternmaker who passed me the tip on the efficient way to use sandpaper (discussed at the end of the chapter on making big ones out of little ones) divulged a further bit of useful wisdom: "Always measure it at least twice before you cut it once." Many times in the years since then, I've been grateful for his good advice, or chagrined that I'd neglected to follow it.

Properly cared for and given occasional applications of light oil at the folding joints, a quality folding rule will serve you well for many years. These have been in regular use for well over twenty years and remain almost as good as new.

The Lufkin steel tape below measures to eight feet, by 1/16 and 1/32-inch graduations, with feet numbered every 12 inches.

Many times around the shop, you'll find yourself wanting a closer, keener look at some item or phase of an operation. At such times, a simple magnifying glass can be extremely helpful and, at times, absolutely indispensible, if you can remember where you put it the last time you had to use it!

Beyond the delightfully inexpensive yardsticks and metersticks, we have the folding rules and retractable steel tapes. I still have a pair of Lufkin folding rules, souvenirs of the long-ago days when I sold such items to sheet metal shops of eastern Wisconsin. These are of the type called inside reading, meaning that the part you don't choose to unfold remains topside and out of the way. I've yet to think of any reason why I'd want an outside reading version.

Most retractable steel tapes, in the sizes designed to be carried in the pocket or clipped to the belt, extend to six

It takes a bit of training to master the knack of holding a jeweler's loupe, such as these two, in your clenched eyebrow, but these are unexcelled for providing close views

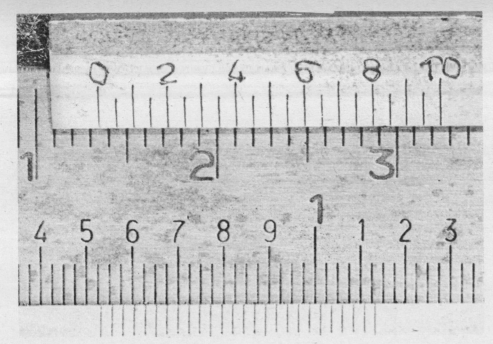

Here are the metric (top) and inch vernier scales of a multilingual caliper calibrated for both systems. The measurements here would be 13.5mm, or .531-inch. Details of the technique for reading vernier scales follow shortly under photos.

feet, or perhaps to eight feet. Beyond that, one usually goes to a cloth tape, of larger size, with a hand crank on the side for winding it back into the case again. Such cloth tapes go to fifty feet, some to considerably more. One six-foot steel tape that I particularly prize and appreciate goes to six feet and it's graduated on one edge in inches to the sixteenth and, on the other edge, in millimeters and centimeters. Thus you've a choice of using either unit of measure and, as frosting on the cake, you've an instant conversion chart back and forth between the two. Seventeen inches is quite close to either 43.2 centimeters or 432 millimeters; ninety centimeters is 35-7/16 inches, and comparable conversions are lightning quick.

Another measuring instrument I'd rate as indispensible is the vernier caliper. I've accumulated a few of these, including one that's my favorite and I go out of my gourd when I can't put hands upon it. I'm not going to try to set forth the principles of its use here, because it can be done much more simply and clearly by means of captions beneath photos. The point is that the vernier, a good one, enables you to measure down to about .001-inch (one-one-thousandth of one inch), which is close enough

Here's our same little slab of wood, from a few pages back, being checked with a well worn and inexpensive Stanley No. 136 pocket caliper, which puts its size at just a hair under ¼-inch. Now check photo at right.

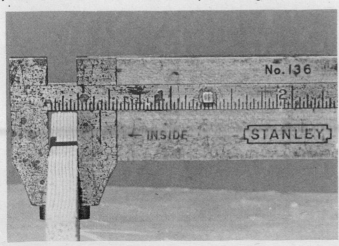

With the vernier calipers, we can pin the thickness down to just .241-inch, close enough for most common needs. The zero is just past the line of .225, not quite to .250, and the vernier matches lines at 16: .225 + .016 = .241"

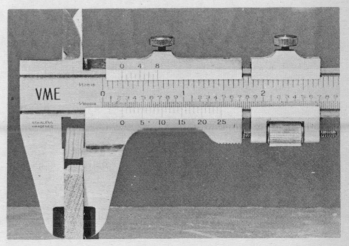

The principle of the vernier caliper is that only one of the lines in the long scale at the bottom lines up exactly with the line above it and the corresponding number on the lower scale is the number of 1/1000″ to be added to the dimension to the left of the zero-line. Upper scale is in 1/16″ and fine graduations are 25/1000″ each or .025″, as usually given. So we have here .475″, plus a trifle over halfway to the .500″ line. On the vernier, line 20 aligns exactly, so it's .475 + .020″, for a total net dimension of .495″. Now, we'll give it a tiny twitch and try it again in the photo at the bottom of the page.

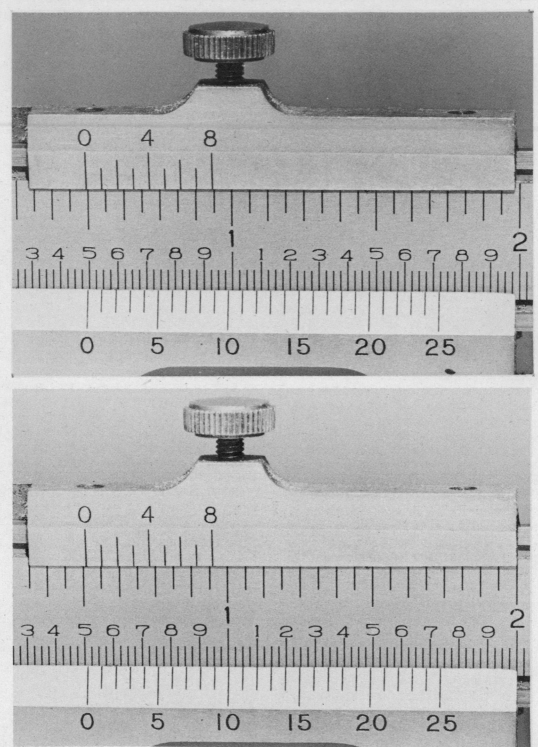

Here, the zero-line is just past the .500″ mark, but not to the one that would represent .525″. Line 10 is close, but line 11 is dead on the money, so we add .500 + .011″ and arrive at our actual dimension of .511″. Fairly simple, isn't it?

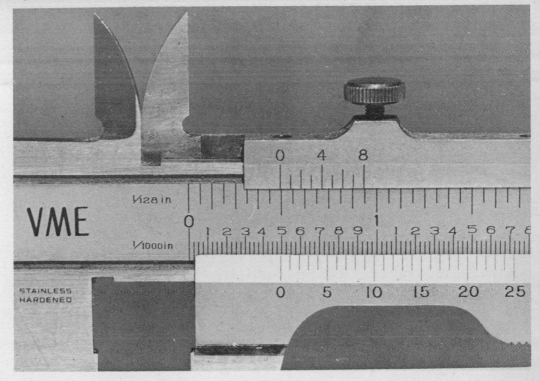

Here's an overall view of the calipers at the same setting shown on the upper photo, opposite page, to help clarify where we were getting that figure of .475" plus a little, as our starting point. Now let's zoom in for a close look. See photo below.

for just about any woodworking operation, as well as for a lot of metalworking.

In addition, the vernier caliper measures outside diameter, inside diameter and functions as a depth-micrometer, for good measure, all as illustrated in the accompanying photos. A comparable model is graduated in both inches and metric scale, enabling measurement to the nearest one-tenth-millimeter (about 1/254-inch).

If you've reached that dubious point where "your eyes are just fine, but your arms are too short," a jeweler's loupe or similar magnifier can be of great help. In fact, once you master the minor challenge of learning to hold the loupe in place with your eyebrow, it becomes yet one more of those absolutely indispensible items around the shop, reducing you almost to tears if you can't recall where you put it the last time you used it. Curiously enough, though I'm almost ambidextrous in the hands (out of sheer self defense), I'm strictly right-eye-browed. I can hold the loupe in the right eye with ease, but I'm totally unable to do it with the left eye.

If you prefer not to have to keep track of loupes or magnifiers, dial-type calipers are available with a little needle that goes around and around, pointing to the appropriate number, all the while. Provided your arms are long enough to let you read the numbers on the dial, you've got it made.

In the chapter on making a table, we touch briefly upon the use of the vernier caliper for precision fitting of wooden dowel joint reinforcements. The probe was used to determine the exact depth of the corresponding holes and the two depths were added to serve as the ideal length of

We had said that line 20 was the one that came closest to matching the line above it. Take a careful look and see if you don't agree. Both lines 19 and 21 are visibly just a tiny tad short of a perfect match.

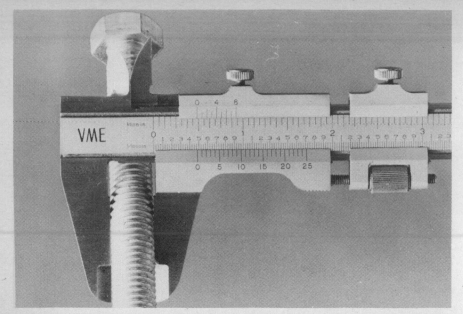

Here, we're checking the outside diameter (OD) of a bolt with ½-13 National Coarse (NC) threads. The diameter appears close to .485".

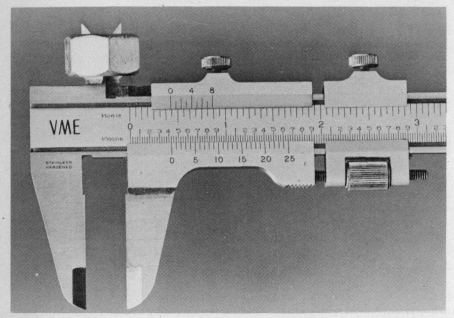

Checking the inside diameter (ID) of the nut that fits the bolt above, it looks like .425" or perhaps .426". This would correspond to the minor thread diameter and the figure for the bolt would be the major diameter, if you're a bit confused because they vary.

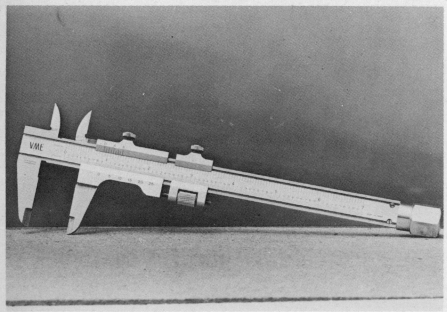

The caliper is in use here to check the depth of a hole by means of the projecting probe at the end. Depth is dead on the money at .900".

A closer look at the business end of the calipers when used as a depth gauge in the bottom photo, opposite page. The item being measured is one of the handmade acorn nuts turned out on the small Edelstaal Unimat lathe from aluminum hex stock.

the dowel section. The total of the two lengths was set up on the vernier caliper and that, in turn, was used as the guide for scribing the thinnest possible mark with a knife edge on the side of the dowel, for cutting to size with the table saw. After cutting, the net length was checked again with the vernier calipers and it was shortened slightly by holding the end of the dowel piece against the belt sander, if necessary. That was a case where it was permissible to be minus the specified length by a thin trifle, but any excess length was unacceptable, since it would have served to keep the major joining surfaces slightly out of contact.

When tolerances are not too screamingly obsessive, I mark and lay out the lines and dimensions with a pencil. I tend to prefer the Venus Col-Erase for this purpose, and I keep them in several appropriate colors, all together in a tin can that's supposed to stay in one place and no other. I have a small and rather battered mechanical pencil sharpener, with a vacuum mounting base that's actuated by a half-turn of a little lever to lock it immovably to any smooth surface long enough to put a fresh needle point on the marking pencils.

The thing about pencils for layout lines is that a pencil mark has a perceptible width; nearly always at least .025-inch and often considerably more. If you can live with tolerances of that magnitude, a pencil will serve the purpose well. In the example of the nicely fitted dowels, .025-inch was unacceptably gross, so I used the finest knife-edge mark I could manage.

As discussed in the text, here are the two scratch awls, with the purchased one at the top and Grennell's handmade version with the Maple Avenue maple handle and a bit made from .125'' music wire by the technique that is described.

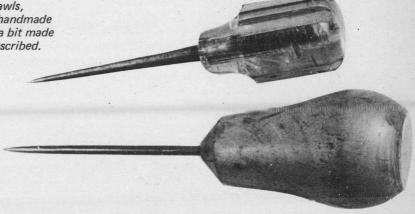

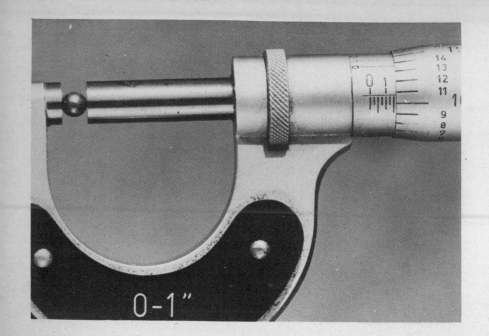

A micrometer, such as this 0-1"
model, is hard to beat for precision
measurement. We have this little
ball bearing and it looks to be
.160" not quite .161". The question
is: How much bigger than .160"?

Another useful tool for precise scribing is the scratch awl, which leaves a hair-fine line and doesn't require frequent re-sharpening. I have two of these, stored side by side, in their prescribed (unintentional, unavoidable pun; please forgive?) places. One is a perfectly serviceable store-bought item, with sturdy shaft and plastic handle. The other has more personal origins and, probably because of that, it's the one I usually tend to grab when such a tool is

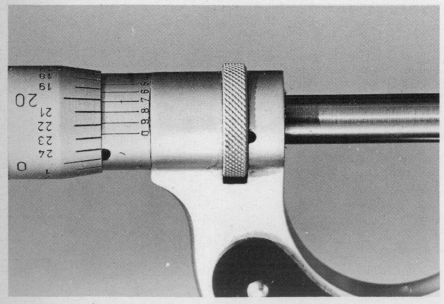

So we roll it over and take a look
at the vernier scale etched on the
shaft, part of which is visible in
the photo above. It's the 8 line that
matches, so we add .0008 to the
.160" for a total diameter of .1608".

Here's the same "mike," set at a pretty doggoned close approximation of ¼" or, as we'd say in decimal parlance, .2500". We check and make sure the vernier stands at 0.

And here, we've dollied in for a still closer look at the scale, same setting as photo at left. Each little mark on the barrel is .025" and the collar is graduated with 25 numbered lines. One revolution advances .025", exactly.

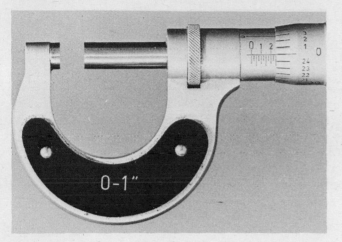

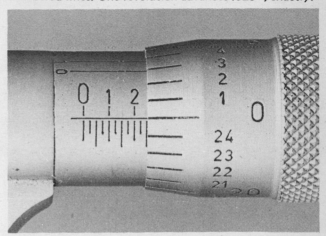

needed. A lot of years ago, I lived in an improbable Midwestern community, on a quiet cul-de-sac called Maple Avenue, with a lovely rock maple tree growing next to the driveway. In the spring, it supplied us with super-luscious syrup and, in the storms of summer, an occasional branch would blow off. I'd salvage those and trim off the larger pieces for patient seasoning and conversion into useful raw materials for the big Delta wood lathe that lurked in the basement.

So the second scratch awl has a handmade handle of genuine Maple Avenue rock maple, with a bit created by cutting off a short section of .125-inch music wire, chucking it into the ¼-inch electric drill and rotating it against the side of the grinding wheel while it was spinning also, thereby creating a nicely symmetrical, tapered needle point. Music wire, in assorted useful diameters, is stocked

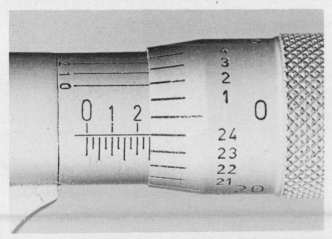

Here, we're just .0010" short of .2500" which would make it .2490" or .2250" + .0240" = .2490"; fairly simple, right?

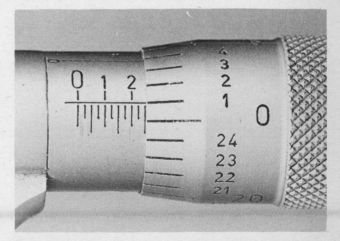

Turning the collar to .0010" in the other direction gives us .2500" + .0010" to total out at .2510"; see how easy?

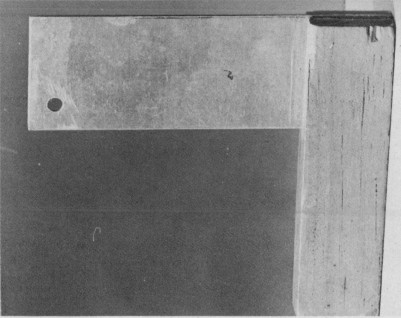

Here's the little homemade square, mentioned in the text. A piece of .064" aluminum was fastened into a saw cut in the piece of wood, using aluminum paste and a drafting triangle to assure a 90-degree fit.

Checked against a plastic drafting triangle, the square shows no detectable amount of angular variation on a flat surface.

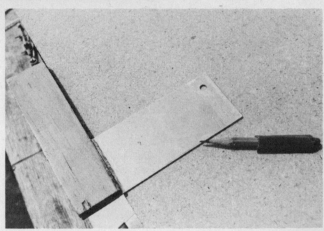

A further way to verify that a square is really square is to use it for ruling a line, as here, then flop to rule another line.

Left, the two lines, ruled as above, with a blue Col-Erase pencil on a piece of particle board are as close to parallel as one might desire, suggesting that it passed the test.

Above, using a pair of dividers to pick up a dimension off the steel rule for transfer to the workpiece. Would you believe it's our old friend, 29/32"? Hey, would I kid you?

This is the homemade center scribing tool which, as discussed, seems to be a bit off, but three lines from it will enclose a triangle and the center of that can be judged.

and sold by stores specializing in model airplanes and allied supplies. You can do a lot of useful things with the stuff.

My original point was that tools you make for yourself tend to see a considerable amount of use through sheer, unadulterated chauvinism. I've never gone all that far overboard on the home toolmaking kick, but the few I've made seem to get a lot of use, even when there is a comparable commercial item nearby that looks nicer.

Another of the few examples of such artifacts is a tiny square I constructed out of a scrap of .064-inch aluminum sheet and a scrap of nominal one-inch board. I scrounged up a circular saw blade with a kerf close to .064-inch, cut a slot midway through one end of the piece of wood scrap, and used aluminum paste to secure the blade in place, as positioned by a draftsman's triangle. Down the many years since then, it has continued to turn out ninety-degree angles within tolerances I regard as acceptably close and — you guessed it, eh? — I tend to use it quite frequently.

It's not at all uncommon to find yourself confronted with the problem of locating the precise center of a circle; on the end of a piece of wooden dowel, for example. There are various commercial devices for the purpose, such as the one from Stanley, illustrated here, and they seem to work quite well. Another homemade solution to the recurring problem is illustrated, also. The latter, I blush to admit, never seems to get a line quite through the center of a round workpiece, but you can scribe a few lines and they will outline the center with sufficient precision to let you stab a guide-mark with the scratch awl (guess which one?)

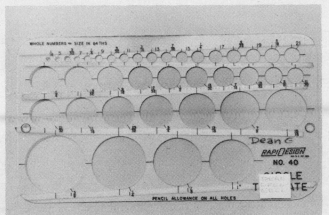

Here's another item used by draftsmen that often proves handy around the shop for laying out circles and checking ahead of time when planning to drill a hole of given diameter to make sure that it's just where wanted. At that point, the lines can be marked to pinpoint the center of the circle. A small prickmark with the scratch awl at that point will aid in getting the point of the drill bit exactly centered.

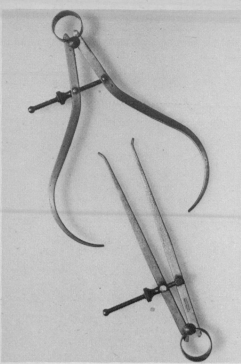

A set of inside and outside calipers can be used to pick up a dimension from a workpiece for measurement against a steel rule, micrometer, or similar tool. Calipers can reach a great many places not readily accessible to rules.

A bevel gauge can be adjusted to any desired angle and locked at that setting. Here's it being set at an angle of 45 degrees, against that angle on a draftsman's triangle.

right in the middle as a point to hit with the descending drill bit on the drill press.

It's a sad fact to contemplate, but all your hard-quested precision goes for nothing-much if you measure and mark with deadly accuracy and then proceed to cut or drill in a slovenly, "shipslod" manner to the line or point. Mindful of all that, some while ago I purchased one of the little student reading lamps, directing a concentrated light beam of fairly fierce intensity upon a small area. I located this on the main workbench, just to the left of the movable table on my venerable and battle-scarred drill press. When the time comes to sink a hole, the first thing I do is to switch on the little light to bathe the workpiece in a more-than-adequate illumination. That strategy is predicated upon the fairly plausible trusim that, "if you can't see 'em, you can't hit 'em."

I wistfully wish that, somewhere amid all this pot of message, I could pass along the innermost secret of achieving total-zilch tolerances, every week in the world. Alas, I'm still questing for that particular elusive grail, myself. As a purely personal point of pride, I try to work wood with the precision of machinists working with metal,

Left, Grennell's drill press vise was handmade, several years ago, by Bob Faber, a tool & diemaker friend mentioned elsewhere here. It finds countless uses around the shop.

and try to go on to superior, more sophisticated precision when working metal. I don't succeed at either goal, even half as often as I'd like to, and all I can pass along, at this point, is the concept of the elusive will o' the wisp, and the fun of chasing the slippery little so-and-so. If you grasp that, however precariously, we will not have wasted our mutual time in this chapter, you and I.

I've an old, good and valued friend who works as what he terms a metrologist for a company that builds trucks. It is a company whose name is a legend in the field. That's all I can say as an aid to your guessing. No, not Peterbilt. A metrologist is not to be confused with a meteorologist. He doesn't predict the coming weather. He just measures, real fine. To Woody, as we refer to him, a thousandth of an inch is a coarse and monstrous thing. He deals, quite routinely, in millionths, ten-millionths, hundred millionths and, for all I know, on down to the wavelength of a sodium light beam, a nanoAngstrom, whatever. I think of Woody, oftentimes, as I struggle and strain to get two pieces together, acceptably by my own vastly more tolerant standards. It doesn't make me feel a bit better, but it keeps me trying, so it's not a total loss, viewed from that aspect.

A small reading lamp is positioned to illuminate the table of "Chuck," Grennell's old and faithful Atlas drill press. You may disregard the notice on the front edge of the platform, or you may follow it, if desired.

Chapter 5

Drilling, Tapping, & Threading Metals

The Tru-Tapper precision tap guide from B-Square is an invaluable aid in assuring that the threads will be tapped absolutely square with the workpiece, here held in the drill press vise illustrated and discussed in another chapter. Photos at right show how the upper shank retracts and extends as the tapping progresses.

PLEASE DISREGARD THIS NOTICE

The Ability To Cut Your Own Threads Opens Many Useful Possibilities

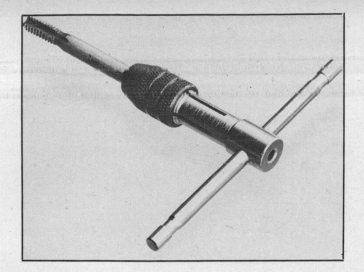

This inexpensive tap wrench is designed to be used freehand, which can be a severe challenge, but it has a hole at the top of the shaft to accept a guide pin, if you can figure out where and how to hold such a pin.

THREADED HARDWARE — bolts, nuts, wing nuts, and the like — is a most useful aid in assembling construction projects made of wood, metal, or a combination of the two materials. The more common forms of such things are readily available at nearby stores, but the time may come when you need something out of the ordinary; something that simply isn't to be had.

Let's assume that you're engaged in designing and building some manner of needed device and you wish to be able to loosen parts, move them to a new location and tighten them securely back into place. At one level of Spartan expedience, you might be able to get it done with a simple assembly of a bolt, washers and a nut or perhaps a wing nut. The trouble with that approach is that you'd have

to dig up a crescent wrench or open/box-end wrench to hold the head of the bolt every time you wished to loosen, adjust and tighten it. The inconvenience of that should be obvious.

As an illustration of the problem and solution, there are pictures of a vertical camera copying stand and another gizmo, built quite a number of years ago, that was originally intended to serve as a low-level camera stand. In actual practice, the latter has served yeoman duty for a host of chores and has been used only rarely for the purposes for which it was designed; by no means an uncommon state of affairs. It's infinitely adjustable as to height and angle over its modest dimensions and I've used it many times for supporting subjects to be photographed, for but one example.

Both devices make extensive use of what I guess we can term an anchored bolt, for lack of a better name. Let us take a thoughtful look at the anchored bolt, since its useful applications are quite widespread, even if you have no use for photo accessories, such as the ones shown.

Most hardware stores or builders supply outlets stock a generous assortment of threaded rod in a number of diameters and thread pitches, as well as in popular lengths such as eighteen or thirty-six inches. You will usually find them in steel and perhaps in brass, as well. The cost is so modest that it serves little purpose to try to make up threaded rod on your own, unless forced to do so by unusual conditions.

The two sizes of threaded rod for which I've found the

Taps and dies vary both in diameter and pitch, which is the number of threads per inch. The small tap at the top here has a pitch of 36 threads per inch (tpi), while the others are 32 tpi, but of varying diameters, to serve different applications

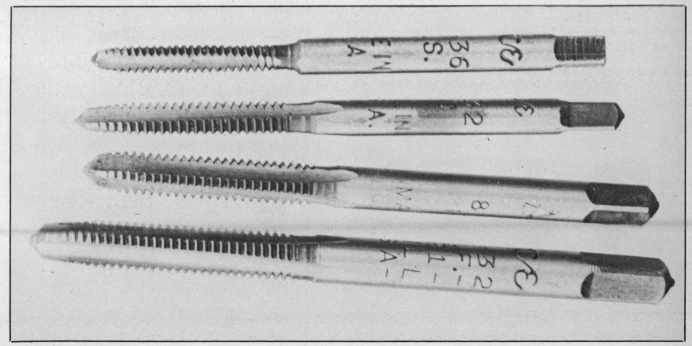

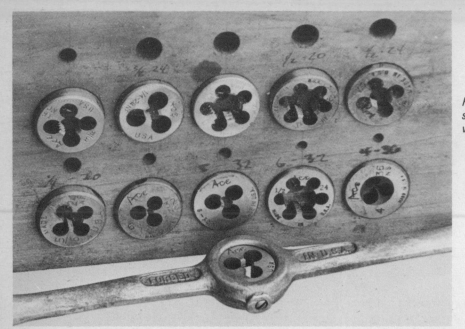

Here are threading dies in several sizes, with an inexpensive die wrench with which they can be used.

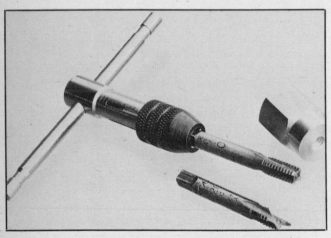

Taps are devilishly easy to break, especially the smaller sizes, if they are not used according to directions, as reproduced at right from the bubble pack in which a tap was sold. Too much has broken off the tap above, but the other was salvaged to serve as a bottoming tap. It is shown below next to an unbroken one and an acorn nut.

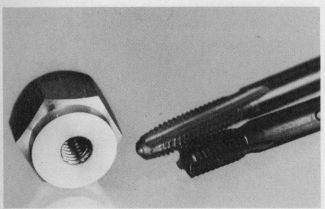

HOW TO USE A TAP

A tap is used to cut an internal thread. First a hole is drilled in the piece to be threaded (drill size on shank of tap.) The tap is held by the square in a tap wrench and is made to enter the hole by turning in a clockwise direction for regular threads. Turns of from ¼ to ½ revolutions should be made and then the action reversed to break the chips. This allows the tap to cut freely and prevent breakage.

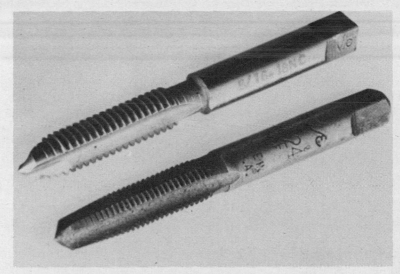

Above, a 5/16-18 National Coarse (NC) tap and another for 5/16-24 National Fine (NF) threads. The latter requires a larger hole, since the threads are not as deep as the NC.

Both sides of the homemade locking joint of the stand illustrated below. Left, a die in its pack.

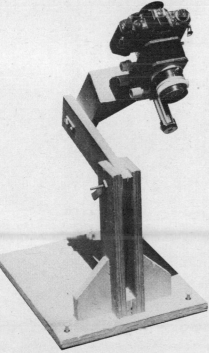

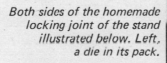

Originally built to serve as a low-level camera stand, this double-adjustable mount has served a great many other purposes. It employs two of the anchored bolt systems. Levers are tapped flat steel.

Details of a camera copy stand made almost entirely with homebuilt hardware, except for the threaded rod and hex nuts. Rod is threaded into the ¼" aluminum bar below.

Here's the anchored bolt that makes adjusting the crossarm a one-handed and easy operation.

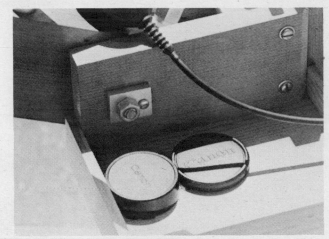

Above, three of the "super wing nuts," made from aluminum hex stock and steel rod as discussed. Below, another holds camera.

A small fluorescent light makes it easy to turn color slides into black and white negatives, in dim light.

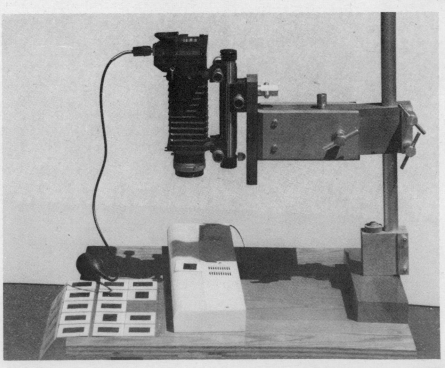

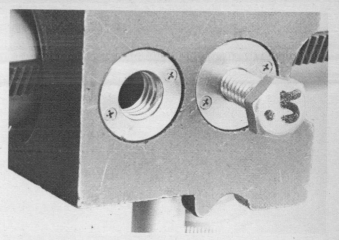

Underside of Canon Type FL bellows shows the two sizes of tripod threads. Larger is a metric size, smaller is the common and popular 1/4-20 size, making it a simple matter to construct custom equipment for camera mounting.

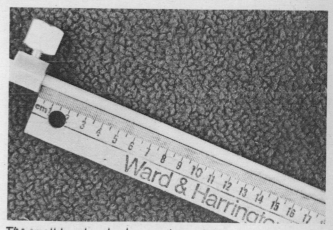

The small handmade clamp at lower left is in use here as a specialized depth gauge, fastened to a piece of ¼" birch dowel to measure depths limited solely by the length of rod or dowel that happens to be available in the diameter.

most use are ¼-20 and 3/8-16. While the intermediate 5/16-18 size might prove useful at times, it simplifies things to select between the two mentioned, thereby reducing the inventory a bit.

The tool used for cutting threads in a drilled hole is called a tap, while the one that cuts threads on a rod is called a die. To make a hole of the proper diameter for the ¼-20 thread, you'll need a No. 7 drill (.2010-inch diameter); or a 5/16-inch drill for the 3/8-16 thread, if you decide you need homemade hardware that sturdy.

A drill press and a drill press vise are extremely helpful, both for drilling the holes at a perfect ninety-degree angle to the workpiece and for guiding the tap when starting the thread. In the absence of a drill press, one of the

A close look at the little clamp, made of aluminum hex stock about ¾" across the flats. Central hole is 3/8" and the piece of common threaded rod is 1/4-20 NC.

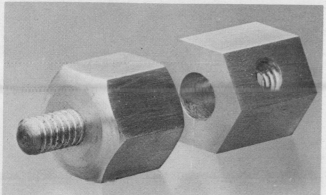

inexpensive plastic or metal drill guides — such as the two shown in the accompanying illustrations — can be substituted to reasonably good effect.

Even if you get the hole at a perfect ninety degrees, it is an extremely difficult challenge to start tapping, freehand, to end up with a true and concentric thread. I suppose there are people who can do it, but I'm not one of them.

Tapping in the softer metals, such as brass or aluminum, is considerably easier than tapping in steel, and the harder alloys of steel present a formidable challenge. Various specialized lubricants are available to ease the effort of tapping and improve the accuracy of the finished thread, as illustrated here. It is well to study the instructions on the can or container of tapping lube, since some are not intended for use with certain metals or other materials and should not be used with them.

It does not take a lot of muscle power to break a tap, since they are made of extremely hard steel that is rather brittle. It is a good policy to wear eye protection when tapping, since fragments of a broken tap can pose a serious hazard. The portion of a broken tap that remains in the workpiece may be difficult, impossible or impractical to

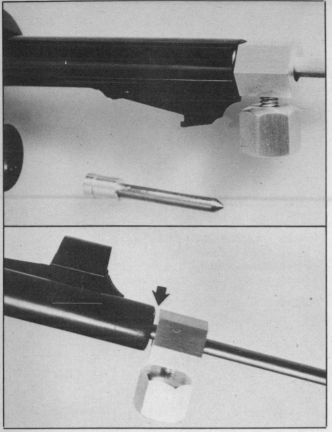

Here the small clamp on the previous page is being used to determine the distance a bullet can move out of the cartridge case before it engages the rifling in the bore. In the upper photo, the clamp is loosened, the dowel is moved down to touch the bullet of the chambered cartridge and the clamp is re-tightened. In the lower photo, the small punch pressed the bullet alone into firm contact with the rifling and the gap (arrow) shows the amount of net "free jump" available. This is a specialized application, for which no readymade equipment is commonly available. A 1/4-20 hole was drilled and tapped in the knob and a short section of threaded rod was turned in and secured by a drop of Loctite thread sealant; a reliable technique.

remove. As a result, all your work to that point will have to be done over, along with purchasing a replacement tap.

The tap in the nearby photo was broken when I grabbed a No. 14 drill, thinking it to be the usual No. 7, and tried to start the thread, puzzled over the difficulty being encountered. It was not a total loss, apart from the education, because enough of the full-diameter portion of the tap remained so I was able to put the shank in the chuck of the little Unimat lathe and, while it was turning, I put a green grinding wheel in the Dremel Moto-Tool and ground off the jagged part of the break, leaving the end perfectly flat. The result: a bottoming tap that has proved quite serviceable for extending the threads to the bottom of a blind hole, as when fashioning the little handmade aluminum acorn nuts that find so many handy uses around the shop.

The secret of trouble-free tapping, apart from accurate drilling, alignment and lubrication, seems to lie in reversing the tap as you commence to encounter noticeably greater resistance. Reversing the tap breaks loose the curling chips being carved by the teeth of the tap. If you are tapping a hole to any considerable depth, it is well to back the tap entirely out of the hole, periodically, to remove the chips and debris from between the flutes of the tap.

It should be noted that a small item called a Teenut is widely available in various popular thread sizes. Instead of an anchored bolt, such as we've been discussing, the Teenut serves as an anchored nut, so that a thumb screw or a bolt with some manner of lever-like handle on the end of it can be tightened or loosened with one hand and no wrench, much in the same manner.

The Teenuts are extremely handy things to have on hand

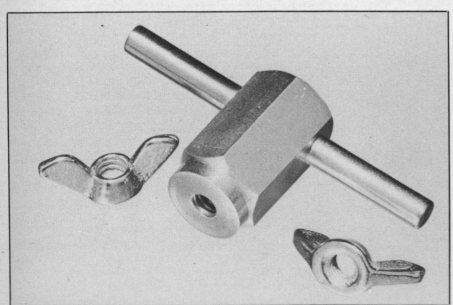

A pair of commercial 1/4-20 wing nuts, with one of the handmade ones having its steel shank fastened into place with Loctite sealant.

Perhaps you might call this a king size, or extended wing nut. It's another example of the unlikely hardware that can be built to meet a special need, but can't be purchased.

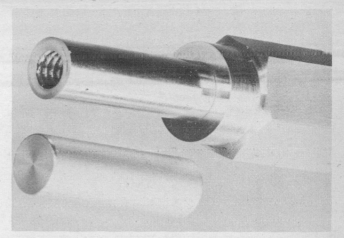

The shank was cut from a piece of 3/8" aluminum rod, drilled full-length in the little Edelstaal Unimat lathe, and threaded before seating in the handle with Loctite.

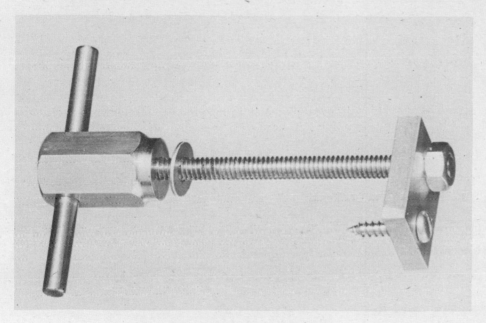

An overall view of the super wing nut and anchored bolt system, shown at lower right as disassembled.

In this set, the anchor plate was made from 1/8x3/4" flat aluminum stock and two holes were provided for screws.

This one has the anchor plate of 1/4x1" aluminum, with a single No. 8x3/4 sheet metal screw to prevent rotation.

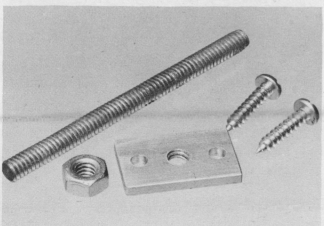

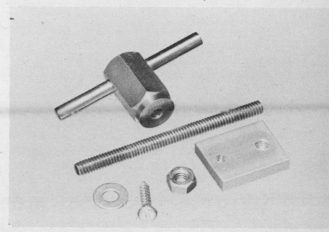

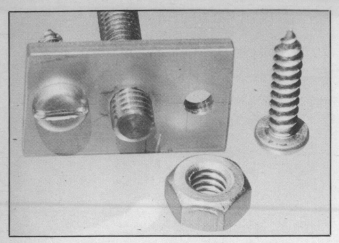

A close look at the anchor plate, with the threaded rod turned in, ready for the securing hex nut, installed and tightened below. Holes for screws are not threaded.

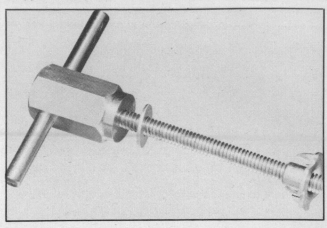

Here's a reverse approach, with a "super thumb screw" and a 1/4-20 Teenut. It can be selected as an alternate if it appears likely that it will work out better in use.

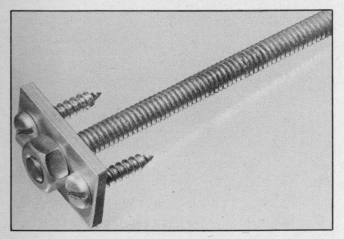

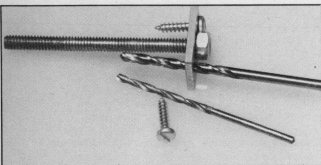

A No. 18 drill gives the right size of hole for the No. 8 sheet metal screw and a 1/8" is used to drill into the wood to give a good grip on the threads of the screw.

for meeting the demands of construction projects. In effect, they enable the workshopper to install a durable steel thread in a workpiece of wood or similar, softer material. I use up a lot of these in ¼-20 — my favorite size, as noted — and keep a few of the other sizes on hand against the event of unexpected need. Accompanying photos show the procedures for installing one of the ¼-20 Teenuts in a piece of one-inch board so that the project can be mounted on a common camera tripod. Most cameras intended for sale in this country carry ¼-20 tripod sockets, usefully simplifying

construction of accessories for use with them.

Thus, in an all-out pinch, you can make do in a fairly satisfactory manner by installing a Teenut of appropriate size, cutting a length of threaded rod and adding a suitable lever to the far end, perhaps by jam-tightening a hex nut against a wing nut. The problem is that most wing nuts do not provide a large amount of leverage. A better approach is to drill and tap a hole in one end of a short length of flat band stock, and turn enough of the threaded rod through it so a hex nut can be jam-tightened over the exposed end of the threaded rod to hold everything in secure assembly. If desired, a few drops of Loctite thread sealant, added before jam-tightening the nut, will keep everything together for a long, long while; forever plus six months, perhaps.

The jam-tightening technique and concept deserves a bit of discussion. There are several approaches to the problem

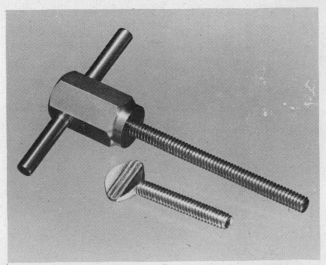

The super thumb-screw is just a super wing nut with a length of threaded rod held in place by a dab of Loctite. It's shown here next to a commercial thumb screw of the same thread. Advantage in leverage is quite obvious.

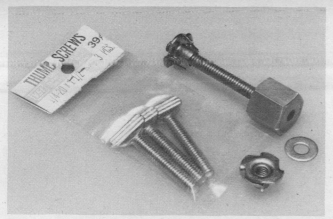

Store-bought and homemade thumb screws, latter without extension handle rod, with a Teenut and a flat washer.

In the usual applications, a thumb screw exerts pressure with its tip, rather than holding by the flange, although a washer, used as shown, will work in a reasonable fashion.

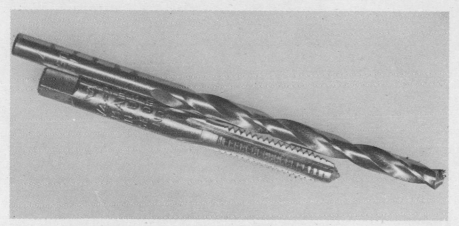

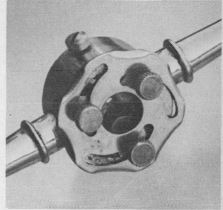

Left, a 1/4-20 tap with the No. 7 size drill that is prescribed for drilling the holes to be tapped with that thread. Right, a somewhat more sophisticated die holder equipped with three adjustable guides to aid in centering and squaring the thread.

Below, two views of another alternative choice available at most hardware stores. It is usually termed a cap screw and it has a hex socket to accept the appropriate size of hex wrench, shown in use at the right, with a 1/4-20 thumb screw.

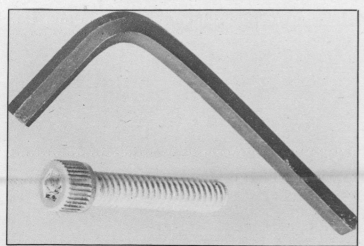

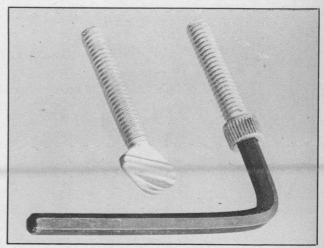

METRIC SCREW CHEK'R NO. 1 (R) — BROWNELL'S Gunsmith Tools, Montezuma, Ia. 50171

70 60 50 40 30 20 10

| M M DIAMETER | | | INCH DIA. | M M PITCH | |
FIRST CHOICE	SECOND CHOICE	THIRD CHOICE		COARSE	FINE
2 •46			.079	.4 •52	.25 •50
DRILLS→	2.2 •43		.087	.45 •50	.25 •48
			.098	.45 •45	.35 •43
2.5 •39			.118	.5 •39	.35 •37
3 •31					
DRILLS→	3.5 •28	U.S. PAT. 2728145	.138	.6 •32	.35 •30
4 •21			.157	.7 •30	.5 •28
DRILLS→	4.5 •16	OTHER PAT. PEND.	.177	.75 •25	.5 •22
5 •8			.197	.8 •18	.5 •16
		5.5 •7/32	.217		.5 •10
DRILLS→			.236	1 •8	.75 •4
6 •					
© RUELLE BROS. 1974		7 •J	.276	1. •B	.75 •D

Above, the incomparably handy Teenut fasteners, available in several popular thread sizes, enable you to put steel threads in wood that can perform countless things not easily possible otherwise. Left, Brownell's has their Screw Check'r in both inch sizes and metric, as shown.

Screws are available in many types and sizes to meet a host of specialized needs, of which several are shown here.

COMMON SCREW TYPES

Slotted Head

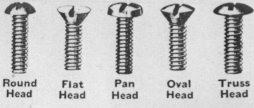

Round Head | Flat Head | Pan Head | Oval Head | Truss Head

Phillips Recessed Head

Oval Head | Fillister Head | Pan Head

Also available with Round, Flat or Truss Heads.

Hexagon Head

Washer Head

THREAD CUTTING SHANKS

TAPPING SCREWS

TYPE A— GIMLET POINT

TYPE B— BLUNT POINT

Available with slotted, Phillips or hexagon heads.

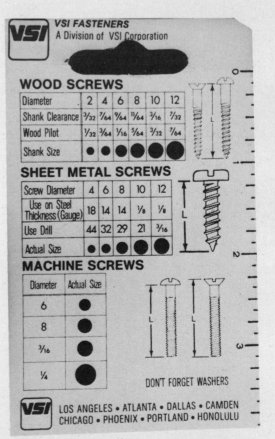

VSI FASTENERS — A Division of VSI Corporation

WOOD SCREWS

Diameter	2	4	6	8	10	12
Shank Clearance	3/32	7/64	9/64	11/64	3/16	7/32
Wood Pilot	1/32	3/64	1/16	5/64	3/32	7/64
Shank Size	•	•	•	•	•	•

SHEET METAL SCREWS

Screw Diameter	4	6	8	10	12
Use on Steel Thickness (Gauge)	18	14	14	1/8	1/8
Use Drill	44	32	29	21	3/16
Actual Size	•	•	•	•	•

MACHINE SCREWS

Diameter	Actual Size
6	•
8	•
3/16	•
1/4	•

DON'T FORGET WASHERS

VSI — LOS ANGELES • ATLANTA • DALLAS • CAMDEN CHICAGO • PHOENIX • PORTLAND • HONOLULU

Handy data often is given on the backs of packing cartons, such as the example reproduced here. The standard pan head sheet metal works well for wood-to-wood, or for wood-to-metal applications.

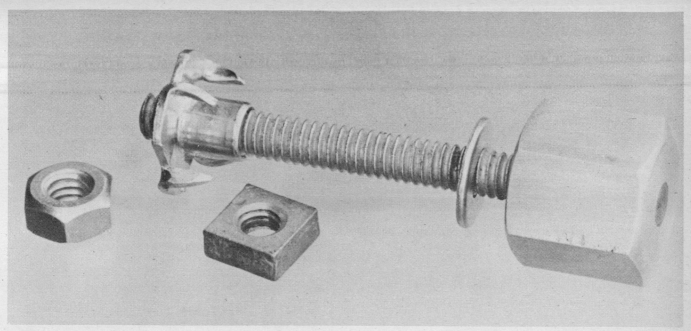

Here a short piece of aluminum hex stock has been drilled and threaded, with a length of 1/4-20 threaded rod sealed into it with a drop of Loctite. By this approach, one can make up thumb screws of any desired length, quite easily.

of keeping nuts from coming loose due to impact, strain or vibration. There are various types of lock washers, for example, as well as patented nuts that incorporate a tightly fitting segment of fiber or nylon at the outer end, designed to minimize or eliminate unwanted loosening. At the far end of such systems, there is the old aircraft approach of using a castellated nut — one with notches in the outer surface, reminiscent of turrets on an old castle — with transverse holes drilled through the end of the bolt. In use, the nut is tightened so that a pair of the notches line up with the hole and a length of wire, called safety wire, is

slipped through the notches and hole, to be wrapped tightly around something nearby.

All of these approaches work more or less well, depending somewhat upon the materials of the assembly and the application. Lock washers may work just fine on an all-metal assembly that is incompressible, once tightened securely. The same lock washer, used to hold pieces of soft wood together, can loosen through compression of the wood, due to strain and vibration.

The advantage of the jam-tightened, double-nut system is that the first nut can be snubbed down to any desired

Left, a Teenut has been installed in this piece of board to serve as a socket for fastening it to a camera tripod. The ¾" flange was countersunk below the opposite surface and a short piece of ¾" dowel was glued in place, sanded flush.

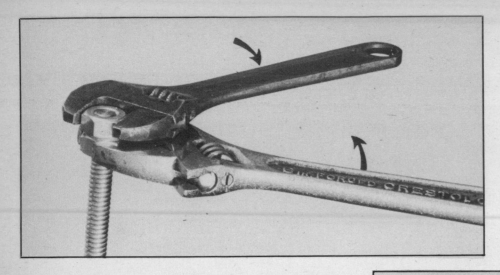

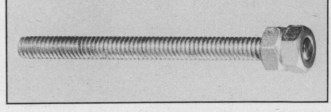

A simple technique for putting a temporary or permanent head on a piece of threaded rod is to "jam" two opposing nuts of that size, as shown. If absolute permanence is desired, seal with Loctite. If an anchored stud is the goal, turn into a 7/32" hole in wood and remove the nuts.

tension and, when it is held motionless and the second nut is torqued tightly against it, the result is a pair of nuts that can be counted upon not to move until deliberately disengaged from each other at a future time.

The anchored bolts illustrated here are just a modification of the jammed-nut approach, with the inner nut handmade to provide a larger flange that can be drilled to accept one or more screws, strategically located. Nearby photos show one made from 1/8x¾-inch aluminum band stock, a section of ¼-20 threaded rod, a ¼-20 hex nut and a pair of No. 8x¾-inch sheet metal screws. If this offends anyone's purist soul, round head wood screws can be

A simple rack, fitted with a 1/4-20 Teenut for holding it to a tripod, can be used for making novel photos through a telescopic sight, or for calibrating the sight. It's usually necessary to back off a scope eyepiece until camera is in focus on scope reticle at 15 feet or more, according to the distance scale on the camera lens. Most scopes are set for 4 to 6 feet when received, as checked this way.

substituted. Personally, I use a lot of sheet metal screws in wood because they're available in hundred-packs at modest cost and they can be made to do jobs such as this extremely well.

A No. 18 wire gauge drill bit (.1695-inch diameter) makes a hole in the band stock that accepts the No. 8 sheet metal screw for a nice fit. If no No. 18 drill is on hand, an 11/64-inch (.1719-inch) will serve about as well. If you wish to drill a hole in the wood to accept a No. 8 sheet metal screw, a 1/8-inch (.125-inch) drill will do nicely.

Once the anchored bolt is made up and installed, with an appropriate amount of its length extending beyond the parts you want held together, it merely remains to fashion what I call a super wing nut to install at the other end. A

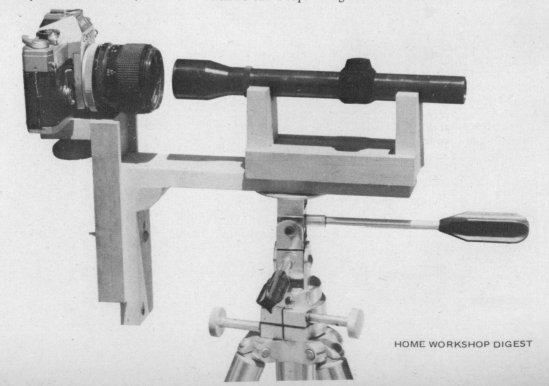

SHEET METAL SCREW DATA				
SCREW SIZE NO.	MAJOR THREAD DIAMETER	MINOR THREAD DIAMETER	SUGGESTED DRILL BIT SIZE	
			FOR METAL	FOR WOOD
4	.110″	.085″	No. 34	No. 45
6	.140	.112	28	33
7	.156	.120	5/32″	31 or 1/8″
8	.169	.125	18	1/8″
10	.194	.135	9	29
12	.218	.161	7/32″	20
14	.253	.187	F or 17/64″	13 or 3/16″

Suggested drill bit sizes should produce a hole that will allow the screw to pass through the metal, being slightly larger in diameter than the major thread diameter, meanwhile providing full engagement for the threads in the hole drilled in wood at close to the minor thread diameter. Bit sizes are listed in wire gauge series or inches of diameter. This chart assumes you're fastening metal to wood.

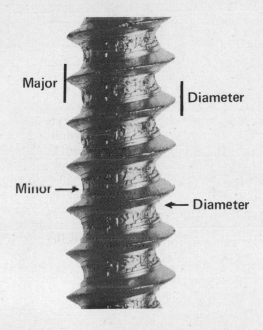

Major — Diameter

Minor → ← Diameter

The Portalign tool, right, and the Black & Decker drill guide, below, can serve as rudimentary drill presses, at least assuring that drilled holes will be at right angles to the workpiece. Notches accept round dowels for drilling.

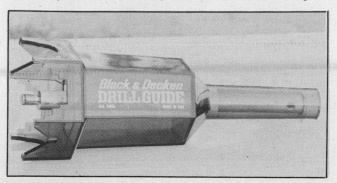

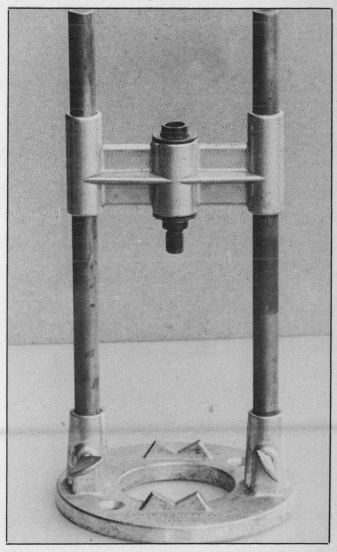

A 10x32NF die, fastened in a die wrench, viewed from the opposite of the starting side.

Cutting fluid can ease the work and improve results, but read the directions! Material below is not suited for aluminum.

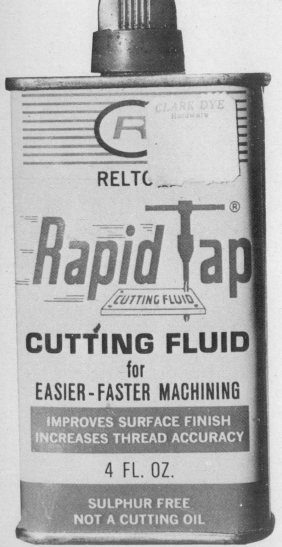

CLARK DYE
Hardware

RELTO

Rapid Tap®
CUTTING FLUID

CUTTING FLUID
for
EASIER - FASTER MACHINING

IMPROVES SURFACE FINISH
INCREASES THREAD ACCURACY

4 FL. OZ.

SULPHUR FREE
NOT A CUTTING OIL

DIRECTIONS

Apply a few drops to tool as it contacts work and as pressure builds up. Rapid Tap immediately breaks down surface tensions, and adhesions. Improves surface finish, by eliminating skuff marks, produces cleaner truer thread, releases stuck taps and stops tool breakage. Quick evaporation leaves a clean surface.

EFFECTIVE ON
Stainless Steel
Beryllium Copper

Renee 41	Hestaloy B
Brass	Chrome-Molly
Monel	Chromium
Iron	Titanium
Inconel	Tungsten

DO NOT USE ON
ALUMINUM OR PLASTICS
manufactured by
or under the supervisory control of

RELTON CORPORATION
ARCADIA, CALIF. 91006
U.S.A.

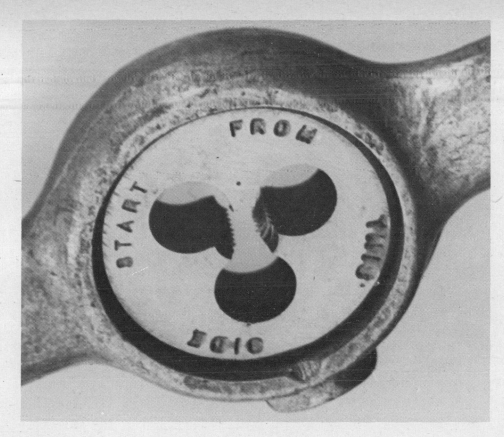

The die on the opposite page, as viewed from its other side, is marked to indicate the side from which to start the threading.

Brownell's Flute Juice resembles thin, pink yogurt in general appearance, but it is quite helpful for tapping in all of the materials listed on the back label, including aluminum, and seems helpful in metal drilling, too.

Instructions

A soft, adhering compound that can be applied as shown or brushed over entire tap. Non-Toxic, Water Soluble, Does Not Stain. For tapping in steel, cast iron, die castings, nickel alloys, aluminum, stainless steel and other metals encountered by gunsmiths.

TO FILL SQUIRT BOTTLE
Remove top, squeeze sides, stick neck into Flute Juice, release sides. Bottle fills itself.

Although the flat cut steel washers above are designated as 3/16, they fit a 1/4-20 bolt quite nicely, as here and work well for use with that size. Sheet metal screws, such as the two sizes below, are relatively economical, particularly when purchased in the plastic bulk packs. They are uncommonly tough for their size, with deep threads, and work well in wood.

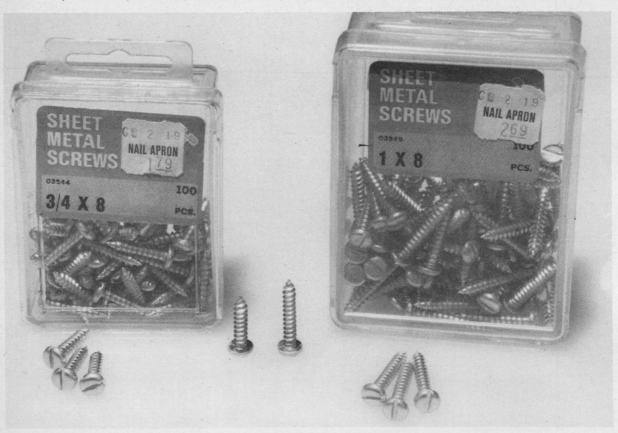

DECIMAL EQUIVALENTS OF FRACTION, WIRE GAUGE AND LETTER SIZE DRILLS

Drill Size	Decimal	Drill Size	Decimal	Drill Size	Decimal	Drill Size	Decimal
80	.0135	42	.0935	13/64	.2031	X	.3970
79	.0145	3/32	.0938	6	.2040	Y	.4040
1/64	.0156	41	.0960	5	.2055	13/32	.4062
78	.0160	40	.0980	4	.2090	Z	.4130
77	.0180	39	.0995	3	.2130	27/64	.4219
76	.0200	38	.1015	7/32	.2188	7/16	.4375
75	.0210	37	.1040	2	.2210	29/64	.4531
74	.0225	36	.1065	1	.2280	15/32	.4688
73	.0240	7/64	.1094	A	.2340	31/64	.4844
72	.0250	35	.1100	15/64	.2344	1/2	.5000
71	.0260	34	.1110	B	.2380	33/64	.5156
70	.0280	33	.1130	C	.2420	17/32	.5312
69	.0292	32	.1160	D	.2460	35/64	.5469
68	.0310	31	.1200	1/4	.2500	9/16	.5625
1/32	.0312	1/8	.1250	E	.2500	37/64	.5781
67	.0320	30	.1285	F	.2570	19/32	.5938
66	.0330	29	.1360	G	.2610	39/64	.6094
65	.0350	28	.1405	17/64	.2656	5/8	.6250
64	.0360	9/64	.1406	H	.2660	41/64	.6406
63	.0370	27	.1440	I	.2720	21/32	.6562
62	.0380	26	.1470	J	.2770	43/64	.6719
61	.0390	25	.1495	K	.2810	11/16	.6875
60	.0400	24	.1520	9/32	.2812	45/64	.7031
59	.0410	23	.1540	L	.2900	23/32	.7188
58	.0420	5/32	.1562	M	.2950	47/64	.7344
57	.0430	22	.1570	19/64	.2969	3/4	.7500
56	.0465	21	.1590	N	.3020	49/64	.7656
3/64	.0469	20	.1610	5/16	.3125	25/32	.7812
55	.0520	19	.1660	0	.3160	51/64	.7969
54	.0550	18	.1695	P	.3230	13/16	.8125
53	.0595	11/64	.1719	21/64	.3281	53/64	.8281
1/16	.0625	17	.1730	Q	.3320	27/32	.8438
52	.0635	16	.1770	R	.3390	55/64	.8594
51	.0670	15	.1800	11/32	.3438	7/8	.8750
50	.0700	14	.1820	S	.3480	57/64	.8906
49	.0730	13	.1850	T	.3580	29/32	.9062
48	.0760	3/16	.1875	23/64	.3594	59/64	.9219
5/64	.0781	12	.1890	U	.3680	15/16	.9375
47	.0785	11	.1910	3/8	.3750	61/64	.9531
46	.0810	10	.1935	V	.3770	31/32	.9688
45	.0820	9	.1960	W	.3860	63/64	.9844
44	.0860	8	.1990	25/64	.3906	1	1.0000
43	.0890	7	.2010				

conventional wing nut may serve your purpose fairly well and, if so, it simplifies things quite usefully. Wing nuts are readily available, nearly everywhere, in the common sizes, at modest cost. They do not provide a lot of leverage, as noted.

The flossier examples of super wing nuts illustrated here were made up on the little Unimat, using hexagonal aluminum stock that measured either ¾ or 11/16-inch across the flats. For applications where a lot of easily

Chart on previous page gives progressive sizes of drill bits available in fractional and wire gauge sizes. Below is a list of drill bit and diameter for drilling holes for tapping.

THREAD	BIT SIZE	DIAMETER
0-80	3/64	.0469
1-64	53	.0595
1-72	53	.0595
2-56	50	.0700
2-64	50	.0700
3-48	47	.0785
3-56	45	.0820
4-40	43	.0890
4-48	42	.0935
5-40	38	.1015
5-44	37	.1040
6-32	36	.1065
6-40	33	.1130
6-48	31	.1200
8-32	29	.1360
8-36	29	.1360
10-24	25	.1495
10-32	21	.1590
12-24	16	.1770
12-28	14	.1820
¼-20	7	.2010
¼-28	3	.2130
5/16-18	F	.2570
5/16-24	I	.2720
3/8-16	5/16	.3125
3/8-24	Q	.3320
7/16-14	U	.3680
7/16-20	25/64	.3906
1/2-13	27/64	.4219
1/2-20	29/64	.4531
9/16-12	31/64	.4844
9/16-18	33/64	.5156
5/8-11	17/32	.5312
5/8-18	37/64	.5781
3/4-10	21/32	.6562
3/4-16	11/16	.6875
7/8-9	49/64	.7656
7/8-14	13/16	.8125
1-8	7/8	.8750
1-12	59/64	.9219
1-1/8-7	63/64	.9844

Both of these charts are reproduced here through the courtesy of Hornady Manufacturing, Grand Island, Nebraska.

applied torque was desired, a hole was drilled through the outer end and a short section of steel rod was cut off with a hacksaw, its ends rounded with a flat file as it was spun in the drill press or lathe and it was installed in the hex stock with a dab of Loctite.

Examining the artifact built to serve as a low-level camera tripod, you will note that it was made in the days before I had the Unimat, forcing me to adopt a different approach for the super wing nuts.

If you forage through the hardware stores, you may encounter a version of steel bar stock (band stock) that measures about 5/8-inch wide by 3/16-inch thick, with its two edges more or less semicircular in cross-section. It may be bare, uncoated "black iron," or it may be galvanized (dipped in molten zinc, for rust-resistance). This doesn't seem to be stocked everywhere, but if you find a place that has some, splurge for a three-foot piece or two, because it's handy for many applications.

Fasten your length of the stuff in the bench vise, measure and mark it for the desired length, and cut it off with a hacksaw; the 32-tooth blade will do a fairly quick job and leave a smooth cut. Fasten the cut piece back in the vise and use a flat file to smooth both ends, rounding the sharp corners and edges.

Assuming you wish a tapping hole for ¼-20 in one end, or in the center, measure it, mark it, use a center punch to establish a biting-place for the No. 7 drill bit, make the hole and tap it, as described and discussed.

Once that's done, put the tapped section back in the bench vise and use a Crescent wrench or Vise-Grip pliers to bend it to the cross-section you have in mind, so as to provide suitable clearance for fingertips in use. Slip a flat washer over the exposed end of threaded rod, then turn the homemade lever or super wing nut onto it, snub it down and you're in business. Pictured examples show various approaches, or think up a fresh one, if you wish.

A further possibility is to cut off, finish, drill and tap the hole lengthwise in a short section of nominal 3/8-inch aluminum rod, available in six-foot lengths as a common hardware store item. Leave a bit of solid stock at one end and you can drill a perpendicular hole there to install a short section of steel rod (cut from a spike with a hacksaw, if need be) with its ends rounded, cemented in place with Loctite, and you have yet a third possibility. If it seems more advantageous, you can secure the short section of threaded rod solidly into such an affair, with Loctite, and install one of the Teenuts at the other end, as an equally effective approach.

Minor notes on dimensional discrepancies: The actual diameter of the six-foot section of 3/8-inch aluminum rod currently in the shop stockpile is .365-inch, rather than the .375-inch that would equate to the Real World 3/8-inch. The cut flat washers sold as a nominal 3/16-inch size make a pleasantly precise fit for ¼-20 bolts and the like, whereas the duly labeled ¼-inch washers are a rather sloppy fit. Well, as we often have occasion to remind ourselves, no one ever said it was supposed to be simple, right?

A chart of the correct drill bits to use for the various thread configurations closes out the discussion at hand. You might wish to dog-ear that page, because you can expect to refer to it fairly frequently in the course of tap-dancing your way through future projects.

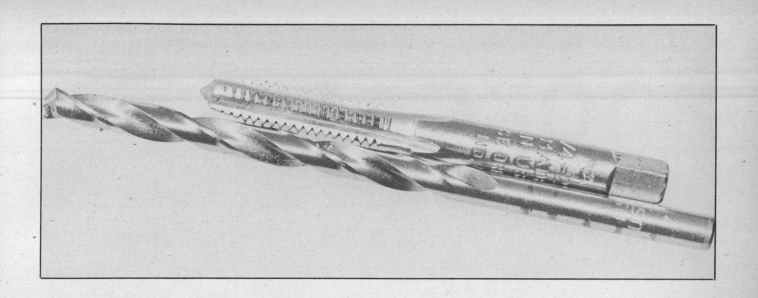

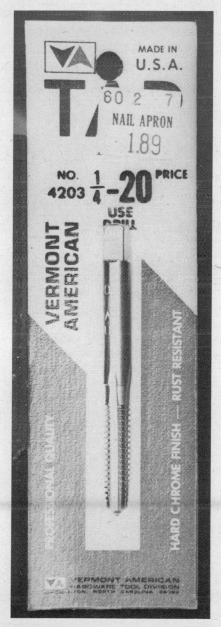

The bubble-packs in which taps are sold usually specify the proper size of drill to use, visible after removing the tap. A 1/4-20 tap with matching No. 7 drill bit is shown above for comparison.

Chapter 6

BOOKCASES

Here's The Basic Approach — With A Few Crafty Kinks And Wrinkles — For Making Bookcases, Or Several Other Comparable Items

Grennell's oldest son Chuck completes the preliminary assembly of the sides and ends, using eight of the handy corner clamps. Once clamps are adjusted, they will be loosened from the sides and left attached to each end as the glue is applied to mating surfaces and re-attached for the final curing of the glued joints as the basic assembly.

Make sure your boards are all of the same width! As seen here, two nominal 12x48 pieces, from different sources, vary in width by a full ½-inch; a potential problem source!

Bookcase to be discussed here will require five pieces of 12x48 particle board. Solid lumber, ¾-inch or more in thickness can be used in the same manner and will work even better, if you have it and prefer to use it. Left, the two sides and two ends, after the ends are cut.

THERE IS HARDLY any such thing as too many bookcases. Even if you don't have a large number of books, they remain a conveniently accessible storage facility for all manner of other small items.

Book storage shelves can be improvised at a primitive but functional state of the art by purchasing the required footage of boards sufficiently sturdy to resist sagging under the load, and using concrete blocks, bottles, separating supports constructed of glued wood, or a similar approach. This method has the virtue of being easy to knock down and move to a new location, as desired. It has, on the other hand, the disadvantage of lacking something in all-out elegance; particularly if you employ empty half-gallon scotch bottles or quart tequila bottles as the shelf spacers.

Convenience for purposes of moving from house to house deserves thoughtful consideration if your lifestyle involves frequent moves. An alternative and somewhat less Bohemian solution involves slotted rails that can be screwed to the walls to hold especially designed brackets that support the basic shelves. If you rent your house, however, it can trigger spirited dialog with the landlord when you

leave, due to the unsightly holes in the wall when you unscrew the vertical support rails.

In parts of the country where a lot of houses are built with two or more floors, local lumber yards offer stair tread in lengths of six or eight feet, at costs per running foot that are not unduly ruinous. Such lumber usually is about 9¼ inches wide, with a semicircular cross-section on one edge, a full inch or a bit better in thickness, and it makes a highly satisfactory bookshelf, barely sagging beneath foot after foot of the most massive tomes.

If you have no fierce objection to saddling yourself with unitary bookcases of conventional size and design, they can be constructed at gratifying moderate cost, with the ubiquitous particle board as the prime ingredient, without offending the eye unduly. I have constructed several such works and the burgeoning of the private bibliotheque is such that I need to build a few more, so there's ample justification to produce one so that step-by-step photos can be made to illustrate its progress toward completion.

Let us assume that we want a bookcase about four feet high, two feet wide and one foot deep; a convenient size

Combined thickness of two boards is 1½ inches. This is subtracted from desired height of case to determine length of side pieces. Intended height here is 46 inches.

Here the specified 1½'' has been subtracted from 46'', leaving 44½'', aligned against lower edge of the side.

Pencil is used to mark cut line at end of the Lufkin Red End No. 966 inside-reading folding rule; a handy item!

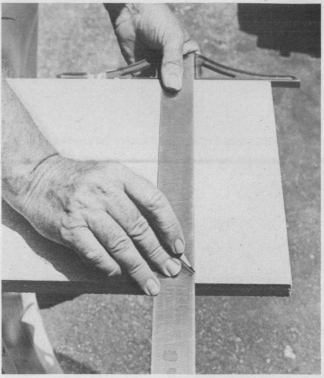

As discussed elsewhere Grennell puts no more than limited trust in carpenter's square, preferring to use a draftsman's T-square. He has satisfied himself that it is sufficiently close to an actual 90-degree angle. With the T-square held in place, the cut line is ruled across the end of the board, per discussion in text.

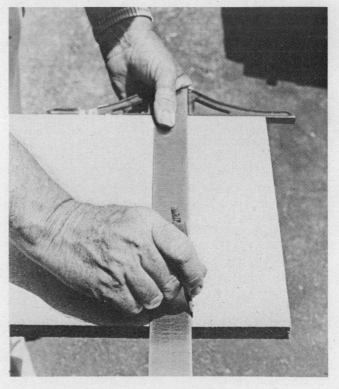

Here's a close look at the teeth of the saw blade, tipped with tungsten carbide to resist wear from the abrasive ingredients in particle board, which ruins steel blades.

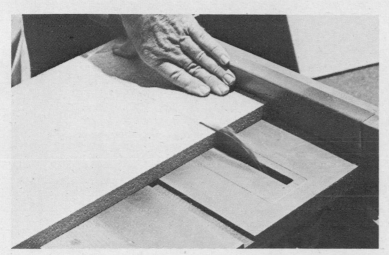

While the guard is not in place, for clarity of illustration, blade guards supplied with table saw should be left in place, if at all possible and practicable. Rip fence has been set up so that the kerf (saw blade cut) comes right up to the ruled pencil line, as shown in closeup photo at right above. This blade cuts nearly 1/8" of kerf and that's enough distance to result in a visibly cockeyed construction project, if not given suitable attention and allowances!

that will set you back around $80 if you purchase one, ready-made, at a typical office supply store. If we don't set too high a figure for our hours of labor, we can do considerably better than that. With one-by-four pieces of ¾-inch particle board going at about $1.50 apiece, we're looking at a cost of materials of around $7.50 for the particle board, plus another buck or so for the two-by-four-foot sheet of masonite that covers the rear surface, and a bit of handmade stripping to mask the ugly raw edges of the particle board in front. Call it close to ten bucks for materials and you can credit your personal cabinet shop with the remaining seventy or so.

The nominal one-by-four piece of particle board may actually be a full forty-eight inches in length — check it to make certain — but it's apt to be only 11¼ inches wide and it may be only 5/8-inch in thickness instead of a full ¾-inch. Try to hold out for the full three quarters stuff, because the five-eighths will sag alarmingly if an adolescent house fly chances to land upon it.

If you plan to have a top and bottom, with four shelves in between, you'll need five pieces of one-by-four particle board. It helps usefully to buy them all at once, from the same place, perhaps measuring to make sure they're all of uniform size.

Select the piece that's going to comprise your top/bottom, measure it carefully, draw a fine pencil line to divide it into exact halves, and cut it so that the saw blade kerf (cut) goes right down the center of the line.

At this point, it will be enormously helpful if you have access to eight of the right-angle gluing clamps, so that you can put the entire outer enclosure together as a single operation, one clamp at each of the eight corners. Use

Note that Grennell is wearing a plastic face shield. When cutting particle board, one's face is peppered with stinging shrapnel and such shields are a must. Above, adjusting miter gauge with a draftsman's triangle.

Left, with the miter gauge of the table saw verified at a 90-degree angle, the two ends are carefully cut to the pencil line, with the kerf evenly divided between the two. Above, eight corner clamps permit simultaneous setup. Clamp is shown below with bookcase lying on its side.

aliphatic resin glue, such as Elmer's Professional Carpenter's, or Titebond, applying moderate amounts to each contacting surface and smoothing it to uniformity with a fingertip. Keep a bucket of water and a sponge or old towel handy for getting the stubborn stuff off your fingertips after spreading it about. Make firm contact and alignment between all of the mating surfaces. This is a butt-glue operation, rather than a mitered joint. The raw edges of cut particle board are woefully lacking in strength when glued. Butt the ends of the sides up against the bottom of the top and the top of the bottom pieces. Make sure that the ambient temperature is 65 degrees Fahrenheit or better, and let it set up for a generous length of time, because the project is wobbly and very fragile at this stage of construction.

In placing the glue clamps, plan to let the raw edges of the top and bottom pieces project beyond the surfaces of the sides by a tiny amount, about 1/32-inch, so that you can sand it flush to the sides, later.

If you feel a need for added strength, mark the spots

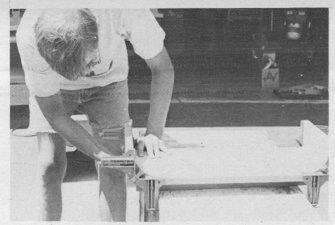

Chuck is using short pieces of scrap to set up the clamps on the piece that will be the bookcase bottom. It's easier, at this point, than trying to keep control of a 4' board!

With sides in place and glued at the lower edges, Chuck runs a bead of glue down the upper edge and spreads it out into an even layer, then applies top piece and clamps.

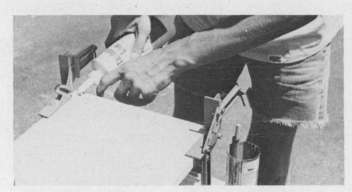

Lower edges of the top also get a thin bead of glue and it is smoothly distributed before making final assembly.

Below are two more views of the rather messy process of applying and distributing glue to the edges of the p-board.

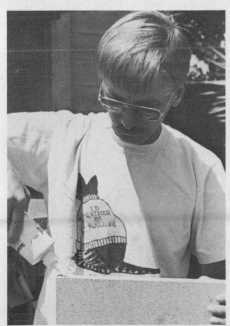

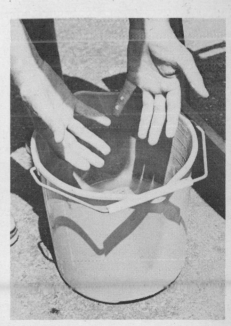

After all that, a bucket of water for washing glue from the hands is a much-appreciated luxury!

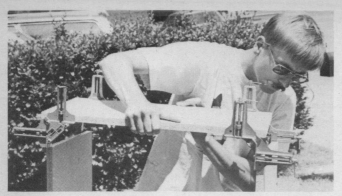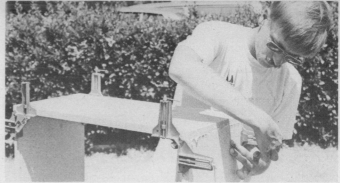

Left, upper edges of sides and lower ends of top have been coated with glue and the loosened clamps are being put into place. Right, once installed, the corner clamps are retightened. Oozing surplus glue will be cleaned up.

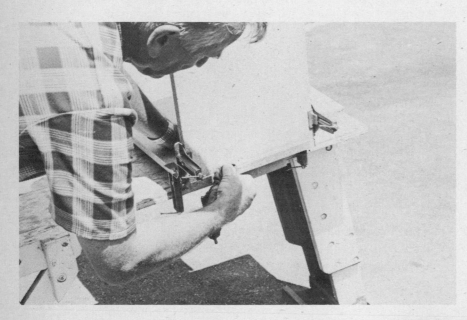

The yellow aliphatic resin glue is water soluble, simplifying cleanup. A damp rag is being used to clean the outside corner and, below, a putty knife removes surplus from the inside corner. Removing excess glue while still soft saves a lot of time and bother in final finishing. Bottom, a line has been scribed on the end of the top piece to show the center of the side piece as a guide for drilling holes to take dowels.

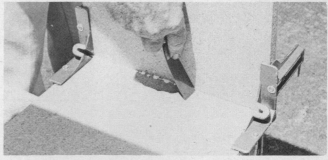

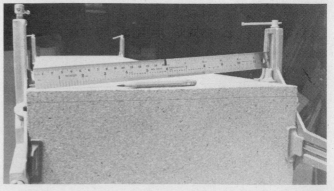

carefully to center into the vertical sides and drill 3/8-inch holes directly downward and upward into the joints to a depth of about 1½ inches from the surfaces of the ends. You can do this while the clamps are in place and the glue is setting up. Cut pieces of 3/8-inch hardwood dowel, about 1-5/8 inches long, run glue into the drilled holes and tap the dowels in with a mallet. The end of the dowel will project a trifle above the surface, but you'll sand that down flush after the glue sets up. About three equally-spaced dowels for each one-foot (or 11¼-inch) joint is about right.

When you figure the glue is well set, give it another half-hour or so for good measure, remembering the dubious strength of glue on the scruffy raw edge of the particle board, then remove the clamps (with crossed fingers, if you like). Lay the assembly on its side on a fairly low workbench and mark the location of the four central shelves on the edges of the vertical members — which will be horizontal for the present.

At this point, there are two approaches, depending upon whether or not you have access to a router with a ¾-inch bit having tungsten carbide cutting edges. If you try to rout particle board with ordinary steel bits, you can plan upon buying a new bit about every two or three cuts.

If you do not have a router with a carbide bit, use a

Left, a 3/8" Irwin Speed-Bor bit is in the ¼" Black & Decker No. 7014 electric drill, with a strip of white tape as a guide for drilling to uniform depth. Below, drilling three holes on the scribed line for reinforcing 3/8" dowels.

A small amount of glue is put into each hole and the pre-cut pieces of dowel are tapped into place to set.

Depth of hole and length of dowel were set up to leave about 1/16" protruding above surface. Later, this will be sanded down flush as part of the final finishing.

Holding strength of glued particle board is a bit marginal, which is why we've doweled the corners.

carpenter's square or draftsman's T-square to scribe pencil lines across the inner surfaces of the vertical members (sides) for positioning of the support cleats that will be glued into place to provide support for the ends of the shelves.

If you do have a router with a ¾-inch carbide bit, rout grooves to a depth of about 1/8-inch into the inner surfaces of the sides to accept the ends of the central shelves. It works well to C-clamp a draftsman's T-square into position and use it as a guide for the router. It requires a bit of finagling to get the square located precisely. Refer to the accompanying photos for details.

Be sure you have adequate eye protection when you perform the routing. The flying particles of particle board have the velocity of tiny bullets; a hazard far better avoided!

With the routing, or installation of support cleats, completed you are ready to cut and install the central shelves. With the outer assembly still on its side on the low

Stanley Swirlaway sanding head can be set to swivel or be rigid. It's set for flexible use here and fitted with 5'' 3M sanding discs in coarse grade for rapid removal of excess.

Here are three of the dowels after being sanded flush. If given a coat of paint, they'll be quite inconspicuous, or the top of the case can be covered with Formica.

The sanding disc in the electric drill makes quick work of sanding protruding ends of the dowels down flush.

Remember that we let the ends of the top and bottom protrude over the sides by a tiny margin? Now we're ready to deal with that. All it takes is a few deft, whirring wipes with the Stanley Swirlaway sander and the exposed edge is nicely flush, smoother too. Photo below shows sanded edge, ready for painting.

Left, another view of the remarkably useful Stanley Swirlaway sanding disc with its flexible coupling shaft. Two of the dowels have been flush-sanded, one to go!

The 3/8" router bit above was of high-speed steel, but it didn't last long when routing particle board. The more expensive bits with tungsten carbide blades are the only ones that can stand up to the abrasives in particle board.

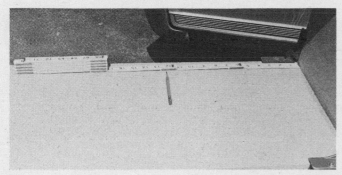

It was decided that we want 12" of clear height for the top shelf, so we've measured down and made marks at 12" and 12¾" as guides for the router. Right, draftsman's T-square is aligned with the pencil lines and clamped down.

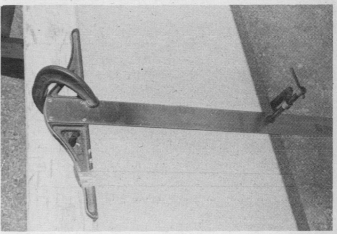

workbench, use a yardstick or, better, a meterstick to measure the exact distance between the two surfaces and transfer it with all possible precision to the piece from which you plan to cut the shelf. The pencil or other scribe should be sharp, to keep the line as fine as possible. When you make the cross cut, keep the near edge of the kerf centered in the scribed line as precisely as you can manage. This is one instance where accuracy pays off most helpfully.

I'd suggest that you cut, fit and attach one central shelf at a time, because any slight departure from intended length can affect the dimension needed for the rest of the shelves; especially if you get one of the first ones a hair too long.

If you have no router and are using support cleats, rub a thin coat of glue on the top of the cleat on each side, with a little more on the mating surfaces of the shelf, and a bit more on the ends and where they make contact. Turn the assembly right-side-up to affix each shelf and wipe off any excess smears of glue with a wet rag. Weight it down, or clamp it, and let it set up thoroughly before installing the next shelf.

If you're gluing the ends of the shelves into channels routed on the inner surfaces of the sides, you'll perceive a problem in getting a uniform and useful deposit of glue between all of the mating surfaces. Take heart, because there is one of those elegant solutions to this particular problem and I'm about to lay it upon you.

What you do is to run a moderate bead of glue along the

Here the router is being used to cut a groove about 1/8" deep, being guided against the edge of the T-square. This is another operation where the plastic face shield is a good idea, or safety glasses as an absolute minimum measure.

As the Black & Decker router completes each groove, it is held in place and switched off before going on to the next cut. Note the plastic face mask to protect the eyes.

With all the grooves for the ends of the shelves routed (we even routed one too many, by mistake!), Chuck holds the meterstick to determine the exact length to which the shelves must be cut to assure a perfect fit in the grooves.

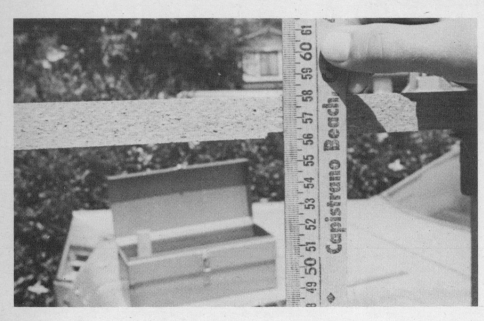

Here's a closer look at the meterstick. It indicates the distance from groove to groove as 56.3 centimeters. That would be about 22-5/32" but 56.3cm is an easier, simpler number to recall and duplicate in layout.

Here, as discussed in the text, we've run a bead of glue down the center of the upper edge of the shelf. We set it aside for a moment, but do not spread it with a fingertip.

Here, we've run a similar bead of glue down the center of the lower router groove, again leaving it as deposited.

Here, the glue-beaded upper edge of the shelf has been positioned carefully in the upper router groove and the dry lower edge is being nudged toward the glued lower router groove. When it drops in place, both are glued.

In this photo, the lower edge has been guided into the router groove and a small amount of glue can be seen to ooze from the joint. Excess is cleaned up with a damp rag.

At left, a plastic mallet is being used to tap the edge of the shelf into perfect alignment with the two sides before the glue commences to set up. In the photo below, a pair of pipe clamps have been positioned and tightened to put some pressure upon the joint. This adds to the resulting strength.

channel of the lower side and not spreading it with the fingertip. Then put a similar coating along the edge of the shelf that will be on top.

Now then, with great care and delicacy, move the glue-beaded upper edge of the shelf toward the unglued upper router slot, meanwhile letting the unglued lower edge of the shelf move toward the glue-beaded lower groove. Introduce the upper edge into the upper router groove and then, gently and tenderly, bump the lower end of the shelf with the heel of your free hand until it pops down into the lower router groove, right on top of the deposit of glue that you put there.

Amazingly simple, once you know how, isn't it?

Above is a close look at one of the shelf joints after the glue has set. Lacking a router for cutting the grooves, one could glue a supporting cleat to inside, below shelf.

Particle board is fairly hard, so there's little need for protective pads of scrap wood, as long as you don't turn down the pipe clamps with an excess of enthusiasm.

It's a bit out of logical sequence, but here's how we took care of the groove that, somehow, got routed in the wrong place. A 1/8x¾'' strip of facing wood fills it nicely.

The last of the three shelves is installed and the glue is curing. You'll note that we've still not removed the corner clamps, as there was no need to and particle board glued joints benefit from all the curing time you can spare.

Use a non-marring mallet to tap the edges of the shelf and sides into perfect alignment and then it's helpful if you use a pair of pipe clamps to apply pressure upon the joint, front and back. Allow a generous amount of curing time for the joint, based somewhat upon ambient temperature.

Once you get all of the central shelves attached, in one of the manners described, flop the assembly onto the work surface, front-down and back-uppermost, depositing a well distributed coating of glue over the edges of the sides and shelves. If you desire maximum strength, you will have positioned the assembly over the piece of masonite that will serve as the back and used a pencil to outline the contacting area of the back, so as to apply a thin, uniform layer of glue to the masonite back, as well.

At any rate, with one or two surfaces coated with glue, position the backing sheet of masonite and use gluing weights to hold it in firm contact with the assembly of sides and shelves until the glue takes firm hold. Again, temperature is the factor. You may wish to drive a few small brads into the joints as further reinforcement.

Ideally, the backing sheet of masonite will project beyond all the edges of the sides and top by a small fraction of an inch. It is a simple matter to cut it flush, using a trimming bit in the router — assuming you have a router, of

All clamps are off now and we're tracing the outlines of the back edges on a 2x4' piece of 1/8" Masonite or hardboard that will form the back.

This is an edging bit for the router. The small ball-bearing rotor rides against a flat surface as a guide and the blades of tungsten carbide trim away excess covering projecting.

Cutter at left is installed in the router here. This is about the setting that was used to go around after the Masonite was glued to the back, trimming it neatly flush with sides.

course. At about this same time, you can use a good, brisk sander to flush away the excess protrusion of the top and bottom beyond the side pieces and, if you reinforced the corners with dowels, to flush down the protruding ends of the dowels.

That leaves us with the basic assembly, which will hold books and perform similar services quite nicely. We still have a problem, however, in the exposed edges of raw particle board on the front surfaces of the sides and shelves; a really revolting spectacle. We can do something constructive about that, too.

If you have access to a table saw, you can install a smooth-cutting blade, such as a hollow-ground planer blade, and adjust the rip fence to cut thin strips of about 1/8-inch thickness, from pieces of clear (knot-free) pine boards of about ¾-inch heft. You will need two pieces at least four feet long, and six more a bit over two feet. That may enable you to work around a few pesky knots in your basic stock.

With a sufficient quantity of the stripping cut and on hand, measure, mark and miter the ends for the two sides to forty-five degrees, apply glue to the two mating surfaces, and weight it down to set up. Cut the same, carefully

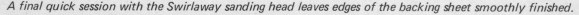

A final quick session with the Swirlaway sanding head leaves edges of the backing sheet smoothly finished.

In order to hide the rather unsightly edges of the exposed particle board, ¾'' strips of board have been cut to a thickness of about 1/8'' on the table saw, using a planer blade. The first strip has been measured, mitered to a 45-degree angle on each end, cut and glued in place. The five lead gluing weights were cast in a GI mess kit cover and weigh about six pounds apiece; quite handy for such uses. Covering strips will be glued to all of the exposed edges.

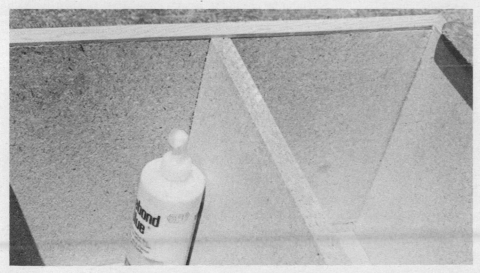

A closer view of the mitered strips being glued to sides and top edges. Shelf edge is still exposed, here.

It's best to let the glue for the first strip set up for a bit before trying to fit mating surfaces of the second strip, as we're doing here.

This shows the mitered joint of the strips of wood that cover edges of the sides and top. After the glue dries, a sanding block will be used to smooth out the joint.

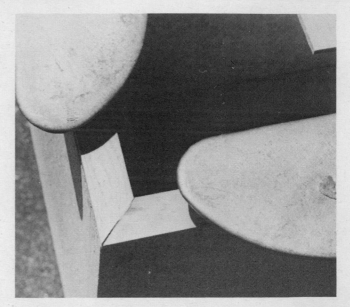

adjusted forty-five-degree angle to one of the ends of the strip to go on the top or bottom edge, hold it in place and scribe a precise line for cutting it to exact dimension. As before, apply glue to mating surfaces, position and weight it down to set. Do the same for the other end, to complete facing of the enclosure.

In covering the exposed edges of the central shelves, try to cut the facing strips perhaps 1/128-inch too long, so you can apply glue to all of the mating surfaces, including the ends, and squash them into place with gluing weights for a super-hairline joint.

At this point, if all went according to plan, you have a basic bookcase, closed on the back with a strengthening ply of 1/8-inch masonite, its unsightly front edges of raw particle board discreetly camouflaged with homemade veneer, needing but a few rubs with the sanding block to bring all joints into indetectible perfection.

If you feel inclined, you can protect the top surface with a layer of Formica, secured in place by applications of contact cement to the mating surfaces and flushed even all around with the trimming bit in the router, or with a file and sander. Then it is but a matter of applying paint to all of the surfaces where you deem finishing to be necessary. If you don't elect to paint the hidden surface of the back panel, I'll never tell, and that's a promise!

The basic techniques and approaches, discussed in detail to this point, can be employed with suitable modification in the construction of all manner of other enclosures, storage spaces and cabinets. A framework around the front, suitably attached, can be fitted with a door, or doors. With just a bit of modification, the basic procedures can be used

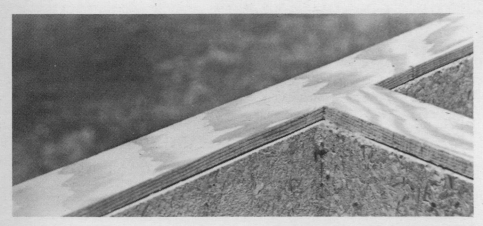

As discussed, when gluing the strips to the shelf edges, the strip is cut a tiny bit too long, to provide a slight compression fit against the side strips.

With all of the facing strips fitted, it's "all done but the finishing." Opaque paint is a better choice than varnish, since the more you hide the surface of particle board, the better the resulting artifact is apt to end up looking!

to build a telephone stand, with shelves for phone books, a sewing stand, a lamp stand, a magazine stand, or you-name-it/you-build-it.

The basic box, constructed in the manner described here, serves as the starting point for innumerable projects such as tool boxes, carrying cases, stackable cube systems, and so forth and so on.

If you do not happen to have amassed a trove of eight of the indispensible corner clamps, discussions elsewhere in the book tell how you can fashion your own right-angle gluing clamps that can be used, together with spring-clamps or C-clamps, for putting together two or more pieces of board as a slower approach toward completing the desired rectangle or square.

We've spoken of using particle board, because of its moderate cost, but much the same procedures work equally well with plywood or solid lumber of nominal one-inch thickness (actually, about ¾-inch). If it pleases your fancy and satisfies your sense of fitness, you can veneer such artifacts with thin strips of suitable woods, sliced on the table saw or radial arm saw. With a bit of additional zeal and application, you can even turn out such covering materials with an electric saber saw.

The point is that the general approaches outlined here can be applied to your own facilities, even down through progressive layers of modesty. A firm grasp of the basic principles will enable you to construct shadow boxes, spice racks, or display racks for collector items such as spoons, with virtually no end to the possible applications. The only limit — assuming for the sake of discussion that one exists — is in your own imagination and ingenuity. With any kind of decent luck, both of those will improve as you go along.

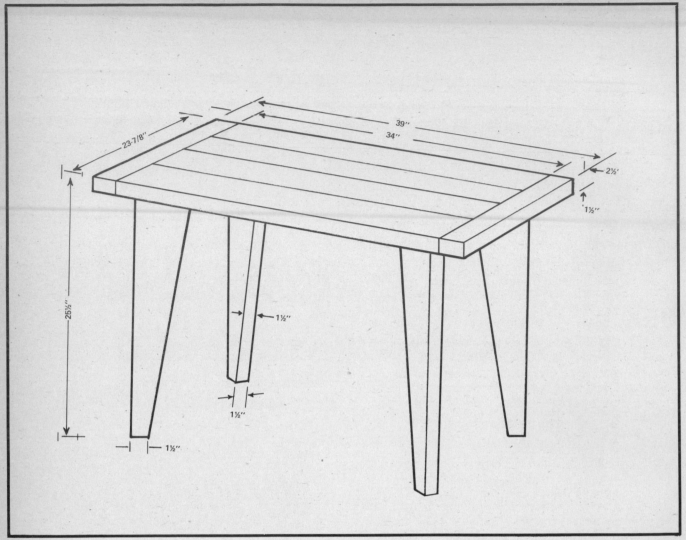

Here is a perspective sketch, with dimensions, of the table discussed here. The tapered legs were made by ruling diagonal lines on 24-inch lengths of nominal 2x8 planks, from marks 1½ inches away from opposite corners, and cut by use of the sawing guide strips discussed in the text. Legs were centered on lines drawn between opposite corners on the lower surface of the table top and the outer edge of each leg was installed at a distance of 4½ inches from the corner.

Building A Table

I T HAS BEEN noted that I tend to wander overboard in favor of the brutally functional approach to design and construction and the resulting works tend to take on the subtle aura of Dr. Frankenstein's most memorable creation, sometimes even complete to the exposed stove bolts jutting out of unlikely places. At times, I reflect ruefully that it isn't really necessary to show such callous disregard for the aesthetic aspects of things. I suppose it's a bit like the traditional situation of the clown who yearns to play Hamlet.

Some months earlier, I had built a small table, intending it as a mount for the little Black & Decker Workmate that has proved itself so indispensible for so many purposes. The first table turned out so handsome and appealing that I decided I wanted it as an occasional table in the den/office, so I ended up having to build another table for the Workmate. You may be certain I built a touch of ugliness into the second attempt, to forestall further such problems.

The first table, nicely covered with homemade stain created by dissolving a little burnt sienna artist's oil

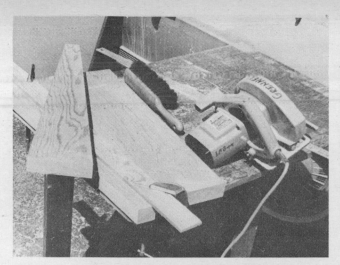

Above, as discussed in the text, 24" sections of 2x8 were ruled to get two tapered legs from each piece and plank was C-clamped to the end of the bench with a wooden straightedge to guide the electric handsaw. Above left, one of the legs is shown after being cut off. Left, the photos of the sections of the top being joined together did not come out well. Here is a view of reasonably comparable procedures for gluing up the top of an earlier project, with pipe clamps and C-clamps in use to put the required pressure upon the joints being glued.

Chapter 7

Here's A Simple, Sturdy Piece Of Furniture, Not Too Hard To Build, With Specifications That Can Be Varied To Your Personal Taste

pigment in some lighter fluid and wiping it on with pieces of paper towel, followed by a few coats of clear gloss Varathane from a spray can, was not entirely satisfactory as an item of home furnishings. The legs, it was painfully apparent, were lengths of 2x4 and the raw end of the braces where the legs joined the top were pieces of 2x4, also, and flush with the table edge. It was a miserable misfit of a table, too pretty for the shop and a touch overly uncouth for the den.

So, another weekend, I decided to gear up and try to knock out yet one more table that the connoisseur's eye might not find too intolerable. As one of the primary specifications, I decreed that it would not have braces exposing the raw ends of a piece of 2x4.

The basic assembly of the table top, itself, progressed rapidly, with the ease that comes with having made much the same thing on several prior occasions. Another hard dictum was that the top of the table would not show exposed knots in the wood. Thus it came down to a matter of winnowing forth lengths of nominal two-inch plank

After the four tapered legs were cut, the raw edges were smoothed down with the belt sander, using a fine grade of sanding belt in it.

Here's another view of nominal 2" planks being joined edge to edge with pipe clamps and a layer of wax paper beneath to prevent the assembly from sticking to the bench.

(actual thickness the usual 1½-inch) whacked out of pieces of 2x6 and 2x8. All edges were dressed to a smooth surface with square edges on the eight-inch table saw, after being cut to basic size on the big ten-incher. True, it's vulgar ostentation to have more than one table saw and I'd planned to sell off the little one when I picked up the big one for a remarkable $199 as a demonstrator at the Builder's Emporium, up in El Toro.

That was before I discovered that, while the mighty ten-inch roars through heavy planks with contemptuous ease, the eight-inch I've been using since 1962 produces a much cleaner, finer cut; even when both saws are carrying a planer blade.

The technique for "making big ones out of little ones" is a useful knack to have. It can produce a lot of handy things otherwise unobtainable. The important thing is to handle one joint at a time, waiting for the glue to set up before going on to the next one. Trying to glue it all up at one time would be a reliable shortcut to disaster, I'm sure. Likewise utterly vital is the placing of a length of waxed

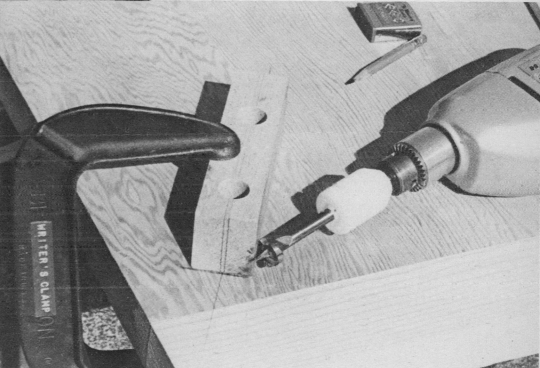

A Black & Decker drill stop was secured to the shaft of this auger-type Stanley wood bit to control the depth of the hole being drilled through the doweling guide into the ends of the legs and lower surface of the top of the table.

The pair of centering lines were scribed on the improvised doweling jig by laying it on its side, with a ¾″ board to guide the pencil, then inverting the jig and repeating the ruling. Here, it's aligned with guide marks on the lower side.

paper beneath the joint, to keep oozing glue from cementing it inextricably to the upper surface of the workbench.

Over the years, I've built up a collection of pipe clamps. Those are accessory items that can be attached to pieces of ½-inch or ¾-inch steel pipe to create king-size C-clamps. They are extremely handy to have around the shop and I use them quite extensively for a host of chores. In building the table top at hand, I took care to make sure that its finished length would be slightly shorter than the reach of my two longest pipe clamps.

In setting up each joint, both ends of both joining pieces are snubbed down to the surface of the workbench with C-clamps, lightly but firmly, to correct any vertical disparities of the joint, at least at the ends. This is done before exerting pressure from the sides with the series of pipe clamps.

A quiet side note is in order at this point concerning the effective use of steel clamps on relatively soft wood. The available leverage is more than great enough to crush the

Doweling jig was secured to the upper ends of each leg in turn by means of a pipe clamp. A slightly greater hole depth was desired here, so a line was marked on the bit shaft (arrow) to achieve a reasonably uniform depth.

In drilling through the doweling jig, the bit shaft was kept centered in the exposed opening to assure that the holes would be perpendicular to the surface of the table top.

wood fibers, creating unsightly dings, divots and declivities in the finished work, should the clamps be tightened with more enthusiasm than judgment. If in doubt, use pads of scrap wood between the clamp jaws and the workpieces.

As the pipe clamps are tightened, glue will come oozing out of the exposed parts of the joint. I was using my usual adhesive, Elmer's Professional Carpenter's Wood glue. It's an aliphatic resin glue that I buy by the quart and decant into pint bottles that used to hold Titebond, a closely similar glue no longer obtainable locally. I prefer the Titebond dispensers because they're cylindrical rather than flat. Thus they are not as apt to be knocked over by a gust of wind or an incautious elbow.

While the glue is setting up — roughly forty-five to sixty minutes at 80 degrees F — all of the visible excess is cleaned up with a small putty knife and a piece of dampened paper towel. That is a great help, later, when you work over the surfaces with power sanding equipment because it keeps the

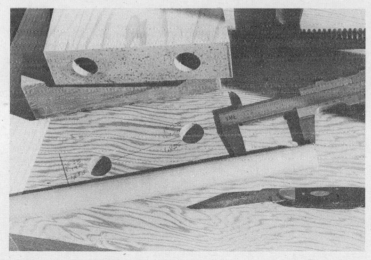

Left and above are two views made during the process of cutting the sections of ¾" hardwood dowel to the proper length. The vernier caliper was used as a depth gauge to measure each pair of holes and measurements were added. The caliper was then set for the total length and the knife was used to scribe a fine cut line on the dowel to the nearest .001", after which it was cut off on the table saw.

sandpaper from getting clogged with glue that is still only partially hardened. Any residue of glue will also prove a real headache when you come to apply the final finish, since the absorbency of the wood is changed where covered with glue.

When the joint is unclamped, the protective waxed paper is peeled away from the lower surface and that is cleaned up with the putty knife and wet paper towel in the same manner before going on to the next joint. This is just

another of the many precautions you learn to take, after having to endure the consequence of neglecting such things on an earlier project.

While assembling the top, I snapped several photos of the work in progress, showing the clamps and everything in position. Galling to say but, when the film was developed, it turned out that it was one of those times when the otherwise faithful and highly competent little Canon A-1 had elected to go into a state of snit and over-expose each

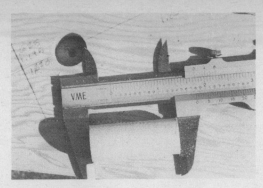

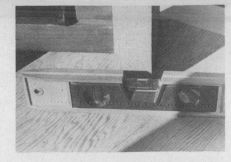

Below, after cutting and fitting, dowels were marked as to location to avoid confusion.

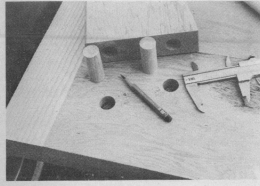

Above left, length of the cut sections of dowel was checked with the caliper and reduced as necessary by holding against the moving belt of the belt sander. Above right, a level was used to align top before gluing.

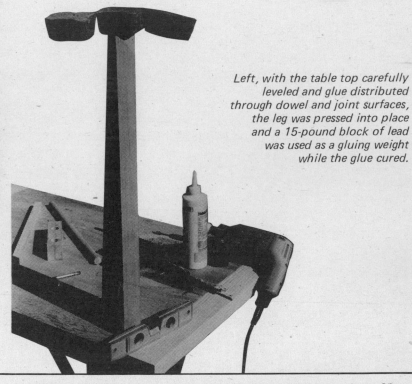

Left, with the table top carefully leveled and glue distributed through dowel and joint surfaces, the leg was pressed into place and a 15-pound block of lead was used as a gluing weight while the glue cured.

Before installing the legs, the belt sander was used to remove the layout lines from the surface.

frame by about four f-stops. It seems to do that perhaps three times in the average year and this was one of them. No one ever said it was supposed to be simple, right?

After the longitudinal (lengthwise) pieces of plank were all joined, I clamped a straightedge guide to the ends with C-clamps, having laid out a cutoff line with the draftsman's T-square, and used the electric handsaw to trim the ends dead square and flush. A 2½-inch strip of plank, the same thickness, was glued to each end, one piece at a time. Such strips serve at least two useful purposes. Not only do they cover the exposed ends of the planks, but they help greatly in preventing the planks from developing cracks at the end or from separating at the joints.

Minor irregularities between adjacent pieces of wood were trued up at this point, using the belt sander with a coarse belt followed by more work with a fine belt in place. It could have been done with a Stanley Swirlaway sanding head in the electric drill, but it would have taken quite a bit longer on a job of this size. The belt sander is a wondrously

handy tool, but it demands skilled and practiced use. If you get inattentive, especially with a coarse belt installed, it can and will create gullies that are just about beyond hope of eradicating.

With the top all joined and semi-finished, some legs were in order. I decided that I wanted the top of the table to end up 25½ inches above the floor, on the possibility that it might end up as a typing table. As the top was 1½ inches thick, the legs needed to be 24 inches long. I wanted the legs to be tapered in at least one dimension, rather than the starkly parallel sides of my usual procedures. That meant cutting a taper more or less from corner to corner of a 24-inch workpiece.

It is at least theoretically possible to improvise a taper-cutting jig for a table saw but I didn't care to tackle it for a piece that size, even on the ten-inch saw. What I did was to employ a touch of craft and guile to attack the problem from a different side.

I cut twenty-four-inch lengths from a nice, clear 2x8

Left and above are two procedures used to nudge a pair of the legs into the desired 90-degree angle while the glue was setting up. The leg above needed a bit more guidance, hence the use of the spring clamps and homemade wooden angle brace.

plank (nominal dimensions, actually 1½x7¼ inches) and made marks at opposite corners, 1½ inches from the edge. Ruling a line between each pair of marks produced the basic cutline. The workpiece was C-clamped to an end of the workbench and a guiding straightedge was clamped atop the workpiece at the correct distance from the cutline. One easy pass with the electric handsaw separated each pair of legs quite neatly and it took just a few wipes with the belt sander to render the resulting cut as smooth as a baby's cheek.

As I'd gone to the bother of creating tapered legs, I didn't fancy attaching them parallel to either the sides or ends. It was the sort of carefree and easy approach that I was trying to avoid. Instead, I used a long straightedge to mark lines on the lower side of the table top from opposite corners. I measured off 4¼ inches from each corner and made a crossmark on the layout lines at that point. Making a small mark in the center of each narrow side of the leg, at the top, I lined up those marks with the lines from corner

to corner and outlined the contacting surfaces on the lower surface of the table. Stepping back for perspective to eyeball the resulting effect, it looked quite encouraging. I toyed briefly with the possibility of trimming the top of each leg to an angle slightly greater than ninety degrees, so the legs would pitch out a bit, but quickly vetoed that idea. I visualized a table against whose legs I'd be bashing toes forever. There is nothing unendurable about a ninety-degree angle, so long as the concept isn't carried to extremes.

I did, however, want the legs to be strong enough to cope with any probable stresses they might encounter, but I was opposed to adding external — and visible — braces for the purpose. The obvious alternative was to reinforce the junctures between the tops of the legs and the lower surface of the table with dowels. That involved making up a doweling jig and it proved to be a fairly clearcut and simple chore. As a matter of fact, I got one that worked, and only on the second try.

The first attempt failed because I didn't manage to get

the guide holes centered precisely in the scrap piece of nominal 2-inch plank I was using. It was clearly visible that the holes were closer to one side than the other. On the second effort, I used a different approach for finding a centerline. I laid the workpiece on its side, held a scrap of nominal 1-inch board against it, ruling the line with a pencil, then flopped the workpiece onto its opposite side and ruled another line in the same way. This resulted in a pair of blue pencil marks, about 1/8-inch apart and it proved an easy matter to guide the point of the drill precisely between the two lines. The holes were drilled in the jig on the drill press, a reliable way to get them perpendicular, with one hole centered at 1-1/8 inches from the end of the jig and the second 4¼ inches from the same end. Held against the large end of one of the legs, it left a useful amount of wood all around each dowel.

The jig was held against the large end of each leg in turn by means of one of the pipe clamps, to keep it from moving during the drilling. With the drill spinning, I ruled a line around the shank of the bit with a felt-tip marker to serve as a guide for uniform depth. With the legs drilled, I installed a depth gauge and centered the jig over the guidelines on the lower side of the table top and held it in place with a C-clamp as I drilled matching holes at each corner in turn to accept the other ends of the dowels. The available depth with the drill stop wasn't quite enough for the legs, which is why I relied upon the mark on the bit shaft, for them.

I had planned to use hardwood dowels of ¾-inch diameter and made the holes with a Stanley auger bit designed for use in drill presses and electric hand drills. As received, the bit made a hole somewhat larger than the desired .750-inch, so I reduced the size of the bit slightly — as discussed in the chapter titled Sharpening Edged Tools — until the resulting holes were a snug fit to the dowels.

I worried a little over the chance that I might have thus used up some tolerance that I'd wish I had back, but the worries proved groundless. Everything worked like a million-dollar wristwatch, only somewhat more noisily, of course.

I used my vernier caliper to measure the depth of each matching pair of holes to the nearest .001-inch, noting both dimensions within the space that would be covered by the joint between leg and table top and adding them together to determine the exact length required for each individual dowel. Setting the vernier caliper for that given length, I used it as a gauge to make a thin knife cut to mark the cutoff point for each length of dowel. The dowel segments were cut to the knife line on the eight-inch table saw, with the planer blade still in place and the resulting length was rechecked with the vernier caliper. On a few, I ended up with dowels perhaps .005-inch too long, but it was easily rectified by turning on the belt sander and holding an end to the whirring sandpaper, rechecking with the vernier to make sure I'd gotten it down to the specified length or perhaps a couple of thousandths shorter. I had dark visions of an overlength section of dowel that might cause a bit of daylight to show between the leg and the top, and took pains to avoid such catastrophes.

With each piece of dowel painstakingly hand-fitted and marked to prevent mixups, I leveled the upper surface of the workbench with considerable care, because the attaching procedure I planned to use would be complicated

intolerably by any trace of downhill slant, or uphill, for that matter. With the table top assembly on the bench, lower side-uppermost, I proceeded to attach the legs, one at a time, letting each joint cure for upward of half an hour in the hot sun before going on to the next.

The attaching procedure went like this: I'd squeeze a small amount of glue into each of the two holes in the top and swozzle one end of each dowel down into it, turning and pushing until the excess was forced up out of the hole. Then I'd put about the same amount into each of the two holes in the top of the leg and repeat the operation on the other ends of both dowels, leaving them in place on top of the leg and applying a little more glue to the flat surface of the top of it, spreading it to a thin, uniform coat with a fingertip. Holding the leg in place, I'd apply and spread a little more glue to the outlined portion on the lower surface of the table top.

Sidenote: Before getting to the glue, I had made certain that each leg, with dowels in place, would mate correctly with the corresponding holes in the lower side of the table top. If they didn't fit, it would be a miserable thing to find out, after everything was smeared with glue, right? Right!

Once the mating glued surfaces and dowels were all brought together, deftly and expeditiously, to avoid

The Stanley Swirlaway sanding attachment, illustrated here and shown in use on the facing page, was used to even out minor irregularities of the upper and lower surfaces of the table top, in progressively finer grades of sandpaper.

dripping glue where unwanted and unneeded, it was pressed into place by hand, as far as possible, after which a fifteen-pound trio of blocks of plumber's lead was balanced carefully on the top end of the leg. The force of gravity, unfaltering for millions of years, quickly extruded any excess glue and brought all mating surfaces into snug contact.

Excess glue was cleaned away with the putty knife and wet paper towel and a small square was used to check the perpendicularity of the angle between leg and top. On a couple of the legs, it proved to be off by a degree or three. In such cases, the square was positioned with a C-clamp to warp the leg back into alignment while the glue set up.

Prior to final glue-up, I'd used the belt sander, with a fine belt installed, to erase the construction guidelines on the lower surface of the top. It was just one more thoughtful touch, since I tend to grade myself on such projects and this was one time when I was grinding for at least an A-, if not higher.

How much time is involved in the construction of such a table? As nearly as I could keep track, not counting minor distractions, it blotted up about five hours of a Saturday afternoon and another six or so the following day. Much of that time was used up in the curing of the glue in the

several joints and I was occupied at other chores, some of them unrelated to the project at hand. That brought the table to the point where it was all put together, leaving only the finishing procedures such as final hand sanding, staining and application of a suitable finish.

The result of all these efforts is impressively sturdy and solid, yet it manifests a degree of grace and style that turns up all too rarely in most such things that I produce. It's certainly true that no one is apt to wonder whether it's a Queen Anne or a Chippendale, but it seems to be shaping into a table that I can live with without need for avoiding painful winces when I happen to look at it. Stifling fatuous smirks may prove to be a greater problem, however.

In the foregoing, I tended to get a trifle prolix with the prose for a deliberate reason. I wanted to give you a fairly hi-fi insight into the thinking that goes on, as well as the purely manual procedures involved in such activities. The resulting artifact may not be quite your particular mug of mocha, but the basic approaches and procedures, modified to taste, can be employed to turn out comparable works in infinite variety. First, you have to decide what it is you really have in mind and then it becomes a somewhat simpler matter to bring the desired thing into existence.

And that's where the fun comes in...

Chapter 8

Having Your Own Sawmilling And Re-Joining Facilities Can Confer A Lot Of Useful Advantages

MAKING Big Ones
OUT OF Little Ones
AND VICE VERSA

NOMINAL one-inch lumber usually measures quite close to ¾-inch in thickness, and nominal two-inch is about 1½ inches thick. The discrepancy between termed and actual thickness is that in finishing it down smooth, about 1/8-inch is planed off of each side, but they still refer to it in terms of original dimensions.

Those are the two thicknesses of solid wood most apt to be readily available to the home workshopper. In the course of working on various projects, down the way, it may become highly desirable to obtain solid wood in thicknesses such as 1/8, 3/16, 1/4, 5/16, 3/8, 1/2, 5/8 and even larger. Generally speaking, you just can't go out and buy wood in such thicknesses but, if you happen to own a table saw or radial arm saw, you can sure as heck make your own, as we'll be discussing here.

Moreover, once you've produced a suitable quantity of thin planks of the desired dimension, it's a pleasantly simple matter to go on and join them, edge-to-edge, to produce larger boards of the intended thickness.

An illustration that appears nearby shows a carrying case that measures about 17¼x12¼x3½ inches. The entire project was made from a single piece of nominal 2x4, six feet long, in red Western cedar, at a cost of $2.40 from the local Nail Apron, and there was a reasonable amount of wood left over. The sides and ends are made of pieces about ½-inch thick, mitered at the corners and glued together.

The carrying case at left, assembled but not yet cut apart, was made from a six-foot length of 2x4, such as the one it is resting upon, by cutting the wood into strips and gluing them together, using the techniques described here.

A closer look at one of the corners, with an arrow to indicate the joint between two of the strips that were joined to make up the large sheets for the top and bottom.

Here the ten-inch Rockwell table saw has its rip fence set up for slicing wood into strips about 3/16" in thickness. Depending upon the design of the saw, it may be necessary to remove the blade guard and, if so, exceptional care must be exercised, as discussed in the text. If possible, the blade guard should be left in place. You may have to fiddle with the adjustment of blade and/or rip fence to get the slices to a uniform thickness on each edge, so make the first few trial cuts with leftover scraps of wood.

Here the two side pieces are being glued to the framework of the case, with two pieces of particle board to protect the workpiece from pressure of the C-clamps on three sides. A pair of pipe clamps have been pressed into use, also, as the supply of large C-clamps was exhausted.

The larger of my two table saws, a ten-inch Rockwell, has a maximum cut of about 3-3/8 inches; not quite enough to deal with a nominal 4x4, which is 3½ inches in each dimension. A nominal 2x4 is about the same maximum width and that means that I can take about 1/8-inch off the edge of a 2x4 and then stand it on edge and pass it through the saw, with the rip fence adjusted to produce planklets of any reasonable desired thickness.

My smaller table saw, a vintage 1962 Atlas eight-inch, has a bite of only 2¼ inches with an eight-inch blade installed and, what's more to the point, when it's trying to chew through that much thickness, it's terribly slow going. It's pushed along by a ½ hp motor, and that can seem painfully diffident, at times.

The big Rockwell has a motor rated at 2½ hp, and it whirs the ten-inch blade at fairly close to the rated maximum of 4200 rpm, which seems to figure out to a net tooth velocity of 183.26 feet per second.

When I first got the ten-inch Rockwell, I bought a few ten-inch planer blades, but found their performance rather disappointing. An eight-inch planer blade, in the old Atlas, left a cut as smooth as a baby's cheek. The same sort of blade, in the Rockwell left a fair amount of gouges and chatter marks.

I finally ended up with a Fire Tooth rip/combination blade in the Rockwell and I've come around to the

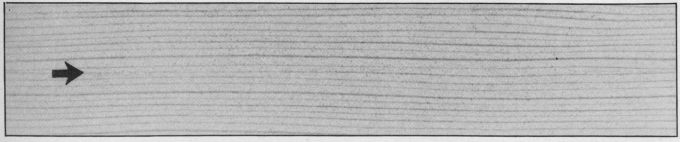

About at midpoint of the photo, as indicated by the arrow, is a joint between two pieces of redwood, at slightly larger than life size. Both pieces are from the same 2x4, so that grain and pattern match closely, making the joint hard to spot.

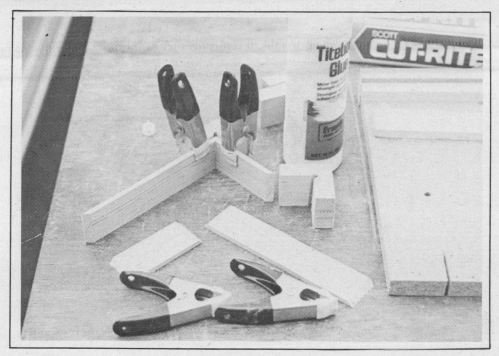

Here, four pieces of approximately ¼" strip have been mitered and are being glued together to form the framework of a small box. The corner clamps were homemade from scrap and the inside corner relieved to prevent oozing glue from adhering to the clamp while the glued joints set up.

viewpoint that it's about the best possible blade for my usual purposes, in that saw.

Planer blades have no set at all, meaning the kerf (saw cut) is absolutely at exact blade thickness. If there is any warping strain in the wood, itself, the kerf may pinch at the rear to bind the blade rotation, unless offset by a judiciously inserted wedge at that point.

The ten-inch Fire Tooth rip/combination has a generous amount of set, meaning that it carves a kerf wider than the minimum thickness of the blade. It gnaws briskly along cuts as thick as 3-3/8-inch, goaded along by the 2½ hp motor.

The resulting cut is by no means as baby-cheek smooth as one might wistfully wish. There is an easy solution to that problem, however. Just cut the planklet a tiny bit thicker than you had in mind in the first place and then dress it down with a belt sander, using a medium-grit belt for initial smoothing and a fine-grit for the end finish.

Regardless of the sort of saw being used, you'll probably be well advised to slice a hunk of scrap wood at first, to check for an absolutely parallel cut. The first planklet may be 5/16 on one edge and 3/16 on the opposite one, which dictates an adjustment of the angle of either the blade or the rip fence, or perhaps of both. Another indicated precaution is to make certain the rip fence is absolutely parallel with the blade, front-to-back. If there is a bit of toed-in angle, the wood may wedge against the side of the whirring sawblade, hanging up operations. If they veer apart, even slightly, you may not be able to hold the uncut

Here, a larger board, roughly 10x16¾x5/16", has been assembled from three strips of fir that has a novel, rippling grain pattern.

The improvised joining board in use to glue six strips together. The two strips at right are glued to the piece of particle board to form a straight and sturdy vertical surface. Strip at left is movable and somewhat curved, with its concave surface positioned against the left strip to maintain pressure throughout the length. A small block was used behind it to get the jaw of the pipe clamp a bit lower. Note the piece of wax paper beneath the strip to prevent adhesion to the joining board. Only a moderate amount of pressure is exerted at this point, to prevent the strips from popping upward. Refer to the next photo.

stock against the rip fence for the full length of the cut.

It shouldn't need saying, but I'll say it anyway: This is an operation that requires the greatest possible care and attention to safety precautions. In some of the accompanying photo illustrations, the guard has been removed from the saw for an unimpeded view of what's going on. If at all possible or practicable, the guard should be left in place and, if it's removed, never forget that those razor-sharp teeth are traveling at speeds in the range of air gun pellets. They may slow down while cutting woods, but they'd never even *notice* a finger!

If small planks at the maximum cutting width of your saw will serve your needs, a simple dressing down with the belt sander — or a Stanley Swirlaway sanding head in an electric drill, if you don't have a belt sander — will complete the home sawmill operation. With care, practice and the right blade, you can turn out some remarkably thin stock, if that's what you want, down to 1/16-inch or finer. That gets into the category of veneers, and you can dress up a project in common wood by applying thin layers of carefully fitted veneering over the exposed surfaces.

If you require working stock in widths greater than you

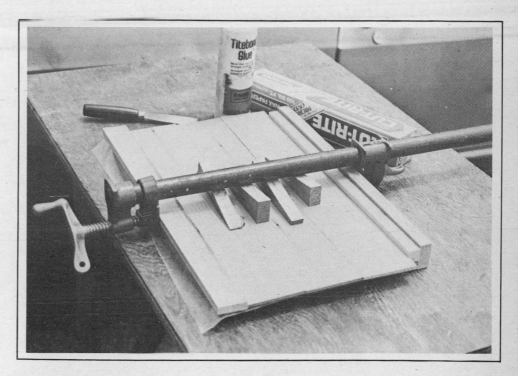

This isn't the same assembly, but it's closely similar and four of the little wooden wedges have been placed between the pipe and the strips with moderate pressure to prevent the pieces from bowing upward when the pipe clamp is tightened.

can saw, you'll have to glue the strips edge-to-edge, but that's not at all difficult. Nearby photos show a small edge-gluing table I knocked together out of a leftover piece of particle board and some scrap strips of wood. Sneer at particle board if you feel so inclined, but it has the one saving virtue of being awfully close to dead-flat and it tends to stay that way, rather than warping about as the relative humidity changes. The ledge at the rear provides a straight and solid edge against which the first strip can be anchored while the rest of the strips are being pressed into place. If you need to work with larger assemblies, the gluing board can be made up to any desired size, up to 4x8 feet.

You'll note, in the photos, that we tear off a strip of wax paper and lay it on the particle board as a foundation. That's to spare us the annoyance and frustration of having oozing glue cement the assembly inextricably to the base board. One of the little dispenser rolls of wax paper, available from any supermarket, is one of the handiest items around the shop, especially if you can find where you left it after using it last!

Our glue for the operation is Elmer's Professional Carpenter's Wood Glue, bought in quart containers and redispensed into Titebond bottles for convenience, since they're not as apt to blow over in a gust of wind as the flat bottles used by Borden. Those who do all their work indoors can stay with the flat and teetery bottles, but they can't hose the sawdust away down the sloping drive at the end of the project, right? Similar and comparable creamy-yellow glues (aliphatic resins, to be technical) are available in additional brands such as Gluebird or Wilhold; perhaps others with which I'm not familiar. They share a useful virtue: If properly applied, the resulting joint usually is stronger than the wood itself. Proper application involves

In the photo at left, three pipe clamps are in use, with the wedges positioned to force the strips down flat against the particle board for better alignment of the mating edges.

In this assembly, there is a marked discrepancy between two of the strips (arrow). You can push down firmly at such points, before final tightening of the pipe clamp, and wipe it all smooth later, when using belt sander for finish.

clamping to put the joining surfaces into close and intimate contact, thereby greatly increasing the strength of the joint.

Somewhere along the way, a scrap of wood turned up with a fairly pronounced warp in its narrower dimension, though it's nicely flat the other way. There is a use for nearly everything, if only you can find it, and this warped hunk of scrap wood turned out to be just perfect as a movable backing strip for gluing strips of wood together. A single pipe clamp is positioned between the middle of the warped strip and the back brace of the gluing board and tightened down gently. That straightens the warped wood against the strips being joined and maintains a considerable degree of pressure down the full length of the workpiece, both ways from the center.

If desired, a few more pipe clamps can be located in strategic places to further increase the pressure. Judicious is the pertinent word, here. A good sturdy pipe clamp can exert a force of a few hundred pounds, if savagely torqued; more than enough to damage the wood, in a lot of instances. The goal is to exert enough force, but not too much.

That gets even more pertinent if you're joining several strips of wood that are quite thin in the first place. Here, we'll take "thin" to mean anything less than around 5/16-inch. Exert a bit too much pressure and suddenly it will bow in places and snap upward in crazy angles and you've got the whole job to do all over again. As so often is the case, a bit of shrewd strategy forestalls the whole problem in the first place.

When you install the first pipe clamp, in the center of the assembly, just snub it down to easy contact and then slide in a few wooden wedges between the pipe and the surfaces of the different strips, so as to forestall any bowing-up movement on the part of the fragile strips. Wooden wedges, such as those shown in the photos, are another super-handy item to have around the shop. They can be made up from scrap wood, rather than throwing the precious stuff away. Just set the crossbar of the miter gauge on your table saw a bit askew and convert the scrap to wedges by flopping the board after each cut. The resulting wedges can be used to cure the teetering tendencies of four-legged items on uneven footing. Two, of the same angle, can be positioned point-to-point to form an adjustable squeezer with parallel sides that can be used to hold a lot of low-strain components being assembled. Toss your accumulation of little wedges into a handy box and you'll find yourself reaching for them constantly.

As you snug down the pressure, the inevitable excess of glue will ooze from the joints, both from the upper surface and the lower, as well. That's why we were so crafty as to put down a piece of wax paper beneath it. Excess ooze from the top can be cleaned up with a putty knife at this time, which gets around the need for removing it with sandpaper, once it hardens. The yellow, aliphatic resin glues, once fully hardened, have the virtue of clogging sandpaper little if at all. Several other glues, including the original white glue that dries clear, tend to soften under the heat of friction and use up a lot of sandpaper in the process.

Paper towels are endless in demand around the shop, particularly for cleaning up after gluing operations, and the holder shown here was constructed from leftover scraps. The plate at left was a cutout left from making a large hole in a piece of ¼'' Masonite with the Pawood circle cutter. A length of 1'' hardwood dowel makes up the shaft on which the towel turns, and the right-hand end plate is held in place by the little pin of ¼'' dowel inserted in the hole visible here.

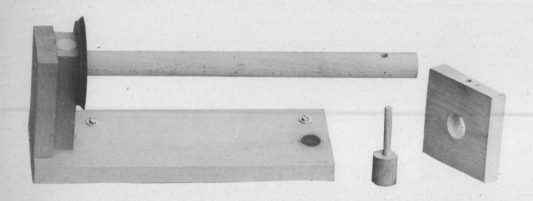

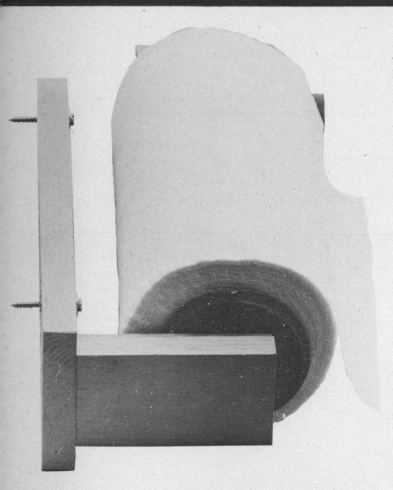

The usual aliphatic resin glue was used for assembling the pieces and the end of the dowel is glued into a 1'' hole drilled about 1'' into the end brackets. Right, after trying several different brands, Grennell prefers Bounty for use in the shop, due to its superior wet strength and absorbency.

Another view of the paper towel rack with the retaining plate and peg in place. Two No. 8x1½ sheet metal screws and washers hold it to the vertical studs of the shop wall.

Aliphatic resin glues set up slowly if at all when the temperature is at or below the readings shown at right.

You'll want a bucket of water handy, with a shop rag for getting the stubborn glue off the putty knife and your fingertips, with a roll of paper towels nearby for drying, wiping and general cleanup. If wax paper is indispensible around the shop, paper towels are even moreso. When my present shop had been in service for a year or so, I found myself going slightly bananas, eternally in feverish quest of the roll of paper towels, so I devoted an entire Sunday afternoon to the fabrication of a marvelous paper towel holder that is immovably attached to one of the studs. I've never had trouble putting hands upon a paper towel since. For shop purposes, Bounty seems to be the best of the brands currently available, being strong and notably absorbent.

Once the strips have been set up for gluing, they should remain for a suitable length of time, somewhat inversely proportionate to the ambient temperature. The critical temperature for aliphatic resin glues is about 65F/19C. Below that point, their curing time approaches infinity, asymptotically. It's hard to pinpoint, and it depends upon the given application, but a rough rule would be one hour at 70F, half an hour at 80F or fifteen minutes at 90F. That brings the glued joint to the point where it will endure modest strains without coming infuriatingly apart. Double the specified times if you're working with materials such as Masonite or particle board, rather than solid, tree-grown woods.

When the elapsed interval has come to an end, loosen and remove the clamps and lift the assembly from the supporting board. The wax paper will come with it, to the sound effects of a hissy crackle. If you left it a bit too long, prepare to be really astounded at the tenacious grip the aliphatic resin glue can get on even so unlikely a medium as wax paper! You'll have to peel it away gently and, in extreme cases, you'll have to scrape and sand stuck strips of wax paper off the lower side. Be very glad you had the forethought to put down the wax paper, right?

If you didn't wait overly long, the oozed glue on the underside can be cleaned up usefully with a putty knife, and the wax paper won't cling too badly. Be cautious about scrubbing it off with a sopping paper towel, because the water will raise the grain of the wood and could even resoften the glued joint, in extreme examples. Better to let it get good and dry so you can cope with it by means of sandpaper.

At this phase in its development, your assembly may not present quite the smooth appearance you really had in mind. Not to fret. Sandpaper, that utterly indispensible stuff, has the ability to cloak a multitude of constructional shortcomings. Minor irregularities, on the order of 1/128 to 1/16-inch disappear rapidly under the abrasive magic of rapidly moving sandpaper.

Here is the improvised holder for the Black & Decker Workmate, for holding items being belt-sanded at various points of the operation. A short length of 2x4 has a small piece of scrap glued to the opposite end, projecting about 1/8" above the surface, to serve as a stop for sanding strips or small assemblies. At the near end, here, another short piece of 2x4 was glued to the longer piece, both upper surfaces flush with each other. In this photo, the framework for the small wooden case is in the process of being sanded. The inner surfaces, of course, must be sanded smooth before assembling with glue.

My belt sander is a Black & Decker Model 7451, using a 3x24-inch sanding belt at a no-load speed of 1200 feet per minute (a trifle under fourteen miles per hour). Of all the power tools I'd really hate to have to get along without, the belt sander ranks high on the list. Properly and skillfully employed, it gets work done in seconds that would require minutes or even hours by other approaches. More, it whirs the sandpaper in a perfectly straight line, enabling you to get away from the unsightly rotary sanding marks that are the bane of most rotary or oscillating sanders.

Skillful use is the keynote, and that takes a bit of experience and rueful realization, along the way. The belt sander must be kept in motion, especially when using the coarser grits of belts. Let it pause for just a moment and you can create an unsightly gouge that you may (or, again, may not) be able to wipe away before you run out of working stock. Such errors tend to be highly educational.

Using a belt sander to maximum advantage requires that the workpiece be held securely. As the tool develops quite a lot of rearward thrust, at up to nearly 14 mph, an insecure hold can cause the workpiece to come scooting back into your gizzard or groin at the same speed, if it gets loose from

The Black & Decker Model 7451 uses
3x24" sanding belts in various grits,
such as the 40-grit/extra coarse and
120-grit/fine belts illustrated here.
Coarser grades cost a bit more, but
they make short work of the early
elimination of major irregularities.

*In this example, a strip of wood scrap has been C-clamped
to the rear edge of the three legged workbench as a retainer
to hold a fairly large assembly of strips for final finishing.
The upper end in this photo has already been sanded, then
reversed in order to sand irregularities from the lower end.*

Here is the holding block illustrated earlier, before the final crosspiece was added to the opposite end. The block at the near end projects slightly above the 2x4 to provide support for the thin strips being belt-sanded with the Black & Decker.

the holding device. Again, that can be memorably educational. The tractional forces are enough to require a heavy, solid, holding support. My lightweight portable workbench will tip and totter all over the place if I try to use it for belt sanding. The mass of the stand for the Black & Decker Workmate stays put much better, so I've come to favor that.

At any rate, it turns out to be a simple matter to install a coarse or medium belt in the sander and scour away the obvious irregularities, switching to a fine belt for the sleek final finish. Carefully and thoughtfully employed, the techniques described here will enable you to produce sheets of wood in the desired thickness, of nearly any practical length and width.

You may have been wondering why anyone goes to all

this bother to make up pieces of thin wood when they could just buy a hunk of plywood in the first place. Good question! I'll try to explain. Plywood is great stuff, and I employ it frequently when it seems suited to the need at hand. It suffers, however, from the handicap of having an exposed raw edge that is painfully vulnerable to wear and hard knocks. If you wish to miter all the corners to conceal and protect the edge, there is no big problem, in low-wear applications. A nearby photo shows the appalling degree of decrepitude that a utility carrying case achieved after a few years of casual use and banging about. The laminations of plywood came unglued, splintering away to result in an artifact that you feel inclined to carry beneath your coat tails, out of sight of the jeering public.

In reviewing the discussion to this point, it appears that I

A strip of redwood, about 3/16'' by 3-3/8'', after being smoothed down with the belt sander in the holder.

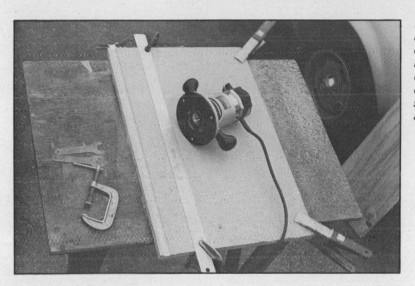

Here's a new and larger joining board in the early phases of its construction. The drafting square has been C-clamped to the piece of particle board and a shallow channel was routed to accept the strip of 1'' board that will serve as a straight surface at the rear.

Assemblies of moderate width can be belt-sanded in the holder by moving them from side to side as work progresses.

Here's a ghastly example of what several years of hard duty can do to a utility carrying case covered with plywood. The thin layers of decorative veneer loosened from the support and were broken off, producing a thoroughly unsightly look.

Here's the completion of the new joining board shown at the start on a previous page. Titebond glue has been applied to the routed channel and to the lower edge of the strip. Five C-clamps apply gluing pressure against protective strip of scrap.

neglected to crank at least one further helpful stratagem: After you've cut what I chose to term "planklets" from the original parent stock, and before your commence to join them together with glue, edge-to-edge, it is extremely helpful to give them a thin edge-trim, on both long edges, to square the edges. Set up the rip fence of the table saw to remove just the merest cat's-whisker from one edge of each of the strips, setting them aside in uniform order for further attention. Then move the rip fence another 1/32-inch or so closer to the blade, checking to make sure fence and blade are dead-parallel, and pick up each piece in turn to trim the second edge. A planer blade works best for this.

It is a somewhat paradoxical axiom of gluing, especially in applications such as edge-gluing, that the least amount of glue holds the best and strongest, provided that there is a uniform distribution of glue.

A joint, set up and glued, with smooth, straight, flat surfaces held together in a sensible amount of compression,

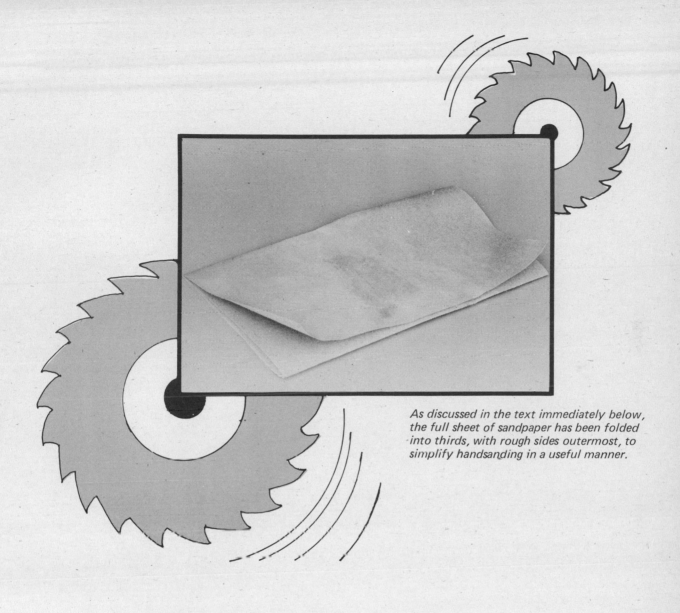

As discussed in the text immediately below, the full sheet of sandpaper has been folded into thirds, with rough sides outermost, to simplify handsanding in a useful manner.

will produce a melding-together that usually is stronger than the wood on either side of the joint. If skeptical, you can prove or disprove this by making up a sample with scrap wood and breaking it at or near the joint.

If you are gluing strips together, it seems the best course to use the strips as they come from the saw — apart from the edge-dressing just discussed — leaving the final finishing with the belt sander, Swirlaway or orbital/oscillating sander, or just plain elbow-grease, in a pinch.

Let me pass along a useful tip on hand sanding, revealed to me by an expert patternmaker, many years ago. If you've ever tried to sand by hand, you notice right off that the friction between the rough side of the paper and the workpiece is much greater than that between your fingertips and the smooth side of the paper. If you try to offset this by folding the paper in half, it will hold on the folded side and slip on the loose side and you won't have gained much, if anything.

The secret, as it turns out, is to fold the sheet of sandpaper into thirds, with rough side out, top and bottom. This gives you a useful grip for your fingers and it will not collapse and distort under strain in reasonably patient, practiced, skillful use.

Small pieces of leftover sandpaper can be attached to bits of scrap wood, perhaps with another bit of scrap for a handle, to make improvised sanding blocks that are almost sinfully handy for small finishing chores. When the sandpaper has lost the last of its bite, you can replace it with another sheet, throw away the entire assembly, or toss it into a box of hopeless scrap for eventual use as kindling for the barbecue pit. A well-run shop minimizes its waste, raw material being as dear as it is. Meat packers used to boast that they used everything but the squeal. In more recent times, they seem to have perfected the technique of selling even that to modern musical groups...

Chapter 9

Natural Art

Train Your Eye To Spot Likely Prospects, Do A Little Finishing And Framing, And You Can Turn Out Some Eye-Arresting Works!

A SWISS psychiatrist, Hermann Rorschach (1884-1922), developed the testing approach that bears his name, the Rorschach inkblot test, in which the subject is asked what each of a series of inkblots suggest to him or her.

You needn't be mentally ill to see pictures in ostensibly random patterns, as witness New Hampshire's celebrated Great Stone Face, a natural rock formation. Cypress knees, in grotesque shapes, sell briskly to the tourist trade in places where cypress knees can be harvested. We've had one such artifact around the house for several years and, to my eye, it looks rather like a rooster who, after being plucked, staggered groggily back to his feet. No, I'm not sure why we've kept it so long; just one of those things you can't quite bear to throw away.

My first effort toward letting Mother Nature express herself came along quite by accident and without premeditation. I happened to notice that a small, cut-off piece of 2x2 lumber in the shop seemed to have a pair of eyes, peering out at the world rather truculently. As I did a

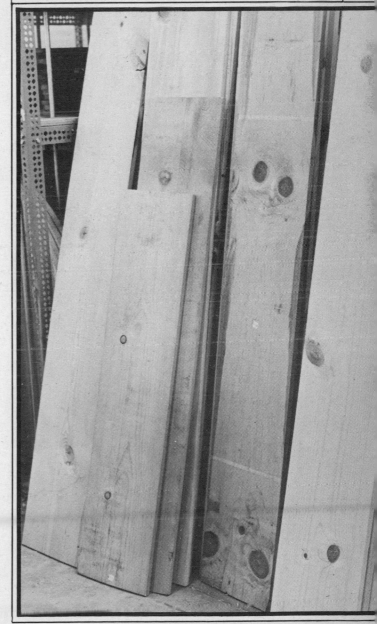

At right is the board bearing the owl's face, as originally sighted in the display of lumber. On the facing page, Ms. Lizzie Eller of the Nail Apron staff, holds it up to give you a better view of the board, as purchased.

The remarkably lifelike hoot owl in the photo below was discovered quite inadvertantly in a piece of scrap during one of Grennell's too-rare shop-cleaning sprees.

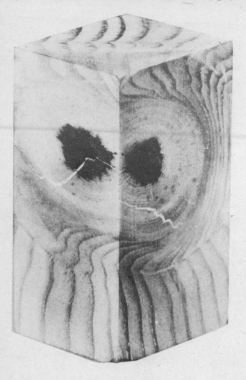

double-take, the lines of the grain seemed to form the head and face of some species of owl; the barred owl, *(Strix varia)*, I'd say, often called the hoot owl for its marrow-curdling night cries. The hoot owl has the huge, dark eyes, surrounded by concentric circles, closely similar to the owl in the block.

For comparison purposes, I'll include a rather nice portrait of Esmeralda, a full-time, professional great horned owl *(Bubo virginianus),* and a star performer at the San Diego Animal Park. Her expression suggests that she's about to express her opinion of hoot owls, or perhaps of photographers.

I donated the first owl block to the Patti Carpenter Museum of Owlish Artifacts, in which it is prominently displayed. Mrs. Carpenter supports her owl habit by working for *Road Rider* magazine as its women's editor.

The next such pattern that turned up is the one I call "BEM in a Board." Bem, I should note, is a science-fiction fan's handy term for bug-eyed monsters of the sort often featured on the slightly lurid covers of science-fiction magazines. Actually, it looks at least as much like some species of African horned ungulate that I can't quite seem to identify, complete with a string of freckles down the center of its nose. The piece of wood was a nominal 1x12, apparently sawn from about the center of the log. The freckles and dark streak on the forehead are the heartwood at the core of the trunk and the two knots that form the eyes were branches from the tree's early youth.

Not surprisingly, that board tended to warp and curl, so I had to laminate it to another piece to get it flat enough to

By way of supplying something for accurate comparison, this is Esmeralda, the fulltime professional great horned owl. Esmeralda is a star performer at the Birds Of Prey feature in the San Diego Wild Animal Park. Her opinion of photographers is obvious, right?

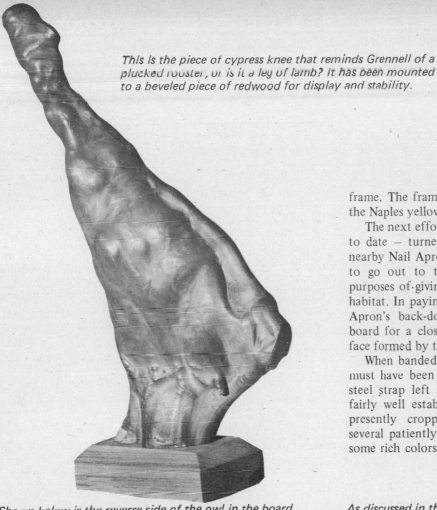

This is the piece of cypress knee that reminds Grennell of a plucked rooster, or is it a leg of lamb? It has been mounted to a beveled piece of redwood for display and stability.

frame. The frame is dark redwood that contrasts nicely to the Naples yellow tone of the board.

The next effort — untitled to the present and unfinished, to date — turned up in a display of six-foot 1x12s at the nearby Nail Apron and I had the unusual presence of mind to go out to the car and return with the camera for purposes of·giving you a view of such things in their natural habitat. In paying for it, Lizzie Eller — in charge of the Nail Apron's back-door cash register — very kindly held the board for a closer view of the curiously troubled-looking face formed by the knots and swirls.

When banded for shipment from the sawmill, this board must have been at the top or bottom of a stack and the steel strap left a mark a few inches above the face that fairly well established the upper limit of the picture. As presently cropped, it measures 9-5/8x11½ inches and several patiently cured coats of tung oil have brought out some rich colors in the wood, increasing the contrast of the

Shown below is the reverse side of the owl in the board, an intriguing image in its own right and only slightly inferior to the obverse side shown at right, below.

As discussed in the text, a mark left by a steel banding strap fairly well dictated the top of the picture, and it was trimmed on the lower edge to Grennell's choice in proportion.

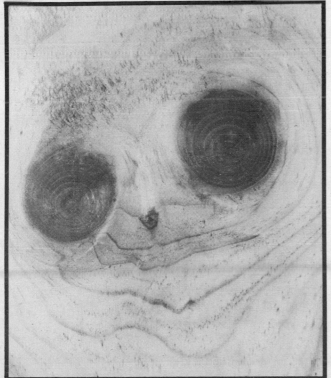

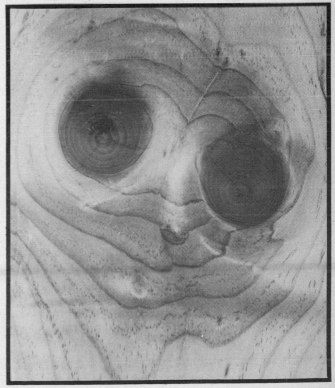

Grennell's "BEM In A Board," was given a few coats of spray Varathane varnish and framed with dark redwood.

grain in the process. Oddly enough, there is almost as good a face on the reverse side, but it has a large rough area above the knots that would require a prodigious amount of sanding to clean up. It would be necessary to remove nearly a quarter-inch of stock from the back to get it smooth, and that wouldn't leave much wood.

My general feeling on such things is that it would be quite unsporting to perform any kind of retouching to augment the effect of the natural image, beyond simple sanding and application of coats of finish, with steel wool rubdowns to prepare it for the next coat.

As a direct upshot of all this, I find myself pawing through the boards at local lumberyards with a fresh and different viewpoint. Previously, I'd been looking for boards with large areas of clear wood, free of unsightly knots. Now, I'm taking a keen and thoughtful look at the knots, too.

Down in the Ozarks, they tell of an old mountaineer who wasn't above giving Ms. Nature a helping hand with her works. His specialty was carving bears from natural wood burls for sale to the passing motorists. Asked how he did it, he replied, "Well, I just look at the burl until I can see a b'ar, and then I cut away the excess wood, and thar's your b'ar."

Examples of unusual configuration or grain pattern, such as those shown, can be handled as pictures in their own right — framed to taste and displayed on the wall — or they can serve as a component of some other artifact; as the face of a homemade clock, for example, a bookend or what have you. The important thing, as I see it, is not to let such curious natural wonders go to waste. If you agree, watch for similar examples at the lumberyards, and good hunting!

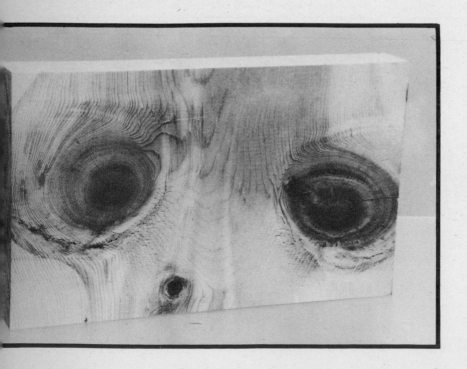

Knot formation at left was sectioned from a piece of nominal 2x12 pine. Various viewers have professed to see a rather bewildering variety of images in the grain pattern of this specimen.

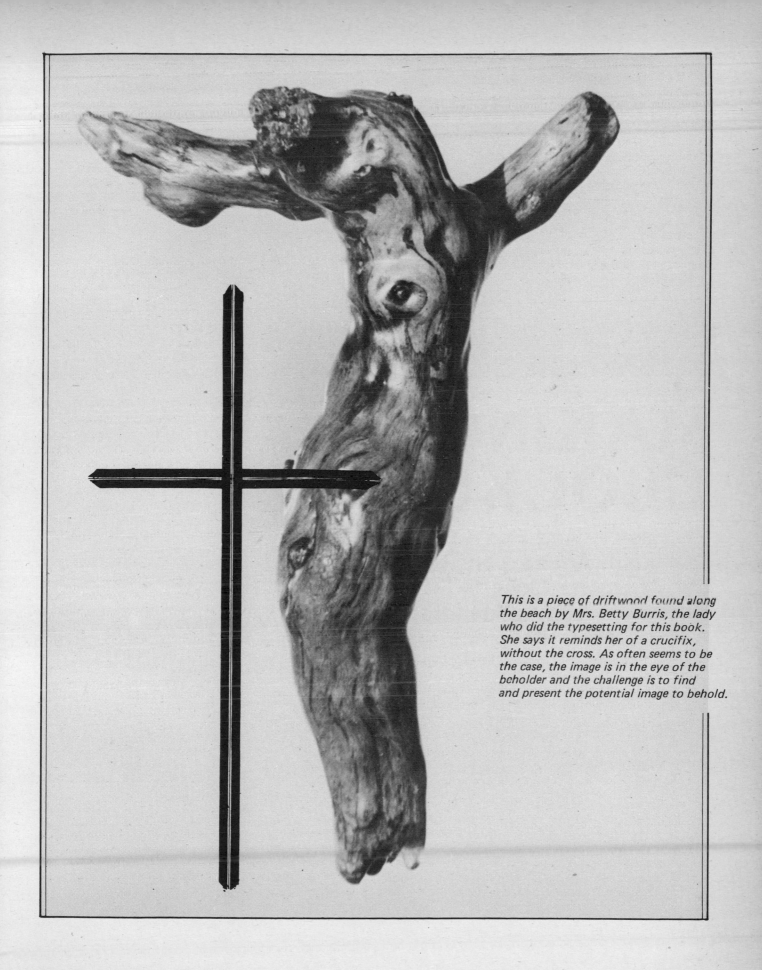

This is a piece of driftwood found along the beach by Mrs. Betty Burris, the lady who did the typesetting for this book. She says it reminds her of a crucifix, without the cross. As often seems to be the case, the image is in the eye of the beholder and the challenge is to find and present the potential image to behold.

MAKING CLOCKS

It's Easy — And Fun—To Transform An Inexpensive Set Of Quartz Clock Movement And Hands Into A Handsome Timepiece

MAKING CLOCKS is by no means the complex and difficult project that you might assume it to be. Expenditure of approximately $10 to $15 puts you in possession of the works, hands and perhaps a set of inexpensive numerals in your choice of Arabic or Roman. After that, all you have to do is to dream up and fabricate some manner of mounting enclosure for the clockwork and finish it to taste.

Ordinary electric clocks, of the type that plug into wall sockets, depend for their accuracy upon the power company's unswerving 60-cycle alternating current (AC). The small movement shown here operates on direct current (DC) which is supplied by a common C-size flashlight battery. Experience with clocks built around similar units indicates that they are astonishingly accurate, and the single battery powers them for well over one year before requiring replacement. The large wall clock, illustrated here, was built by our son Chuck and given to us as a Christmas present, two years ago. It's still keeping precise time on the same, original battery.

The opposite of a stopwatch would be a startclock, I guess, and this is the clock made and presented by son Chuck to fire his sire's enthusiasm for such projects. Its face and frame are of Hawaiian koa wood, measuring 16¼ inches in height and width. A single C-size alkaline battery has kept it running with impressive accuracy for over two years.

Ever since Chuck bestowed the fruits of his clockmaking expertise upon us, I've been experiencing pangs of fierce yen to follow in his footsteps. It seemed as if it ought to be a lot of fun and, as I can now testify, it surely is.

There are mail-order firms that offer clock movements such as the one shown, but I prefer to see the merchandise, pay for it and carry it away, given a choice. I finally found the movements for sale at an establishment doing business under the firm name of It's About Time Clock Company (1238 South Beach Boulevard, Anaheim, California 92804). Ray Taylor, the firm's proprietor, tells me that they will have a catalog listing items such as the movement shown, hands, dials, and similar supplies and equipment for free distribution on request. A self-addressed, stamped envelope would be appreciated, of course.

Thus, we can quote at least one source for the basic ingredients of your homegrown clock, assuming that the firm isn't within easy driving distance. Be it noted, however, that Taylor's shop is but one of a great many emporiums gathered together at a shopping center known as Hobby City, at the corner of Beach Boulevard and Ball Road, in Anaheim. Should your travel plans encompass a trip to Anaheim to take in Disneyland and similar tourist attractions, I'd warmly recommend a detour to Hobby City, a flotilla of firms that strives valiantly — and quite successfully — to be all things to all hobbyists.

To name but a few examples, there are shops for the rock hound and lapidary buff, stores for the model railroad enthusiast, aquarium supplies, a doll museum, model aircraft needfuls and, last but not least, the Flintlock Sporting Goods establishment, operated by Taylor's parents, Ray and Jackie, featuring kits for building black powder guns and countless other items dear to the hearts of primitive Americana aficionados. Few indeed are the collectors and builders who won't find their special interest catered to rather extravagantly at the Hobby City complex and I mention it here on the excuse that, if you ever get a chance to take it in, I believe you'll be grateful for the tip.

But let's veer back to the topic at the head of this chapter. When I returned with my un-Swiss movement, the first thing I did was to install a Ray-O-Vac alkaline C-cell, install the hands and hang the unadorned result from a nail in the wall. That was a mistake and I note it here in hopes of saving you from the consequences. First of all, the minute hand goes over a flattened portion of the shaft and it needs a small retaining nut to hold it in place. I didn't realize that, nor did I get the necessary retaining nut which — as I can now reveal — is threaded 8-32. If you just hang the minute hand in place, as I did, it will have enough play so that it will either hang up on the hour hand or fall clean off, which is what mine did. As it was hanging on the wall above a credenza weighing quite a lot and not easily movable, the first minute hand is not really lost, because I know where it is: It's behind the dingbing credenza.

Chapter 10

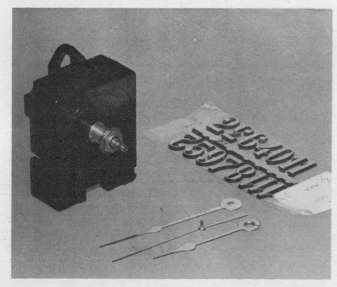

Here is the movement, hands and set of Arabic numerals purchased for well under $20 from It's About Time Clock Company. This particular design of minute hand requires a retaining nut threaded 8-32, as was discovered later.

A piece of koa wood, picked up for 60 cents from remnant table at Gentry Woods was cut into three pieces, its edges dressed on the planer blade in the table saw, whereupon the three pieces were joined with pipe clamps and a joining board, using aliphatic resin glue. With the glue set up, ends of assembly were trimmed to be square with width.

A front-quarter view of the quartz clock movement, with hands installed, but without the retaining 8-32 nut. Loop at left is for hanging completed clock from wall. Central shaft is a tiny bit larger than 3/8-inch in diameter.

A view of the quartz movement from the back, with the C-cell akaline battery installed. Accuracy of this clock has been all but incredible, with somewhat less than one second of departure from "Ma Bell time" over a month.

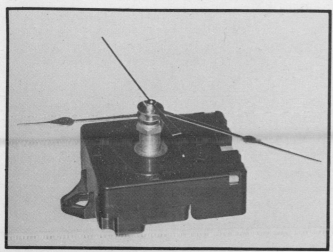

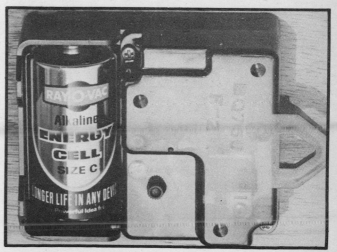

It probably would not have fallen off if I hadn't cannibalized its second hand to put onto Chuck's clock. The original second hand for that one had gotten lost on the way from Chuck's shop — lurking place of his table saw which, gosh help us, is known as Buz Sawyer! — to our dining room. The transplant was quite successful and (sigh) yes, I guess you could say that Chuck's clock now has a second-hand second hand...

Thus it came to pass that the heart and soul of the elder Grennell's first clockly project hung on the wall, with its works all nude and nothing but the surviving hour hand for a matter of some months; a mutely accusing eyesore, every time I happened to glance at it.

The triggering catalyst that finally got me launched into the...uhh...clockenspiel at hand was my happy discovery of a fairly nearby purveyor of exotic raw materials called The

Gentry Woods (23112 Alcalde, Suite E, Laguna Hills, California 92653). Nosing about the place is like a termite's dream of paradise. They have stocks of nearly every gorgeous wood in existence. One they don't seem to have, as yet, is white locust; a special favorite of mine. I rather doubt if many sources offer white locust, because the trees rarely seem to get much larger than four or five inches through the trunks. It is one of the hardest and, I believe, the heaviest of all North American native woods, at around forty-nine pounds to the cubic foot. Belying its name, white locust cures to a rich and vivid lemon yellow, and it works up like elephant tusk ivory.

Despite the lack of white locust, Gentry Woods comes awfully close to offering anything else worth coveting, and every time I visit their seductive stockroom, I get visions of second and third mortgages on the house. For that reason, I

Another view of the face under pressure on the joining board. Note the use of a vertical pipe clamp at the rear to keep the horizontal clamps from bowing up.

Here, the movement has been attached to the face and the assembly rests on the flat saw bed to position first piece of frame so its rear (lower, here) surface will be flush with the rear of the movement, when it's hanging.

ration my visits rather severely. On first encounter, I came away clutching a noble plank of African padauk — rich, reddish chocolate in color and sinfully sensuous to the touch — some zebrawood and a handsome slab of tulipwood. Tulipwood has got to be my prime candidate for the sexiest wood ever grown. It almost makes you want to consign burl walnut to the fireplace; yes, really.

On the second visit, I came away with some slabs of clear birch, and a few hunks of koa that were on their odds and ends table, at sixty and forty cents apiece. The sixty-cent piece of koa ended up as the face of my first clock, cut into shorter sections and edge-glued by the techniques described in the chapter on making big ones out of little ones. I cut my slab of tulipwood up into two-inch strips and mitered the corners to form the outer framework of the clock enclosure. As I wanted the frame to be flush

with the back of the movement, to facilitate hanging it on the wall, I used the bed of the eight-inch saw — commonly known as Euripides — as the aligning surface for gluing the frame, since it's probably the dead-flattest large surface readily available.

The outside diameter of the threaded major mounting shaft of the clock movement was a bit over 3/8-inch. I made a trial hole in a piece of scrap wood with one of the unmodified Stanley auger bits in 3/8-inch size and found to my delight, that it was oversize by just enough to make a perfect fit over the threaded mounting shank.

It was during the course of the mounting activities that I tried a few nuts on the flat-sided shaft that drives the minute hand and discovered that the threads were of 8-32 persuasion. I had a quantity of hex nuts in that size on hand, and installed one, but the effect seemed a touch

A drafting T-square was held against a side and used to align the 3-9 o'clock line of the template as precisely as possible, as shown by the thin, uniform strip of white seen here between the line and the edge of the drafting square.

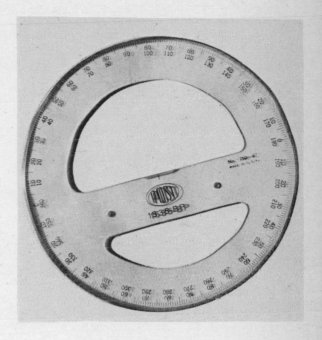

A 360° protractor, above, was used in preliminary dial layout, but a better method is available, as told at the end of the chapter. Left, the arrow indicates shallow hole used to stop dowels at a uniform height. Below, clock installed in mount, before adding the markers to it.

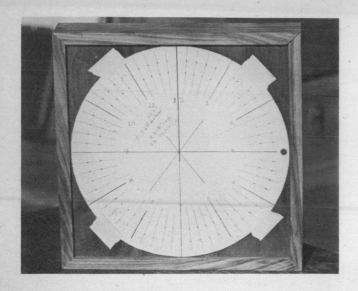

inches in each direction, while the minute-hand was a trifle less than 3½ inches in its swept radius. I decided to set up for a dial on a seven-inch circle, and adjourned to my drafting table.

I will confess that I make up drawings only as a bitter last resort. I hate drafting with a whole-souled passion, a souvenir from the seventeen years spent as a heating/air-conditioning engineer when altogether too many weekends were frittered away at the drafting table, designing systems because there simply wasn't time for such chores that could be purloined from the rest of the week. This, however, was one of those times when a session at the table was inescapable, so I sighed and programmed it.

I set the compass as closely as possible to a 3½-inch radius and drew the basic circle, quartering that with the T-square and triangle, then using a circular protractor to pinpoint the location of the hour marks in between, such as one and two, four and five, et al.

As always, in the throes of such projects, there was the insidious temptation to choose the easy, quick and simple route. With just the hours marked off, one could look at

Left above, the marking layout, on heavy paper, is held to front of the face with strips of drafting tape, after being aligned as closely as possible, and centered. Left, a scratch awl is used to punch marks through the layout into the wood for drilling to install dowels.

overly Gopher Baroque, so I jam-tightened two of the little hex nuts onto the shaft of an 8-32 screw, securing that into the three-jaw chuck of the little Edelstaal Unimat lathe and turned down the flats of the first nut to a nice circular configuration, as shown in the accompanying photo. I've reminded myself, times beyond hope of counting, that the little Unimat isn't much of a lathe, but it's just incomparably better than no lathe at all. Lacking a Unimat, or other lathe, the same chore could be handled by a ¼-inch electric drill, clenched in the bench vise, using a flat file to round off the corners of the nut.

Most of my shop time turns up on weekends and the enclosing of the works, as just described, soaked up all the free time of a Saturday and Sunday. That left the project with the hands held in secure alignment, rotating about a handsome square of koa wood, enclosed by a seductive frame of tulipwood, but with nothing at which to point. It reposed atop the living room television set for the ensuing week, with its second-hand twitching compellingly, meanwhile leaving the viewer a bit bemuddled as to whether it was ten after seven or ten after eight. It became thoroughly apparent that it needed some markers for the hours, at least.

Tentative measurements of the project to that point indicated that the enclosed square was slightly over 9¼

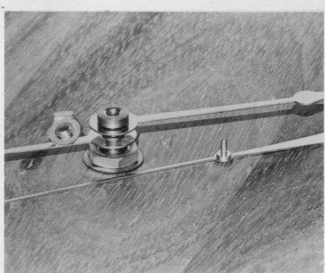

An 8-32 hex nut was rounded in the Unimat lathe, here installed to retain the minute hand, with an unmodified nut just to the left of it, for comparison. The second hand presses into place in the center opening of the shafts.

the clock and tell the time, reasonably well. The problem is that I'm plagued with the conviction that, if it's worth doing in the first place, it's worth doing right. So I sighed again, bitterly, and commenced to grapple with the intricacies of pinpointing locations for the minute marks, as well.

The first attempt involved marking off every six degrees of the circular protractor, but it was apparent, from a casual look at the result that the hand was sloppier than the eye, or perhaps vice versa, or all of the foregoing. Close, but no cigar.

So I muttered something that wild horses couldn't force me to quote here, went out and fetched the vernier caliper in from the shop, checked and found that my circle with the 3½-inch radius was rather closer to 3.518 inches. Switching on the little pocket calculator, it was a simple matter to double the radius for a diameter of 7.036 inches, multiply that times 3.1415926 to get 22.104245 inches as the circumference, and divide that, in turn, by 60 to get .368404-inch as the fairly-exact spacing between each minute marker.

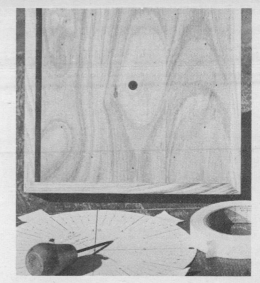

At this point, the twelve marks are punched for drilling holes to accept the ½-inch birch dowels that serve as hour-markers. The holes for minute-markers were added later to prevent confusion.

I set the vernier for .368-inch and used that for setting the points of the small draftsman's dividers, then employed the dividers to mark off the locations for the minute markers around the drawn circle. The results looked a lot more plausible than the graduations derived from the protractor.

I have this series of dicta that I think of as Grennell's Laws. Anything that can go wrong will go wrong. Things that can't possibly go wrong will go wrong also. Things generally stop falling when they get to the floor, and so on. Approaching the moment of truth, I had emmetropic visions of an hour-mark getting made at the fourth minute place, or kindred catastrophes. Refer to the chapter on making book cases and note how, on the one occasion with a large number of readers looking over my shoulder, I managed to rout one groove in the wrong place. That is (sigh!) the way my life is organized. I try to allow for it and cope with it, as best I can manage.

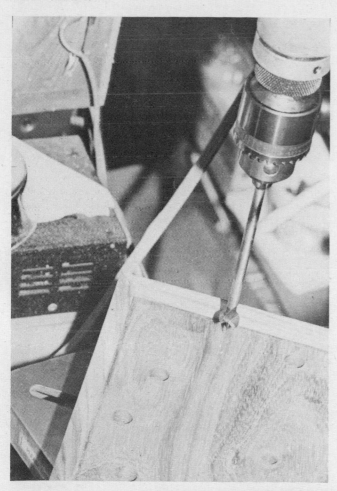

Above, the last of the holes for the hour-markers is being drilled in the drill press, using the Stanley auger-type bit with its central point aligned in the hole left by the scratch awl. Right, with the hour-marker holes drilled, locations of minute-markers have been punched in place.

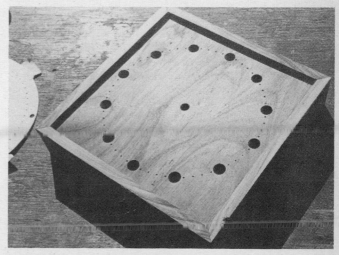

So I marked off and drilled out the places for the hour-markers, first, with the idea that I'd re-position the heavy paper layout against awl-marks to crank in the minute-marks later. As I came to realize, too late, once you drill at the awl-mark for the hour, it's no longer available for re-positioning. Severely chagrined, I was able to re-align the paper pattern by a long, hard squint through the holes in the wood, getting all twelve centered before pressing down on the short strips of drafting tape to secure it. Next time, I plan to make awl-marks at the first and thirty-first minute points...

I decided to use short sections of ½-inch birch dowel as the hour markers and small brass nails with round heads to indicate the minutes in between. The brass nails are of No. 18 diameter and ½-inch in length, about .051-inch in diameter. Checking the supply of small drill bits on hand, I turned up one No. 58 size, at .0410-inch diameter that seemed right to use as a guide hole for the tiny nails. The problem was that it was so petite that the ½-inch Jacobs chuck of the drill press couldn't grasp it. The tailstock chuck in the Unimat lathe held it tightly enough and it turned out that the Unimat chuck and its holding shaft were easily removable by loosening two screws. The Unimat chuck shaft was a bit below ½-inch diameter, so it could be inserted in the drill press chuck for use with the tiniest drills; a handy bit of data to discover and file.

Drilling slightly undersized holes for the brass nails was regarded as a necessity because, if driven into an unmodified scratch awl-mark, the odds seemed quite high that several or all of them would end up with distracting amounts of lean in every possible direction. Actual placement of the brass nails bore out that hypothesis quite redundantly.

The birch dowel hour markers were cut to uniform (hah!) length by making a line on the bed of the eight-inch saw. But they ended up mostly at a painful departure from ninety degrees, also with saw blade burn-marks on the cut portion. I put each piece in the ½-inch chuck of the drill press, bringing the front face of the plug down onto a sheet of coarse sandpaper, then took them over to the little Unimat and clamped them in its three-jaw headstock chuck to chamfer the corner of the front surface with a small metal file. Unconventional, yes indeed, but it worked just fine.

Rounding of the corners made it easier to drive the hour-marking plugs into the ½-inch holes in the face from the rear, after aligning the lines of grain to the center of the dial, for the sake of eye-easing uniformity.

As the last step before tapping the brass nail minute-markers into place, I diluted some tung oil, half and half with lighter fluid and used a piece of Kleenex to swab a coat over all of the assembled woodwork. It brought out the grain of the koa in a manner arrestingly vivid, doing almost as many good things to the tulipwood and the plugs of birch darkened nicely, looking much less like the ends of pieces of dowels. Applying the final finish after setting the brass nails would've been much more difficult, and the results quite a bit less satisfactory. The trick on these projects, I've found, is to try to work smarter instead of working harder.

I had drilled a ½-inch hole to a depth of about 3/16-inch in a piece of scrap wood and used that as a stop for driving the hour-markers into place from the back of the face, by way of assuring uniform height at the front. When I came to placing the brass nails between the birch dowels, I used the flat of the polyurethane mallet as a guide to seat each quartet of nails to exactly the same height as the neighboring pair of birch plugs. All could have been seated flush with the front of the face, but the slight protrusion gives an effect that I find pleasing.

The four slabs of tulipwood that form the outer frame were set up and glued in place against the ground steel top of the eight-inch saw, as noted, so as to be in precise alignment with the rear face of the clock movement. The mounting nail in the wall was given a moderate upward

After establishing desired length of the birch plugs for the hour-markers at about 11/16-inch, a mark was penned on the saw bed to serve as a guide for cutting the twelve plugs. The blade guard should be employed to protect fingers!

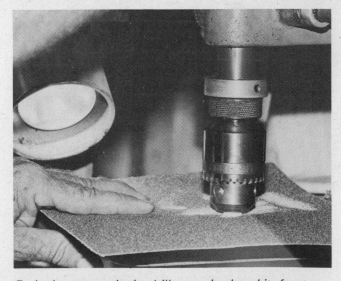

Each plug was put in the drill press chuck and its front surface was held against coarse, then fine sandpaper with the chuck spinning to square off the end, followed by a light rounding of the outer edges in the small Unimat lathe.

slant that proved to be entirely sufficient to hold the finished clock snugly against the wall. If the mounting nail is driven straight-in, the whole clock tends to lurch forward a bit at the top, in an unsightly manner.

A protective covering of glass or Plexiglas could be added, if desired, though there is no obvious need for it and initial setting or such readjustment as may be needed is accomplished by merely moving the given hand with a fingertip, which would be a problem if you added the protective glass or plastic.

Making clocks, in my humble opinion — or "imho," as I tend to abbreviate that phrase — is an immensely gratifying way to expend your time, and the possible variations appear to be infinitely endless. As just one example of the urchin way my mind works, I recently received a catalog from the makers of Heath Kits, listing a unit they have for building a digital clock, with number in light-emitting diodes (LED) about four inches high. Looking at it gave me an idea of the fun one could have in crafting up an exquisitely intricate grandfather clock-type cabinet, installing the Heath Kit to produce what might possibly be the first digital grandfather clock in all of recorded history. I've not built it, and probably will never do so (limitations of available floor space, for one major factor), but if you think you'd like to have a conversation piece of that caliber, you're welcome to the idea: Be my guest, Edgar!

Here, the 12 o'clock dowel has been placed and there are eleven left to go. The squared and rounded front end of the plug was tapped in from the rear of the dial face, to be stopped at a uniform protrusion above face as shown here.

As described at left, the polyurethane mallet was used to tap the plug to just above the front surface, then the little plug-stop was positioned over the end, assembly inverted and the plug was tapped down until arrested by plug-stop.

Arrow indicates the ½-inch hole in the plug-stop used as discussed above to assure pleasantly uniform protrusion of all twelve of the birch dowel hour-markers above the front of the clock dial. Note punches for minute-marks.

Here, all of the hour-markers have been installed and we're ready to drill holes to assure that none of the small brass brads will lean distractingly when we put them in place as the next step. Yup, that's right: getting down to brass tacks!

Since you may not reside within convenient driving distance to Anaheim, I've combed through the most recent issue of a magazine for workshoppers called *Workbench* to compile a listing of suppliers of similar clockworks and supplies. I doubt if this is a complete compendium, but it will give you some sources to check out.

Since we wanted our final finish on the wood, but not on the brass minute-markers, a small amount of Hope's tung oil was cut half-and-half with lighter fuel, mixed and applied to the face and frame, as well as the hour-markers, just before drilling holes and installing the brass brads.

Brass nails have hemispherical heads and a surface that is bright and attractive. Two-ounce box will take care of a lot of clocks, easing cost of nearly $12 a pound considerably.

Heritage Clock Company (send $1)
P.O. Drawer 1577
Lexington, North Carolina 27292

Craft Products Company ($1.50)
2200 Dean Street
St. Charles, Illinois 60174

Selva Borel ($2)
Box 796
Oakland, California 94604

R.D. Thomas (Plans only for all-wood clock, $5)
1412 Drumcliffe Road
Winston Salem, North Carolina 27103

Klockit (50c for sending via first class mail)
Box 629
Lake Geneva, Wisconsin 53147

Fort Products
Drawer 544
Spanish Fort, Alabama 36527

Viking Clocks
The Viking Building
Foley, Alabama 36536

Mason & Sullivan Company ($1)
Osterville, Massachusetts 02655

Newport Enterprises, Inc. ($1)
2313 West Burbank Boulevard
Burbank, California 91506

Turncraft Clock Imports Co. ($2.50)
611 Winnetka Avenue, North
Golden Valley, Minnesota 55427

Cas-Ker Co. ($1)
Box 2347
Cincinnati, Ohio 45201

Kuempel Chime & Clock Works
21195 Minnetonka Boulevard
Excelsior, Minnesota 55331

Two more sources remain, initial cost of catalog not readily ascertainable. Try them with a request and they'll probably let you know if you need to send money.

The Woodworkers' Store
21801 Industrial Boulevard
Rogers, Minnesota 55374

Brookstone Company
127 Vose Farm Road
Peterborough, New Hampshire 03458

Left, the ½-inch drill press chuck wouldn't hold the No. 58 drill bit, but the tailstock chuck of the Unimat lathe would, so it was removed, shaft and all, for use as an improvised pin vise to drill minute-marker holes. Below, tung oil finish left the birch dowels nearly as dark as the dial face.

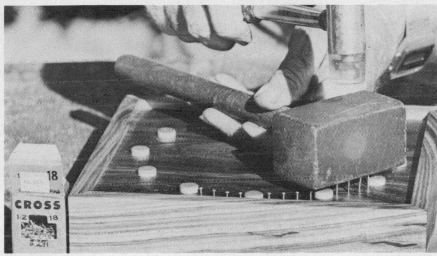

Check the next-to-right brass nail being driven here. See what I mean about the need for drilling the holes first? Side of mallet was used to keep both brads and plugs in line.

A rueful confession, about here: I grappled mightily with the protractor to get the hour-markers located about the circle and it was not until considerably later that it occurred to me that the operation could have been simplified greatly and, probably, made more accurate at the same time.

It's a fairly well-known maxim of geometry that you can draw a circle and, leaving the compass at the original setting, "hexsect" the circumference of the circle. I'm not certain that hexsect is a valid and recognized word, but the radius, marked off around the circle, comes back to the starting point exactly, after marking off a total of six equidistant points.

Thus, it'd be falling-off-a-log easy to establish positions for 12, 2, 4, 6, 8 and 10 o'clock. Setting aside the first compass, with its radius unchanged, use a second compass

to bisect the distance between two of the points established by the first hexsection, set the point of the first compass at that point and do it again to mark off the odd-numbered hours.

As to...uhh...quintisecting the spaces between the hour-marks for the minute-marks, I do not presently perceive a comparably elegant solution. With the twelve hour-marks meticulously pinpointed, there is a choice of establishing the right distance by trial-and-error adjustment of the compass, or by using an accurate measurement of the circle diameter to go the pi and division route previously described.

Trial-and-error division of a circle into any desired number of parts is by no means difficult, and acceptably accurate. It helps if you have one of the compasses or dividers that adjust by means of a small setting wheel,

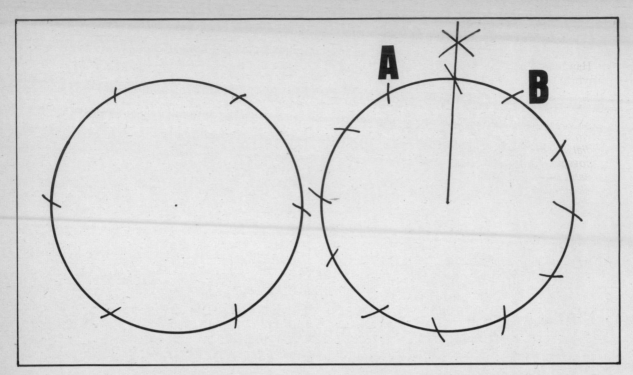

Here is the simpler, inherently more accurate technique for laying out the twelve hour-marks that I (sigh!) thought up just a bit too late to employ on my first clock, but there's no reason why you shouldn't benefit from my 20/20 hindsight, is there? At left the radius (compass setting) is used to divide the circle into six equal parts. Leave the compass setting unchanged and use a second compass to make an intersecting pair of arcs from points A and B. A line from the center of the circle to the intersecting arcs gives you the starting point for your second set of six, resulting in a geometrically accurate division.

rather than friction engagement.

Let's suppose, for example, you wish to lay out a neat five-pointed star. Draw a circle of appropriate size to enclose a star as big as you had in mind. The radius, unchanged, gives a six-pointed star, or hexagon, depending upon how you draw the lines. Obviously, for a five-pointer, you need to increase the radius by a bit. Make a moderate increase and go around the circle once, marking quite lightly. The odds are strong that you'll end up off by a bit. Examine the distance between your starting point and fifth mark, increasing or decreasing the setting, as needed, by one-fifth of the total disparity, as nearly as you can eyeball it. Try it again and you should end up closer, to readjust for one-fifth the difference. Keep it up and, before too many tries, you should be dead on the money, whereupon it's just a matter of connecting every other point about the circle to obtain the desired pentagram, with a pentagon in its center.

Four-pointed stars can be obtained by...well...octasecting a circle by the process described, drawing a second, inner or outer circle of appropriate diameter, ruling guide lines from the eight points to the center and connecting alternate points on the inner and outer circles. Comparable procedures can give you a three-pointed star, similar to the marque of Mercedes-Benz. Quadrisection can produce a two-pointed star, commonly termed a lozenge, an example being the symbol for diamonds in a deck of cards. For a one-pointed star, try a triangle, with two corners rounded.

You might wish to tackle production of a sixty-point star (hexadecagram?) as the motif for a clock face. I've never tried it, but I suspect it could be done.

Which brings up a pertinent and faintly whooshy point: About the time I was well into writing this inlaid footnote to the mass of copy turned in priorly, I took a keen squint at the small electric alarm clock near the typewriter and was roundly consternated to note that it had but three markers between each of the hour points. Had I committed a *faux pas* of truly gargantuan stature? I made a panicky pilgrimage to observe my prototype clock in operation and was vastly relieved to note that its twitching second-hand made one stop, pointing with exquisite precision at each and every one of the twelve birch plugs and forty-eight brass brads. Sojourning to the kitchen, I saw that the little dial clockface on the electric range had four minute-marks between each hour-mark, the same as my clock has.

The obvious inference appears to be that the designers of the upsetting alarm clocks merely shortweighted their graduations by a dozen pips, so as to produce a forty-eight-minute hour. Perhaps that explains why I have trouble getting as much done in a given interval as I'd hoped. Meanwhile, if you'd been planning to write and point out that the graduations of my clock didn't match those of your clock, this might save you the cost of a stamp, no?

As often happens, once an artifact is constructed and lived with for a bit, desirable modifications suggest themselves. One such was the gluing-in of two small aligning blocks, as illustrated, to hold the movement in rigid relationship with the frame, since the small securing hex nut allowed a disturbing amount of slippage. More: When changing time settings, as during a shift from standard/daylight saving, be careful not to scratch the finish of the face with an unwary fingernail!

Speaking of koa wood, as we've been, I'd like to quash a rumor. I don't believe there is a shred of foundation to the reports that Hawaiian forest scientists have succeeded in producing a hybrid between the koa tree and the cocobolo tree. Even if there were the faintest shred of basis to all that scuttlebutt, I simply can't imagine that they'd call the lumber from the hybrid coco-koa.

The very thought of it gives me dys-pepsi...

Below, two small blocks glued to back of dial secure the movement against movement(!). Right, it's a pity it can't be shown in color, since black and white doesn't half do it justice, but this gives an idea.

Just as things were getting nicely rounded up, I glanced at the dial of this clock and nearly went into shock. It has only three marks between the hours instead of four, so that a full sweep produces but 48 minutes to the hour — is it a wonder I'm always behind, working with 48-minute hours?

A frantic canvass among other timepieces soon provided reassurance, including a shot of this stately old clock on the court house in Fond du Lac, Wisconsin — as much a delight to me, right then, as to generations of pigeons!

RIGGING SLR VIEW CAMERAS

Combining Two Systems To Enjoy The Better Aspects Of Both Worlds, With Side Notes On Other Approaches

Chapter 11

NOTE: This is the project mentioned in the second paragraph of the Introduction, on page 6. — DAG

"Gentlemen, start your engines!" — This formation of GH-53 Sea Stallion helicoptors was frozen at 1/1000 of a second by the Canon's focal plane shutter; 135mm lens.

A P-47 propellor, fairly well frozen in full, roaring takeoff. Shutter slit moved upward, catching bottom blade a trifle before it got the top blade, leaving them just a wee bit out of alignment in the resulting photo.

This is the cloth curtain of the focal plane shutter of the Canon A-1 camera. It carries a slit of regulated width from right to left in making the exposure of the film.

This is the smallest of four fixed slits in the Speed Graphic shutter. It zips down in use, catching the bottom of the inverted image first.

A sketch of the legendary Kennedy Monobar 35mm view camera, based upon published photos. The substitute described here costs much less, but it's vastly more convenient and capable than this ultra-rare specimen!

"FOR YEARS 35mm photographers have wished for the swings and tilts of their view camera brothers." The year was 1960, and photojournalist Simon Nathan was writing about a most unusual camera called the Kennedy Monobar in Fawcett's *Good Photography's 35mm Handbook*. Nathan devoted two pages to the wondrous gizmo and I've never seen it mentioned elsewhere before or since, nor have I ever seen one of the actual cameras.

The basic reason for its rarity may have been the fact that the retail price was $875, and those were the considerably more substantial dollars of 1960. The price did not include a lens, and spare film magazines were quoted at $165 apiece. As nearly as I can extrapolate the details of the Kennedy's operation from that brief review, it appears to have been no major marvel of convenience, either. The lens up front (not included, as noted) looks to be one from a small press or view camera, with the usual between-the-lens shutter. It seems probable that the Kennedy did not have a focal plane shutter consisting of a curtain to whip a small slit across the film, just ahead of the film plane, to expose the film.

Taking a photo with the Kennedy probably consisted of mounting the camera on a tripod, opening the shutter by setting the shutter ring to T (for time exposure), opening the lens diaphragm to its largest aperture and peering through the focusing magnifier at the rear of the camera to compose and focus on the subject, using the swings and tilts as necessary to correct the focus. Following that, you took a reading with a handheld light meter to determine the exposure, set the shutter and diaphragm (f-stop) accordingly, cocked the shutter, pivoted the focusing eyepiece away and inserted the film magazine, removing its dark slide or similar arrangement and then, if your subject hadn't grown impatient and wandered off, you exposed the film.

The need for cameras that could produce a good photograph with a minimum of delay had resulted in the development of several systems to permit viewing, focusing and exposure with maximum speed and convenience. One of the earliest examples was the Graflex camera. It had a single lens and a hinged mirror, with a focusing hood that unfolded so that you could peer down at the ground glass to compose and focus.

The Graflex lens had no shutter and exposure was controlled by a focal plane shutter behind the mirror and immediately ahead of the film plane. In the earlier versions, you stopped down the lens diaphragm manually, or perhaps focused at the selected f-stop and pushed down a lever that caused the mirror to snap up out of the way and actuated the focal plane shutter. It was a fairly good system, apart from the fact that the inside of the focusing hood smelled a bit like an abandoned tannery when you put your face down to it. I used to sponge the hoods of the various Graflexes I owned with a dab of after-shave lotion to make focusing more bearable.

Folmer and Schwing, makers of the Graflex, also produced the Speed Graphic and Crown Graphic. The Speed Graphic usually operated by means of a between-the-lens shutter, but it also had a focal plane shutter for use with lenses having no shutter. The Crown Graphic omitted the focal plane shutter for the sake of cost reduction. Both of the Graphics usually had coupled rangefinders matched to a lens of one given focal length and customarily were equipped with a flash gun that tripped the shutter by means of a solenoid so as to synchronize the shutter with the firing of the flash bulb.

It should be noted that the focal plane shutter of the Speed Graphic sometimes is employed for reasons other than the use of lenses that lacked between-the-lens (BTL) shutters. Few BTL shutters offer exposures less than 1/400 or 1/500-second, but the focal plane shutter of the Speed Graphic usually goes to 1/1000-second, making it the indicated choice for handling high speed action. Typical focal plane shutters used with such cameras offered four

Spring-loaded release arm of the Graflock back permits removal of ground glass focusing panel.

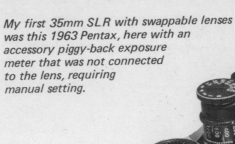

My first 35mm SLR with swappable lenses was this 1963 Pentax, here with an accessory piggy-back exposure meter that was not connected to the lens, requiring manual setting.

With back removed, Graflock latches move sideways and down to hold the various available accessories.

Graflock ground glass focusing panel, with ruled lines to show image size when using 120 roll film in adapter.

The utterly peerless and incomparable 203mm f7.7 Kodak Ektar lens, here at its keen-eyed f22 setting.

Cut film holders. Arrow indicates film code notch. Dark and light sides of slide strips are shown.

A pair of Mamiyaflexes exemplify the TLR type of camera, as discussed.

A TLR Rolleiflex shot this snap of a well-known couple.

176

different slit widths and six levels of spring tension. By combining one of each, the photographer had a choice of twenty-four shutter speeds ranging from 1/10 to 1/1000-second.

You can stop some remarkably brisk action at 1/1000-second. Late in 1945, while assigned to the photo lab at Hamilton Field, I caught a P-47 Thunderbolt fighter in full, roaring takeoff at that shutter setting and it was fast enough to freeze all four of the big propeller blades. That impressed me profoundly at the time and, come to think of it, still does!

A few Speed Graphics were made in 5x7-inch size, but 4x5-inch was much more popular, with the 2¼x3¼-inch and 3¼x4¼-inch sizes following in that order. The usual fodder for the Graphics and Graflexes was sheet film, loaded into sheet film holders, one sheet on each side. Black plastic dark slides protected the film in handling and were withdrawn, once the holder was in the camera. After making the exposure, the dark slide was re-inserted, with the black side of its metal edge outermost to indicate that the sheet had been exposed. Alternatively, there were film packs, used in a special film pack holder and operated by pulling a tab of paper out to expose each of several sheets of film in sequence.

At some point in the Forties, the Speed Graphic's makers introduced their Graphic view camera in the 4x5 size, usually supplied with Eastman's Kodak Ektar f7.7 lens in 203mm focal length. It was a true view camera, with all the swings, tilts, shifts and a lensboard that went up or down. Just a bit later, the same firm came up with what they termed the Graflock back in which the ground glass focusing panel could be removed by depressing two spring-loaded arms to permit the installation of an accessory roll film back for the use of 120 size roll film.

Another camera system that had been widely accepted was the twin-lens reflex or TLR, exemplified by the German-made Rolleiflex and, quite a bit later, by the Japanese Mamiyaflex. The latter featured interchangeable lens pairs and a remarkably lengthy bellows draw to permit close-in focusing. In the TLR, the upper lens reflected its image onto an angled mirror to the viewing ground glass screen, leaving the taking lens with its between-the-lens shutter and diaphragm ready for instant use. It offered a considerable measure of speed and convenience. The image, as seen in the ground glass, was reversed right-to-left, but upright, so that heads were at the top and feet at the bottom. Viewing the ground glass panel of view cameras, press cameras and the like, the image was upside-down, although correct, right-to-left, if you were standing on your head, for example.

A minor handicap of the TLR, at short distances, was the parallax between the viewing and taking lenses, resulting in losing a portion from the top of the image unless you compensated for it.

If not a handicap, it could be termed a strong character trait of the TLR cameras that they tend to be used from down around waist height, due to their system for viewing and focusing. Thus TLR photographers often seem to view their world from about the height of an adult's umbilicus, or perhaps through the eyes of a child around 6 to 8.

The accompanying photo of then-Senator John F Kennedy and his wife is a typical example of the TLR viewpoint. I made it rather early in 1960, when the Kennedys were campaigning in Fort Atkinson, Wisconsin. The camera was a Rolleiflex, with an f2.8 Zeiss Tessar taking lens, usefully unobtrusive for that type of photography.

The single-lens reflex or SLR system, similar to that of the Graflex, had been applied to the 35mm film format and, less frequently, to larger roll film sizes for quite a number of years, with good success, in cameras such as the Ihagee Exacta. Its principle was much the same as the Graflex and its metal focusing hood was entirely odorless, a benefit over the leather hood of the Graflex.

The final developments that put all of the good things into a single package included the introduction of a pentaprism into the viewfinder of the SLR camera. Looking through the viewfinder, you saw an eye-level image that was entirely congruent to the real world, up and down/right to left, but more or less fuzzy if the lens was not focused correctly. After a bit of research and development, they added through-the-lens light metering so that you could determine the correct exposure and focus, simultaneously, while looking through the viewfinder. The culminating touch was incorporation of a miniature computer that, once programmed, would not only determine the exposure but make the proper settings, leaving the photographer nothing to do but aim, focus and shoot. Recent models even added automatic focusing, assuming the target they chose was the same subject you had in mind.

I've not used an auto-focus camera and really don't think I want or need one, but I've had several SLR 35mm versions down the years, culminating with the Canon Model A-1 boasting the automated metering feature. I also have a Canon Model FTb, with match-the-needle metering at maximum lens aperture through the viewfinder and I find myself still using it quite extensively for certain applications where I prefer it to the A-1.

It was early in 1963 when I bought my first 35mm SLR with interchangeable lenses, a Pentax that accepted an accessory light meter that attached to the top of the viewfinder. It came with a 55mm f1.8 lens and I purchased a Kopil Bellowscope, some lens extension tubes and similar accessories to augment its capabilities for close work.

I had owned and operated a 4x5 Speed Graphic since 1948 and had accumulated several lenses for use with it, including one of the 203mm f7.7 Kodak Ektars, about 1952. Compared to the 150mm Zeiss/Jena f4.5 Tessar that had come with the Speed Graphic, the Ektar lens was just plain wonderful, having none of the spherical aberration that was a severe handicap in the Tessar. Spherical abberation, to simplify a bit, means that the focal length of the lens increases as you stop down the diaphragm. At least, that's the way it worked on the Tessar.

You could put the camera on a tripod, open the shutter and use a black cloth and magnifying glass to focus upon the subject precisely, with the lens wide open. Closing down the diaphragm to the selected f-stop and exposing the film, you'd find that the subject had become fuzzy, but portions of the background were crystal-sharp. The only alternative that worked was to stop it down before focusing.

The Ektar, as noted, was gloriously free of that problem and it threw an image sharper than battery acid at any diaphragm opening from f7.7 down to f45, even when focused wide open. For that reason, among others, I came to regard it with intemperate affection and, upon getting the Pentax 35mm SLR, it was inevitable that I began longing to harness the 203mm Ektar to the Pentax by means of the Kopil bellows.

A friend, Bob Faber, was a skilled tool and diemaker and he made a small adapter bushing for me that had Pentax threads to fit the bellows at the rear and threads to fit the Ektar lens at the front.

I still have a print of the first photo I shot with the Pentax through the Ektar lens, of a pack of Lark cigarettes lying on the flaked and blistered paint of our front porch. Shortly after shooting that, our neighbors across the street returned from a shopping trip and I tried it out as a quasi-telephoto lens, again with remarkably impressive success. On developing the film and making a few 5x7-inch enlargements, I felt as if I had been granted a license to steal.

The Kopil bellows pivots the lens on a vertical axis for a short distance either to right or left, giving at least one of the useful capabilities of the view camera.

Let's pause to discuss just what's so special about view cameras, with their swings and tilts, since I've made several mentions here, without further clarification. The focal length of any given lens (of the positive or magnifying type) is the distance between the optical center of the lens and the film plane when it's focused at infinity, i.e., a subject quite far away. The infinity setting, on most lenses that carry a focusing scale, is represented by a symbol (∞) that resembles a figure 8 lying on its side.

If you wish to focus upon a subject closer than infinity, you must move the lens farther from the film plane, by some proportionate distance. In most if not all instances, when the lens is at twice its focal length from the film plane, it will be in focus upon a subject twice the focal length ahead of the lens and the resulting image on the film will be exact life size.

So let's suppose that you wish to photograph a fairly long item at an oblique angle. One end of the subject is closer than the other. As you look through the finder or at the ground glass and rack the lens back and forth, you can see the zone of sharpness on the subject move in relation to the distance of the lens from the film plane. As the lens-to-film distances increase, the image of the nearer portion of the subject gets sharper and vice versa.

With conventional cameras, having their lens and film plane fixed in parallel relationship to each other, about the only thing you can do to obtain a photo of the subject that's as sharp as possible throughout its length — viewed obliquely — is to focus at a point one-third of the distance beyond the nearest part of the subject and then stop down the diaphragm to the smallest aperture practicable. As the diaphragm gets smaller, the apparent zone of sharpness increases, twice as rapidly to the rear of the point of sharpest focus, which is why you focused upon a point one-third of the way back on the subject.

A simple camera can be rigged up with a tiny pinhole substituted for the lens. Since light travels in straight lines, the pinhole transmits an image in much the same manner as a positive lens, although the pinhole has no focal length as such. The sharpness of the pinhole image is rather limited and exposure must be determined by trial and error.

One might assume that the answer for producing a photograph of infinite sharpness, front-to-back, of a subject viewed obliquely would be to stop the diaphragm down to

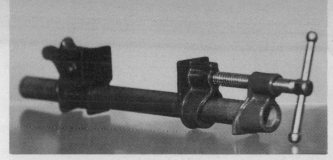

With non-view cameras, oblique subjects are rendered fuzzy at both ends, as in the shot of this pipe clamp.

View camera lens boards pivot from left to right, as above and on the facing page.

Second photo through the first combo of Pentax and Ektar.

First picture through the Pentax/Ektar merger was of subject chosen as a Lark.

Same pipe clamp, same camera setup, but what a change! Lens board has been pivoted to bisect the angle between the subject and the film plane, resulting in an image that is uniformly in sharp focus throughout. Photo below shows the lens board in approximately the angle used for photo.

The 203mm Ektar, removed from its usual 4x4" lens board and installed on the custom adapter in the front of the Kopil bellowscope for use with the Canon FTb.

a tiny f-stop, increasing the exposure time in proportion to the reduced level of light transmitted. If one assumes that, one is incorrect. If the lens diaphragm is stopped down past a given point — typically, around f45, though varying with the given lens design — the entire image becomes detectably fuzzier, although relative depth of field may show a slight increase.

Many people seem to find the entire business of f-stops baffling and incomprehensible. Actually, it's quite simple. The marked f-stop is nothing more, nothing less than a fraction of the focal length of that particular lens, with the figure 1 and the virgule (/) omitted. Thus, at f8, the diameter of the diaphragm opening is 1/8 of the focal length and marked as 8. In the example of the 203mm lens, f8 would give an opening one-eighth of 203mm or 25-3/8mm in diameter, f11 (representing 1/11) would be 18.45mm in diameter, and so on.

The other pertinent fact about f-stops is that each marked stop is either half or twice the area of the one next to it. Thus, if you stop from f8 to f11, light intensity of the image is reduced by one-half; going from f8 to f5.6 doubles the area of the opening and, with it, the light intensity. The f-stops in common use have a numerical relationship in which every second number is half or twice as great, approximately or exactly. In the series of f4, f5.6, f8, f11, f16, f22, f32, and f45; it's obvious that f16 is half of f32 or f8 doubled, while f22 bears the same relation with f11 and f45. No, I don't know why the last figure isn't given as f44.

As the lens is moved farther from the film plane, to focus on closer subjects, the f-stop opening no longer transmits light to the film plane at the same intensity as when the lens was focused at infinity. That requires compensation to assure optimum exposure of the film, since a lens with an eight-inch focal length, focused for a subject sixteen inches away, will be sixteen inches from the film and, at that setting, its focal length becomes sixteen inches for all practical purposes. In that example, a diaphragm opening one-half inch across — f4, originally, and marked thus — is now f8, and must be regarded as such, since the light intensity at the film plane is but one-quarter of what it was at the eight-inch distance. If you don't quadruple the exposure time to compensate, you can expect to get a negative that looks as if it was underexposed by two full f-stops, which indeed it was.

Pre-Anniversary 4x5" Speed Graphic, with 150mm f4.5 Zeiss/Jena Tessar lens which doubled as an enlarging lens at that time and, with all its problems, produced this shot of our babysitter who went on to cop top honors in a Miss Wisconsin competition, many years ago.

Left and near, the 127mm Ektar at f32 and minimum aperture. Latter produces overall degradation of the image sharpness. Next left and near two shots of half-dollar, one sharp throughout, the other showing the usual blurred top and bottom of the closeup photos taken with cameras having non-adjustable lens and film planes. Next left and near, camera as adjusted to correct focus on the half-dollar photos and same camera tilted in the opposite direction. At lower left are two lenses of 192mm and 9½" (242mm) focal length, both set at f11 aperture to illustrate the proportions discussed in the text.

Above, the unlikely hybrid of 4x5" Graphic view camera and Canon A-1 35mm body, connected via homemade adapter, is shown in the process of shooting the photo of the Portra lens depicted on the next page. Note the angle at which the lens board is tilted forward to bring all portions of the tiny subject into equally razor-sharp focus.

An accompanying photo shows a simple cardboard slide rule I made as an aid in calculating the estimated compensation for determining the exposure on extreme closeups when a separate light meter was used. With the shutter still open, I'd squint at the stopped-down aperture, estimate its diameter to be 1/4-inch, for example. Then I'd either estimate or use a tape to measure the distance between the center of the lens and the film plane. Assuming it was ten inches, the f-stop would be treated as f40, regardless of the number next to the diaphragm lever — f32, in the example of an eight-inch lens — and, if the meter called for an exposure of ½-second at f45, I'd set the shutter for ½-second, rather than the ¼-second at f32, the nominal mark for that opening.

By way of assuring that I'd never run out of numbers, I ran my scale of f-stops from f0.7 through f1024 and the time scale from 1/1000-second through 2048 seconds (3600 seconds is one hour).

In pausing to pin down the foregoing definitions and explanations, we've drifted away from the specialized and unique capability of the view camera. In brief, the view camera can be focused sharply upon two or more subjects at different distances simultaneously, *provided that all of the subject(s) form a flat plane* at some given angle in relationship to the film plane.

Light, we noted, travels in straight lines. Increasing the lens-to-film distance brings closer subjects into focus, and vice versa. By varying the angle of the lensboard or the film plane, or both, we can arrange things so that the part of the image with the distant subject is closer to the optical center of the lens and the part carrying the closer subject is farther away. When it's done properly, both will appear sharp and crisply defined, *with the diaphragm wide open!* Then, when we stop down a bit, it produces a photograph of wondrous and mind-boggling clarity.

Which should help to explain what Nathan had in mind when he commented about 35mm photographers yearning for the swings and tilts of the view camera. For certain, I was one of that yearning multitude. In those days, as now, my duties called for a great deal of what I call "nuts &

bolts" photography, or macrophotography, to use the customary term.

There are several approaches available for closeup photography, varying as to efficiency and satisfactory results obtainable. For one, there is a closeup lens that can be attached to the front of the lens the same as a colored filter to reduce the effective focal length of the given lens, making it possible to get closer and obtain a larger image. With few if any exceptions, such supplementary lenses degrade the sharpness of the resulting image to some varying degree.

You can install lens extension tubes between the camera body and the lens to get them farther apart and permit focusing at shorter distances. As you increase this distance, it helps to reverse the lens from its usual position and reversing adapters are available for several popular camera/lens systems, such as the one shown here for the Canon.

You can purchase an especially designed "macro" lens, intended for close work, with its optical equations computed accordingly. As solutions go, this is one of the most attractive. Canon offers a macro lens of 50mm focal length, with a maximum aperture of f3.5 and it can be had with what they call a life size adapter that goes between the lens and body to produce an image on the film up to exactly the size of the original subject. A further option, for Canon users, is their Type FL bellows and the 100mm f4 FL-M macro lens designed for use with it.

I've had both the Canon 50mm macro and the lens/bellows setup just mentioned for the past few years and have used them with absolutely radiant levels of satisfaction. If you can live with a maximum aperture of f3.5, the 50mm macro makes a fine all-purpose lens for normal use, since it's just plain murderously sharp throughout its entire operating range from about four inches to infinity, without the life size adapter.

I still have and use the Kopil bellows, although the Pentax was traded off when I shifted to the first of several Canons about 1969. Canon makes what they call their Lens Mount Converter P, a sort of bushing that combines the

Eastman Portra lenses, offered in different strengths, could be used in filter holders to modify lens focal length to get larger images.

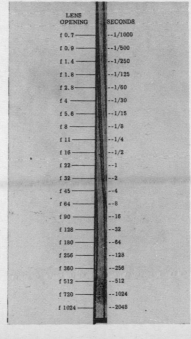

LENS OPENING	SECONDS
f 0.7	1/1000
f 0.9	1/500
f 1.4	1/250
f 1.8	1/125
f 2.8	1/60
f 4	1/30
f 5.6	1/15
f 8	1/8
f 11	1/4
f 16	1/2
f 22	1
f 32	2
f 45	4
f 64	8
f 90	16
f 128	32
f 180	64
f 256	128
f 360	256
f 512	512
f 720	1024
f 1024	2048

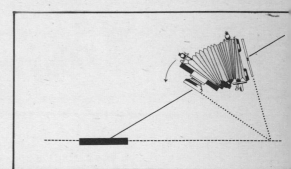

Left, homemade slide rule for coping with the problem of compensating for shifting f-stop values at extreme bellows extension for ultra-closeups. Above, a sketch showing the principle of the Scheimpflug Effect, as discussed.

Here we have a dozen photos giving details on the intricacies of reversing the usual 35mm SLR lens to improve definition when used for extreme closeups. 1. The adapter ring that must have the same thread usually employed for a screw-in filter, 55mm, in this instance. 2. The adapter, installed on the front of the lens. 3. The 50mm, f3.5 Type FD Canon macro lens, normally installed on the A-1 body. 4. The life size adapter, as supplied with the 50mm macro lens. 5. The life size adapter, in place. 6. Macro lens on A-1, here at its infinity setting.

7. Reversed 50mm macro lens on Canon Type FL bellows unit; A-1 body at the rear. 8. Push down catch (broad arrow) so as to move ring and lower stud (curved arrow) as shown. 9. Automatic aperture lever (arrow) in its normal position, as lens is removed from camera. 10. With AAL moved, the diaphragm can be adjusted by turning the lens aperture control ring, when reversed. 11. Camera, as in frame 6, now in focus on the film box, 4" away. 12. Reversed lens on bellows will produce sharp image of ultra-close subjects, highly magnified.

The $20 Speed Graphic, with 127mm Ektar and Canon A-1 body on the most recent variation of the piggy-back adapter, attached via the camera's Graflock back.

Canon Pellix body, Mark II adapter, and the $20 Graphic with 203mm Ektar up front make a thoroughly improbable combo, great pictures.

The same backup, affixed to the $115 Graphic view camera, with the $24 Wollensak 192mm Raptar on the lookout. Still a far cry from the 1960 cost of a Kennedy Monobar — but capable? keep on skimming downward ... counting $229 for the A-1 back, the whole shebang caught this heartwarming snap of a neighbor, pausing in her lawnmowing to amuse her niece, from an unobtrusive 87 yards away.

Canon lens mount converter P takes the place of lens to serve as a light seal for use on homemade adapter.

Pentax body, Kopil bellows and the Tayon 150mm enlarging lens, used hand-held, produced the Lil Tim Tam shot on the facing page.

Left and right, two views of the Mark II adapter, built to couple a Canon Pellix body to the $20 Speed Graphic. The cutaway arc was to give clearance for the lever that advanced the film.

A 135mm lens isn't overly bulky on a 35mm SLR but, at 1/1000-second, it caught the ebullient family group joyously jogging up the beach in crystalline clarity. The 150mm enlarging lens on the Pentax captured the Lil Tim Tam shot which, I like to think, the late Walker Evans might have viewed with zestful appreciation, if he could have seen it.

threading used on Pentax lenses with the bayonet-lock system employed on Canon lenses and bodies.

Some time in the latter Sixties, I bought a 150mm enlarging lens, since I still burned quite a bit of 4x5-inch black and white sheet film in those days. It's a Taylor Tayon, of f4.5 maximum aperture and it cost around $35 at that time, if dimming recollection serves. It seemed remarkably sharp-cutting on the enlarger and I soon developed a yen to find out how it would work as a taking lens on the front of the Kopil bellows. The folks at Koenigs Cameras in Covina, California — my base of operations at the time — were able to rummage up a ring to fit the Tayon's threads and another that matched the Pentax threads at the front of the Kopil bellows. I managed to fasten the two rings together to create an adapter that would hold it precisely in place and, with the Pentax body on the back of the bellows, its performance exceeded my most hopeful dreams, making it a medium-fast 3X telephoto of superb sharpness for the 35mm film format.

This is an appropriate point to note that the diagonal dimension of the given negative is generally taken to be the equivalent of a normal lens's focal length, as an accepted rule of thumb. The image of the standard-frame 35mm camera is usually said to be 24x36mm, though it measures 24.3x35.8mm on a Canon A-1 film window. The diagonal of a 24x36mm rectangle is 43.26mm, and lenses in the 45-55mm focal length range are regarded as normal, with 18-35mm being termed wide angle and greater than about 80mm called telephotos.

The Pentax and, later, the Canon with the converter made a good team with the 150mm Tayon enlarging lens and were by no means as restricted to static subject matter as you might suppose. I was busily engaged in some nuts & bolts shooting, working up on the roof of the office building in Covina and, having a few frames of film left over, took the tripod and camera over to the edge of the roof and focused it at the Orange Julius concession at the corner of Citrus and Badillo. As I was fiddling with the focus to bring every single tiny tile into razor sharpness, a young lady came walking down the sidewalk and, apparently filled to bursting with the sheer joy of being alive, she went skipping blithely around the corner in a hippity-hop gait and I managed to hit the cable release to capture her notable exuberance for posterity. It remains among my favorite photos, rekindling a warm glow every time I look at it, along with the shot of the happy family group loping along the wet sand at Santa Monica (Canon with 135mm lens at 1/1000-second) and the Walker Evans-type study of the

young lady striding past the Lil Tim Tam Cafe, also captured with the Pentax and the 150mm Tayon, handheld.

Walker Evans is one of my personal heroes, a matchless photo technician who viewed our world through a unique and special knot hole, all his own. Encountering his work for the first time, about 1952, was a memorable delight and a discovery that I'd been shooting Walker Evans pictures for years, but just didn't realize it; a bit like the chap who was mind-blown to learn that he'd been talking prose all his life...

It was about 1969 that I wandered into Koenig Cameras and noted that they'd just taken a well-used 4x5 Speed Graphic in trade on something else.

"What're you asking for the old Graphic?" I inquired.

"Ahh...twenty bucks," the clerk responded, and I nearly dislocated a shoulder clawing forth my wallet to swap a steel engraving of Andy Jackson for it. In my book, a $20 Speed Graphic is a great bargain, even if you just use it as a paperweight.

This one proved good for a great many other purposes. It carried a 127mm f4.7 Kodak Ektar lens that turned out to be every bit as sharp-slicing as its 203mm cousin whose capabilities I'd come to appreciate so warmly. In order to really appreciate a lens such as the Ektars, you need to have spent years in tearful frustration, trying to coax sharp pictures through lenses of lesser capability, as I surely did. If you didn't know, one of the most famous photographs of all time went through a 127mm Ektar. A.P. press

The Orange Julius skipper shot: Y'know, the A in hamburgers is still missing, after some dozen years?

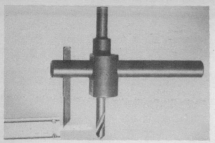

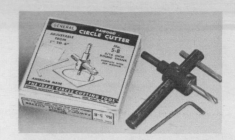

The No. 5-B Pawood circle cutter, left, being adjusted with vernier caliper; above, set screw governs diameter; above right, as supplied; right, in use on drill press. Note clamps and waste stock beneath.

Speed Graphic with focusing hood in place and current adapter back ready for replacing original back.

Here the focusing hood and ground glass panel have been removed, 120 roll film adapter back in use.

The first adapter for the Mamiya was a rather primitive affair, but it worked surprisingly well.

First Kopil/127mm Ektar test shot was this most unlikely juxtaposition of trademarks!

Left thrust-bolt pushes rearward, right acorn nut forward to press aluminum bar and hold camera body.

Most recent mutant: 127mm Ektar on the Kopil bellows assembly, as ruefully discussed in nearby text.

Held as shown, right above, the ¼x1″ aluminum bar presses the SLR body into the recess for light-tight seal, but permits rotation about its optical axis to the extent shown above for convenient control of image.

photographer Joe Rosenthal used that particular lens when he shot the group of Marines raising the flag on Iwo Jima, in the latter part of WWII.

In addition to the 127mm Ektar that was, surprisingly and happily, in perfect tune with the coupled rangefinder, the new/old Graphic boasted a further delight: It had the Graflock back system, mentioned here earlier, and that is pertinent to the current discussion because it was the pivotal point that led to the development of the SLR view camera setup that I've been using with joy and zestful glee the past several years. For here is one 35mm photographer who no longer yearns for the swings and tilts, having achieved them, and it's well worth yearning for, believe it!

I have this uncontrollable itch to find out what would happen if things were to be done thus and such. It has led to assorted joys and occasional spots of trauma. Given that attitude, it's hardly surprising that I was curious to find out what manner of 35mm negative the 127mm Ektar might produce, so I built my first rather crude and primitive adapter to hold a 35mm Mamiya SLR on the Graflock back. It worked out as well as I'd hoped and a bit better. All of which brings up a matter that I note here now with quantities of sheepish embarrassment. I've owned a 127mm Ektar for all these years and have had the adapter for using the 203mm Ektar for quite a bit longer. It was not until I began working on this chapter that it occurred to me belatedly to wonder if both Ektars had the same mounting thread dimensions. Such turned out to be the case. I could have bypassed the construction of that first piggyback adapter and just put the 127mm on the old Kopil bellows. Color my face red, hmm?

At some point in the early Seventies, I encountered a photographer, somewhere up around Burbank, who had a 4x5 Graphic view camera that he wanted to unload for $115, with carrying case and the usual 203mm Ektar lens. I bought it and got acquainted with the power and glory of being able to warp the laws of optics to my own devious ends. The view camera, however, did not have the Graflock back. Most of them didn't. It took a long and patient while to track down and buy a Graflock back for the Graphic view camera, but it was worth all the effort, and then some.

Given the Graflock back, it was a simple matter to install the 120-size roll film adapter to turn out eight 2¼x3¼-inch negatives to the roll of film, with oblique subjects sharp from end to end. The 35mm Mamiya had been sold to a friend in San Antonio, a few years earlier and availability of the Graflock back led me to whip up an adapter that would carry one of the current battery of Canon bodies on the back of the view camera.

The first adapter to harness the Canon SLR bodies to the back of the 4x5 Graphic view camera was hardly more than a qualified success. The adapter plate was made from a piece of pine lumber ¾-inch thick and that set the body a bit too far to the rear for maximum efficiency. In a 35mm SLR, at best, the film plane is nearly two inches behind the front opening in the body, when the usual 35mm camera lens removed. The press or view camera to which you propose to harness the SLR body has some thickness of its own. As a result, lenses much shorter than 200mm in focal length cannot be used with the hybrid setup except for relatively close subjects.

A further design deficiency was noted in the prototype Canon adapter. It had no provision for rotating the SLR

body about its optical axis. You had to tilt the entire large camera to make minor slant corrections and that was a handicap when you were working at short distances, since it moved the lens in the process.

The prototype Canon adapter, pictured here, was relatively simple to make, but it became apparent that a better version was not only possible, but needed.

So I allocated time for a Mark II version, likewise shown in the accompanying photos. Instead of the ¾-inch board, I used a piece of ¼-inch tempered Masonite and put the light-sealing flange in front of the adapter, gaining a bit over ¾-inch of helpful inching-up closer to the view camera lens.

At the same time, I worked out the present holding system that allows a considerable arc of body rotation around its optical axis, without moving the larger camera.

It is pertinent to note that the circles were cut in the Masonite mounting plate as well as the retaining plate of the same material that is glued to the front of it, all by using the No. 5-B Pawood circle cutter, by General, in the drill press.

The Pawood circle cutter is another of those workshop accessories that I've come to regard as awfully close to indispensible. It must be used in a drill press, being quite unsuited and unsafe for handheld operation. Given a drill press, which I've had and appreciated since 1962 — it's made by Atlas and I call it Chuck, in memory of the gent in the leopardskin loin cloth who was once an eighty-seven-pound weakling (me, I was once a 10½-pound weakling) — the Pawood circle cutter enables you to make holes varying infinitely in diameter between one and six inches. It helps to have a good supply of scrap pieces on which to check the diameters as you fiddle the adjustment back and forth in quest of the precise desired dimension.

The larger hole measures 2.475 inches in inside diameter and the Canon converter-P is 2.461 inches in outside diameter; close enough for government work, as some put it. I cut a 1.565-inch hole in a second piece of the same Masonite and glued it in close concentricity to the larger hole. The hole in the center of the converter-P measures 1.606 inches across.

I had a reason for making the hole in the Masonite slightly smaller than the hole in the adapter with its bright metal inner threads. I wanted to keep the diverging beams of light out of the lens from hitting the shiny surfaces of the threads to louse up the purity of the image. The inside of the smaller adapter hole and the front surface of the adapter are finished with flat black paint to minimize any distracting reflections.

A third piece of Masonite was cut and attached to the larger piece, using glue reinforced by small bolts. Small cuts were made on the table saw to provide clearance for the diagonally-sliding flanges of the Graflock back.

The first piggyback adapters had held the SLR bodies by an improvised clamp and wing nut, the wing nut engaging a short section of ¼-20 threaded rod that had been turned into a 7/32-inch hole drilled in the wood. On the Mark II version, for the Canon, I used two opposing pieces of ¼-20 threaded rod, set up as shown in the accompanying photos, to impose stress upon a length of ¼x1-inch aluminum flat stock. The longer end of the flat stock bears against the back of the Canon body to hold it in snug and secure contact with the adapter plate but, at the same time, the

Column-lock knob of tripod was impossibly small and slippery, so "super-wing nut" replacement was made and substituted, solving that.

Relief cut was made in Masonite plate with table saw to provide clearance for Graflock flange, shown immediately below, in use.

Here the A-1 body, with adapter rings, is in place, ready to be held to Masonite plate by the aluminum bar and homemade hex-stock nut.

See that glint of light on the thread? Flat-blacked adapter hole was cut small to shield against reflections. Vertical strips were added as anchors.

As thumbpiece is moved to right, a diagonal slot in the Graflock moves the flange downward to hold adapter. Saw cut, above, provides clearance.

Here, the bar and hex-nut are in place to hold SLR body, as in the photo immediately above this one. System is infinitely adjustable.

Canon body can be rotated through an arc somewhat greater than ninety degrees. That features offers the option of quick and easy changing from horizontal to vertical format, or turning to any desired point in between.

With most of the better modern tripods, there is a lever for tilting the entire camera from side to side. That, however, introduces some amount of lateral camera movement which is a plaguing nuisance when working with subjects only a few inches ahead of the lens. The ability to rotate the camera around its own optical axis is pure, mellow luxury, and more than worth the bother.

I suppose glue alone might have served to hold the mounting clamp to the adapter, but I had no slightest inclination to find out it wouldn't by watching a Canon body plummet to the hard ground. The two small screws add a lot of security and reassurance. The upper nut at the rear interfered with one of the neck chain studs on the front of the Canon FTb body, so I relieved a small amount of metal from one corner of it with an appropriate burr in the Dremel Moto-Tool: another indispensible device for avoiding the consequence of such minor design errors.

The prototype Canon adapter and the Mark II version were built when my entire Canon battery consisted of FTb bodies, but I built a bit of extra provisions into them, just in case. That proved a blessing in mid-1979, when I bought a Canon Model A-1 body. There was no need to buy a lens for it, since I had a good assortment of lenses, all interchangeable from body to body, with appropriate adjustments as covered in the respective operating manuals.

As it turned out, the A-1 body, with just the lens converter P installed as a light seal between body and adapter plate, did not fit perfectly. I ended up adding the thinnest one of a set of extension rings to the converter P,

and that worked out just fine. I had to back out the inboard piece of ¼-20 threaded rod a trifle to compensate for the added thickness of the extension ring, but not quite enough to require cutting and fitting a new piece of threaded rod. To cut and fit a longer piece of rod would pose no difficulties, should I ever acquire a Canon body that's even thicker.

The convenience and simplicity of knocking out photographs with the SLR view camera is downright addictive. The lens up front is always open, since you use the SLR's focal plane shutter to control and make the exposure. You look through the SLR viewfinder and there's your photograph, upright and correct left-to-right. You reach forward, loosening the view camera's holding screws for either swing (horizontal correction) or tilt (vertical correction) if necessary, holding it and maneuvering it gently with one hand as you work either the front or rear focusing knob with the other. A bit of fiddling about and it's fully honed to maximum sharpness, whereupon you secure the holding screw, lock the focus and stop it down until the match-needle system of the FTb or the lighted electrode display (LED) of the A-1 shows the desired setting. That's all there is to it: Your photograph awaits your pleasure.

There are certain special differences in photos taken with the SLR/view camera approach, including a shift in the customary rendering and appearance, as compared to the same subject photographed with a "normal" lens having a focal length about equal to the diagonal dimension of the film image.

The first thing you notice is a marked change in perspective. In drafting, they sometimes develop a drawing of the subject from the blueprint, as it would appear when

To remove SLR body, thrust-bolt is loosened, allowing flat bar to pivot. Hex-nut is not moved unless some other body is being installed instead.

Arrow indicates "peace of mind nut" that had to be relieved with Dremel tool to clear neck-chain stud on the Canon FTb SLR camera body.

Canon Adapter P, plus extension lie atop the view camera here. They fit precisely into the shallow recess of the Masonite adapter plate.

Another shot of the A-1 body set up and in place, with the holding bar being swung into position, prior to tightening thrust-bolt to hold in place.

Combined effect of the unusually long focal length of the lens (203mm, here) plus the focusing correction abilities of the view camera can produce startling perspectives, as in this photo of a shotgun, from about 30 feet away. Text discusses cause and effects.

viewed from an infinite distance. I think the term for this is an isometric drawing, though I certainly wouldn't bet upon it. Such views have no perspective, as we usually think of the term.

Photographs made with lenses of considerably longer than normal focal length for the given film size tend to show a great reduction of perspective, verging toward the singular effect of the isometric rendering. All of this is due, in considerable measure to the fact that the long focal-length lenses force you to make the photos from considerably greater distances than when using a normal lens.

Page back, if you will, to the opening introduction and take a look at the photos of the old coffee table. Those were done on 35mm film, through the 203mm Ektar, at a distance of perhaps twenty-five or thirty feet. They resemble an isometric rendering more than they resemble a conventional photograph. Lines and surfaces at the rear of the subject show little reduction in apparent size from corresponding areas closer to the viewer.

The effect, in its own way, is as singular and arresting as the extreme distortion possible with wide angle lenses, although in the opposite direction. Lenses with focal lengths considerably longer than normal tend to produce pleasing and even flattering effects when used for portraits. This is due, in large part, to a compression of percentages. It can be illustrated rather graphically by comparing photos taken of the same face, on 35mm film, using a wide angle and long focal length lens. With the wide angle, the lens may be but a few inches from the subject's face, so that an ear is much farther from the lens than the nose, in purely percentile proportions. In extreme cases, the ear may be twice as far away as the nose, and the ear appears

grotesquely smaller, in exact proportion.

By contrast, a comparable view through a lens of considerably longer focal length may be made from a distance of ten feet or so. From that viewpoint, the ear is only a tiny bit farther away than the nose, in overall percentage, so that the two features appear in much more natural size relationship to each other.

Since we're still using the viewfinding and light metering system of the SLR camera body, as well as its focal plane shutter, we have no need whatsoever for a between-the-lens shutter in the big lens, up at the front of the view camera. All we need up there is an iris diaphragm and we can get along quite nicely if the diaphragm isn't even graduated in f-stops, provided the SLR body has through-the-lens metering capability.

The great benefit of the system is that we can utilize almost any old lens, up front, discovering to our dazzled delight that some of them produce an image of amazing sharpness and clarity on the film.

Lenses of fairly long focal length, designed and intended for use with the view cameras for film sizes from 4x5 inches and upward, fitted with a between-the-lens shutter, tend to cost an arm, leg and random other appendages, when you check retail prices for new equipment. Having no need for a shutter in the lens gives us a great advantage.

One of the most deadly sharp lenses I own and use cost me just $24 in the last part of 1978. It is a 192mm, f4.5 Wollensak Graphic Raptar, purchased for that figure, plus shipping cost, from Meshna, Box 62, 19 Allerton Street, East Lynn, Massachusetts 01904. It has click stops from f4.5 down to f32, and it's fluoride coated, color corrected, with no slightest trace of spherical abherration that I've ever been able to detect. A large number of the

Above, with lens wide-open, you can see the inverted image of the airplane on the ground glass focusing panel of the Speed Graphic. Right, test shots, at f16 and minimum of about f90, show severe loss of sharpness in the latter, as discussed in adjacent text.

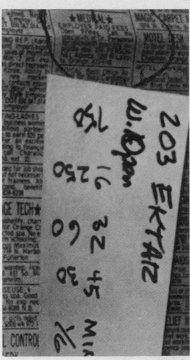

Above, lenses with longer-than-normal focal length tend to produce pleasing effects with portraits, with lifelike, natural proportions. Right, stopped to f32, the $24 192mm lens produces razor-crisp detail on 35mm film for closeup details photos such as this one.

photographs that appear in this book were made with that $24 lens, and they are among the best of the lot, by any technical standard.

To the best of my knowledge, Eastman Kodak stopped making their 127mm and 203mm Ektar lenses some years ago. I still own two apiece, and cherish them tenderly. I paid $55 for the second 127mm Ektar, and regarded it as a bargain, despite the fact that the first had cost $20, with an entire 4x5 Speed Graphic that boasted a Graflock back.

It is an easy and simple matter to conduct a comparison test of various lenses to peg down the exact capabilities of any one in relation to any other, at various settings. Such a test session is considerably interesting and absorbing, costs modestly, and greatly enhances your long-run capabilities. Along the way, it will solidify your convictions and cure the last of your hopeful delusions.

For the test, you need an oblique target/subject, with a lot of fine detail throughout its surface. I used a sheet from the want ad section of the local newspaper, with good results. Lay it out on a horizontal surface and mark your intended focusing point upon it. Lay by a supply of 3x5-inch file cards to put onto the target for recording of data, with a pen capable of making readily visible marks on the cards.

Load your SLR body with a roll of fine-grain film, capable of discerning subtle differences. I used Eastman's Plus-X in 35mm size. Their Tri-X is nearly as good, in my experience, while their Panatomic-X has never displayed any superiority that I've been able to detect and appreciate.

Install the first test lens and make the identifying notes as to lens and f-stop on a piece of 3x5 card, putting that in the foreground. Put your eye to the viewfinder window and focus with care upon the pre-marked point on the want-ad page. Record the f-stop and shutter speed on the card and make the exposure. Continue the procedure, as desired. Change lenses, do it again, until you've covered the combinations of lenses and apertures to be tested.

Develop the film in a quality fine-grain developer. I use Eastman Microdol-X, diluted at 1:3 with water, simply because I've yet to find anything that works better. When the film is dry, make carefully enlarged prints of any negatives you wish to compare.

The resulting test prints will show any difference in performance and sharpness, quite clearly. Since you included the little card of test data in the photo, there will be no confusion as to the lens used and the f-stop at which the particular photo was made.

There is no urgent need to make a separate test shot with each lens at each f-stop, but I'd suggest one at the largest opening, one at two stops down, one at the smallest marked opening and — if the diaphragm closes beyond that point — a final shot at the smallest aperture.

As a general rule, typical lens designs can be expected to deliver optimum sharpness at two f-stops below the largest opening. That is to say, they give the best definition at the exact point on which the lens was focused. They will deliver good definition across a greater distance when stopped on down from that point, but you may be able to detect that the definition isn't quite as icy-keen as it was with the aperture two stops down from wide open.

You can expect that comparison shots at the lowest marked aperture, such as f32 or f45, will be detectably sharper than those made at a minimum aperture even smaller, if such apertures are available. Both the 127 and 203mm Ektars stop on down to approximately f90, producing impressive depths of field at minimum aperture, but with a marked loss of overall definition that is readily discernible.

If I seem obsessed with the quest for ultimate sharpness, it's at least partially due to the value I put upon that quality when working with negatives as small as the standard format 35mm size. To make a 5x7 or 8x10-inch enlargement from a 35mm negative, you're blowing it up by about eight diameters (8X) in the latter instance. Any slight amount of fuzziness will be amplified eight times in the process, and that contributes heavily to the difference between acceptable definition or borderline mediocrity, if not worse.

Using nominally large-format lenses to produce miniature negatives is a real acid test, and I've found it quite educational insofar as gaining an intimate familiarity with the properties and capabilities of the big lenses. The knowledge thus gained carries through most usefully when going back to use the press and view camera lenses on the larger negative sizes for which they were originally designed.

The price you pay for photo equipment — as I discovered long ago, to my profound disillusionment — bears little or no direct correlation to the comparative quality of photographs that you can produce with the equipment. The $24 Wollensak 192mm (7¼-inch) Raptar is a good case in point. The test shots made through it were among the brightest and sharpest obtained with any lens I had. In contrast, a 9½-inch Goerz Artar lens, for which I shelled out $197, in extensively used condition, flunked its test shots in a thoroughly miserable manner. So it goes.

Despite this readily demonstrable fact of life, many photographers cling doggedly to the faith that they could turn out photos every bit as good as legendary workers such as Karsh or Halsman, if only they could afford equipment on the quality level they assume such gifted gentry must use. Inability to afford prestige equipment makes a handy excuse, but it holds water like a bottomless bucket. It is like assuming that Hemingway's books sold well because he tapped them out on a $200,000 typewriter...

The scientific principle that makes it possible for the view camera to work its useful magic by tilting the lens axis or film plane or both, is termed the Scheimpflug Effect and, simply stated, decrees that an extension of the planes of the subject, lens and film must meet at some hypothetical point, in order to assure optimum sharpness of the subject.

In practice, I make the necessary focus corrections by moving the lens, almost exclusively, and rarely move the back of the camera about. The reason is that any tilting of the back is apt to cast a shadow of the adapter plate on the corner of the film, producing a blank area of negative at that point; a defect termed vignetting.

Compared to standard view cameras employed in the conventional manner, the SLR view camera is a wonder of luxurious convenience and ease in use. Instead of a dim, inverted image on the ground glass panel, requiring a black cloth focusing hood to view clearly, and perhaps a magnifying glass, as well, the SLR viewfinder gives you a bright and upright image, with all the fuzzy places clearly apparent. If the subject is at some angle to the film plane, merely loosen the lensboard and move it tentatively toward dividing the given angle in half. Refocus and check to see if both ends have gotten sharp. If they haven't, continue focusing and making minor adjustments in the lens angle until you hit the exact angle up front.

In usual view camera operation, as we've noted, you close, set and cock the shutter at that point, stop down the diaphragm, insert the film holder, pull the dark slide from the holder and then, finally, you're ready to take the photo. That assumes you'd taken a meter reading at some previous point and know the required exposure.

With the SLR view camera, once you've reconciled the focus, merely stop down until the meter in the viewfinder is in proper adjustment and press the shutter button or cable release. The subject remains visible in the viewfinder continuously, except for the interval of exposure when the mirror flips up out of the way and back down after the shutter has closed. A fast flip of the film-advance lever and you're all set for another shot of the same thing, if desired.

When using an SLR body with a built-in, through-the-lens light meter, you need not concern yourself with re-computing the f-stops of the lens up front when making photos of close objects at abnormally long bellows extensions. Since the built-in meter measures the intensity of the light at the effective film plane, it handles any needed compensations automatically and effortlessly.

The advantage of using a bigger camera for such delightful tomfoolery, rather than the Kopil bellows with the 203mm lens, is that it has much more room to contain and absorb the diverging light beams and, as a result, delivers a detectably superior degree of clarity and contrast. A long lens in a small bellows seems to generate what we might term light-echoes, a bit like yelling through a long culvert, perhaps.

I suppose the Graphic view camera could be used in handheld mode; I've never tried it. I've used the Canon on the Speed Graphic handheld, with no major problems. It's not the sort of camera rig you might choose to pack along for a picnic at the beach, or even as compact and handy as either the Kopil or Canon FL bellows, both of which work well in handheld approaches.

The Canon A-1 has a special problem to which you must pay attention or endure the consequence. You may have noted that mine bears a strip of label tape that shouts, "WINDOW." That's a reminder, when I see it, to close the small built-in shutter for the viewfinder window. Any extraneous light that gets into the A-1's viewfinder just croggles its bright little robot brain into a pale pink tizzy, resulting in negatives that are grossly misexposed. When using the A-1, on the view camera, I switch the control dial to the green letter P, for Program, and punch in the little stop that shifts the works to manual mode. When the Canon is taken off the adapter and one of the Canon Type FD lenses — required for full-auto work with the A-1 — is re-installed, you must do one of two things. Either you hold off advancing the film after the last shot out of the adapter or, if you forgot to remember that — I usually do — you have to punch the little stud for double-exposure and work the film advance lever again after installing the FD

In the Canon A-1 SLR camera, the eyepiece shutter lever (arrows) must be used to close out stray light from the eyepiece, if the photographer's eye is not shading it. If not closed, as below, improper exposure will result.

lens. If you neglect that vital step, the next time you prepare to shoot one through an FD lens, the little electronic genie will scream at you. Literally: The LED readout at the lower edge of the viewfinder window will say "EEEE EE," in flashing scarlet letters, signaling, "Ah so! Honorable Yankee photographer-san has pulled another stupid!"

Being screamed-at by a Japanese cybernetic entity is an educational experience. No, contrary to erroneous reports that you may have heard, when you release the shutter, a Canon does not go, "KRICK!"

The chief motive for buying the Canon A-1 body was for use on weird hybrid camera systems such as the ones described here. The built-in meter of the Canon FTb body works fine, over normal exposure ranges. It cuts out, however, at some given shutter speed, depending upon the film speed being used. When the FTb meter is set for film rated at ASA 400, for example, as you rotate the shutter speed dial from 1/15 to 1/8-second, a little red circle rises in the viewfinder window to signal that you have exceeded the scope of the light meter and you're on your own at that and slower shutter speeds.

The Canon A-1, happily, has a metering system capable of working across an extended range, and can cope with exposures as long as thirty seconds or so, although the battery drain is severe on the long exposures. After using it for about eighteen months, I find it highly satisfactory on

Left, for use on the view camera rig described here, the A-1 is set to the green letter P (for Program) in the AE mode window, with mode selector at Tv position. Below, the stop-down lever (arrow) is unlatched and pushed toward the lens, as in right below, to complete preparation of the A-1 body for use with the adapter on the back of view cameras fitted with the Graflock back.

nearly every count. A problem is that it just refuses to believe that any of my Canon Type FD lenses have stops down to f22, although several do. If you attempt to bypass and override its prejudice by manually programming it to f22, in aperture priority mode, it retaliates by delivering extravagantly, flagrantly, heinously overcooked negatives that are all but totally opaque and quite unprintable, as are my comments on such a situation.

Another mistake to avoid with the A-1 is that of clicking the shutter on auto mode with the lens cap in place. The meter beholds total darkness, sets itself for anywhere from six to thirty seconds, wide open, opens the shutter, and hopes for the best. Once the shutter is open, it does no good to remove the lens cap. You can wait it out, losing all that expensive silver oxide battery power or, more practically, just flick the control lever from A (automatic) to L (lock), neatly nullifying the whole problem. The forementioned booboo is apt to happen when you load it with a fresh cartridge of film and try to waste the first two or three frames in your accustomed manner.

It is a fascinating spectacle, however, to watch the little LED readout for the shutter speed count down in the viewfinder of the A-1 as you stop down the lens on the view camera. The LED appears when the shutter button is partially depressed, or a bit of pressure put upon the cable release. With the lens wide open, it usually registers the figure 1000, flashing on and off to indicate that even 1/1000-second would be an overexposure. As you stop down, maintaining shutter button pressure, it changes to a steady 1000, then on through 750, 500, 350 and so on to figures such as 0"7, indicating 7/10-second.

As long as you don't try to force-feed it down to f22 against its will, the A-1 turns out negatives of astounding uniformity. That is a great blessing later, when you're printing in the darkroom. At the same degree of enlargement, you can hold the same print exposures, frame after frame, rarely needing to change the exposure of the enlarging paper.

Almost any SLR camera with removable lenses can be crossbred to just about any press or view camera, although the Graflock back makes the genetic experiment incomparably simpler. As for specimens of the quality of work you can hope to turn out with such a system, this entire book and the last several books I've written are absolutely a-crawl with examples.

To those patient souls, with little or no interest in the mechanics of taking photographs, who've followed this discussion doggedly, learning more about the intricacies of camera manipulation than they really cared to know, I'd like to say that you have my sincere apology, and I promise to stop at once!

MAKING & USING
Screwdrivers

Chapter 12

**Notes On Ways
And Means
For Getting Along
With Our
Threaded Friends**

*There are many ways to make a
screwdriver, and details on the
construction of one such as seen
superimposed over the sheet
metal screw are given here as
at least one possible approach.*

SCREWS OF various specifications are one of the
commoner fastening devices used in the shop, and
many of the small bolts have slotted heads, likewise
requiring a screwdriver to set them. It soon becomes
apparent that a properly fitted screwdriver is a useful item,
and manufacturers seem to delight in supplying screws that
don't quite fit any screwdriver you can put your hands
upon.

It is possible, and not particularly difficult, to
manufacture screwdrivers to custom specifications in a
moderately well equipped shop, so as to turn forth models
that will fit and cope with the manufacturer's practical
jokes in a thoroughly satisfactory manner.

Screws are commonly encountered in three basic
formats: slot-head, Phillips head or cross-point, and

hex-socket or Allen head. There are a few other types, but
they're far less apt to pose a challenge.

The slot-head screw is the most common, by a
considerable margin, and it is the easiest type for which to
fashion a homemade screwdriver. Fabrication of bits for the
Phillips and Allen sockets is rather challenging on the
domestic level, but we'll illustrate approaches for coping
effectively with those types, too. It's even possible to
fashion a screwdriver to handle those faintly trying screw
heads that are intended to be turned with coins.

If you propose to make a screwdriver to handle the
slot-head screws, you will need some suitable steel for the
blade. There is a temptation to salvage some steel from a
common spike of the right diameter, or from some of the
cold-rolled steel rod sold in three-foot lengths by many

hardware stores. I'm afraid you'll be disappointed in the performance of screwdrivers made with blades of either of those materials. The best steel for making up screwdriver blades is what we "Usanians" call drill rod and the British usually term silver steel, although it has no silver content.

You may have difficulty in finding a local source of drill rod, so I'll suggest a mail order source with which I've dealt with satisfaction. It's Manhattan Supply Company, 151 Sunnyside Boulevard, Plainview, New York 11803. They will supply a catalog on request, accepting credit cards such as Master Card or Visa, and they ship via United Parcel Service within the contiguous forty-eight states, with admirable promptness. Their drill rod is stocked in three-foot lengths, diameters by increments of 1/64-inch from 1/16 through 31/32-inch, with ten intermediate diameters between one and two-inch. You've a choice of water hardening or oil hardening alloys, the latter is a trifle more expensive. The cost of one three-foot piece of the ¼-inch, at time of writing, is $1.12 for the water hardening, and $1.53 for the oil hardening; shipping and handling costs are in addition.

Even drill rod is unable to withstand the considerable stresses of such use, as you receive it. After you've formed the blade to shape, you must harden the formed end. Most of the readily obtained steels, such as those used in spikes, or the cold rolled rods, are incapable of being hardened to any useful extent, due to their low carbon content. If you can obtain some masonry nails of suitable size, they are quite hard indeed, as received, but they can be formed on a good grindstone, with care and patience. I've heard of workshoppers who used the masonry nails for making small wood turning tools and the like, with good success.

Let's take up the forming of the blade first, discussing the hardening in logical order. The first step is to decide upon the length for the blade, allowing a suitable amount for the distance it will be seated into the handle. Measure it off on your length of drill rod, marking it with a felt-tipped marker. Put the rod in the vise and cut off the workpiece with a hacksaw — a thirty-two-tooth blade is recommended — and a drop of Tap Free cutting fluid will ease and speed the operation usefully, if applied to the cut, once it has been started.

With the workpiece cut, you need to true up at least the end that will be exposed; truing the end that goes into the

A metal lathe, such as this small Edelstaal Unimat, is helpful in producing handles from hex-sided aluminum bar stock, although there are other possible and workable approaches for the workshopper who does not have one.

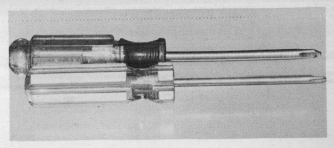

Above, two of the commoner sizes of screwdrivers for use on cross-point or Phillips head screws. Below, many sizes of slot-head screwdrivers are needed in shop use.

handle is a matter between you and your conscience.

The sample screwdriver shown under fabrication in the accompanying photos has a blade that mikes .2025-inch in diameter, after completion. The rod from which it was cut was given to me by a friend when I expressed a hankering for a hunk of 3/16-inch drill rod. That would be .1875-inch and presumably this's nominal 13/64-inch (.2031). Mindful of the cost, I'm not about to complain over a minor discrepancy such as .0151-inch: *If it's free, the price is right* has always been one of my bedrock beliefs.

I faced off the working end of the blade in the Unimat metal lathe, then chucked it into the drill press to bring the end of the blade down against a piece of 400 grit 3M WetOrDry paper to which a drop of honing oil had been applied, moving the paper about a bit, as the blade spun under mild pressure against the grits. I did not go on to 600 grit, because the fine, concentric swirls left in the steel by the 400 grit are used to establish the exact center later, when you get to grinding the two faces. Use a jeweler's loupe to check the progress and, with the center visible, you can arrive at an admirable degree of symmetry between the two faces.

Most store-bought screwdrivers are forged, with a straight taper between the two working faces. The taper will encourage the blade to work its way out of the screw slot and scar up the top of the screw, soothing the temper hardly at all. To avoid possible semantic confusion, that refers to the temper of the workshopper, not to that of the screwdriver or screw. By hollow-grinding the faces of the blade, as shown here, the part of the blade in contact with the screw slot is either dead-parallel, or perhaps a trifle turned-back-out. Such a blade tends to grip the screw slot in a much more secure and slip-free fashion than does a tapered blade.

The blade can be ground freehand on the whirling stones of a bench grinder, if one is available. I usually use a small grindstone, 1.550-inch in diameter by .550 in width, mounted on a ¼-inch shank and turned in the drill press. Such stones are available from Brownell's, Incorporated, Route 2, Box 1, Montezuma, Iowa 50171. The diameter

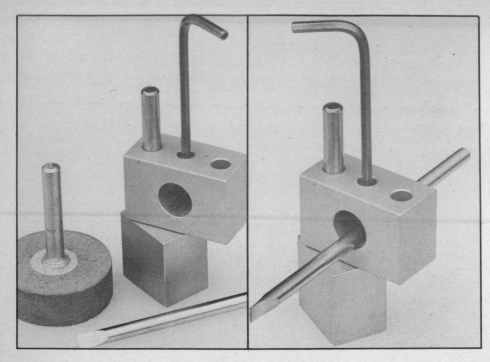

As discussed in the text, here is the small mounted grindstone and the B-Square Blade Maker used to grind hollow faces uniformly on both sides of the screwdriver bit.

A C-clamp has been used to secure the drill press vise to the bed of the drill press, with the vise holding the Blade Maker in the desired alignment to the grindstone.

Note that the blade is at the lower side of the securing hole here. It is necessary to raise small-diameter blades slightly when working on this side for even contact.

Here the blade is at the top of the hole for grinding the other side and the carrying block rests upon the base. Honing oil on the stone helps to keep the pores free.

matches the assortment of bits in the sets they provide for their really excellent magnetic handle kit, enabling the user to re-grind worn bits.

The small appliance shown here in use to hold the blade in exact alignment while grinding is the B-Square Blade Maker, from B-Square Company, Box 11281, Fort Worth, Texas 76109; a catalog showing this and a number of other handy items is free on request, from them.

The Blade Maker consists of two small anodized aluminum blocks. One positions a steel pin and the other holds the blade in place by means of an Allen head screw and the supplied wrench. There are two pivot holes, exactly equidistant from the central hole, and you slip those two holes over the support pin of the first block, in turn, to grind the two faces awfully close to dead uniformity.

I shifted the driving V-belt on the drill press to a fairly high rotating speed, and applied honing oil to the whirling grindstone occasionally during the forming, to get the accumulated metal particles out of the pores of the stone.

That approach is fast but messy, due to centrifugal force. Dress accordingly, or don an apron or shop smock, if you have one (I don't).

Change from side to side on the workpiece, by installing the top part of the Blade Maker on one hole or the other, alternately. As you work your way in, take a close look through the loupe at the little reference swirls you left in the end of the blade, to keep everything fairly even. Avoid overheating the workpiece, which could ruin its metallurgical properties.

As you get close to the form and dimensions you had in mind, ease off on the finger pressure you've been applying

Hardening and tempering of the finished blade is a vital step, though by no means a simple one. This book, as discussed in the text, offers helpful suggestions for it.

while grinding. Move the upper part of the Blade Maker up and down the supporting shaft on the lower part to smooth-up the ground surfaces a bit further.

When it appears to have achieved the desired shape and size, check it against a few typical screw slots of appropriate head diameter to make certain that the blade thickness is not a trifle too much. Do this *before* you remove it from the clamping holder!

So now, our blade is formed to taste and need. Let's harden it before we make the handle to make a logical order of discussion, for a change.

Hardening/tempering/heat-treating metals is most definitely an art in its own right, and but one of a great many arts in which I wish I commanded a lot more expertise. There is a helpful book on the subject — *Hardening and Tempering Engineers' Tools* — available from Brownell's, among other sources, devoted to the general topic. If you are working with steel of unknown provenance, as I am here, the situation gets a trifle

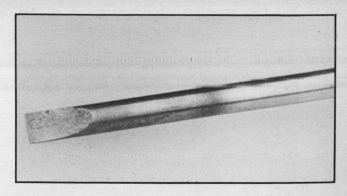

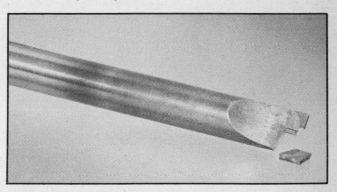

Discoloration of the end of the blade is clearly visible after heating to a cherry red temperature and quenching in water. Leaving it too hard to apt to result in such disconsoling damage to the blade as illustrated below!

confusing. I'm not certain if the drill rod on hand is of the water or oil hardening variety.

In brief theory, you heat the working end of the blade to the point where it turns a moderate cherry red, quenching it by plunging it into a container of the appropriate cooling medium — water, oil, or perhaps brine — then polish away the blued finish left on the heated portion, and re-heat it until it turns a soft shade of straw yellow, quenching it again in the same medium as before. That should do it, and you can then polish away the second set of stains, if you feel inclined.

In brief, that's the prescribed regimen. In practice, I followed it faithfully with a matching screwdriver I made from a piece of .3128-inch — presumably 5/16 (.3125)-inch drill rod supplied by the same friendly Bob Young who, among his other unlikely distinctions, runs a swimming pool service that maintains the pools of such legendary lovelies as Esther Williams and Doris Day; yes, really.

The 5/16-inch screwdriver did not turn out to be as hard as I'd hoped it might. I bent the blade slightly on a moderately taxing usage, but got it restored to its original shape by judicious adjustment of the bench vise to hold it for warping in the opposite direction. I plan to make another try at re-hardening it properly, Real Soon Now.

With the screwdriver of smaller diameter, shown here in production, I secured the blade in a pair of Vise-Grip pliers, fired up the propane torch, and heated the working end until it was a moderate cherry red in subdued light, then plunged it into a small can holding straight tap water, followed by polishing off the blue stain that resulted. Since that time, I've used the finished tool several times, occasionally under a fair amount of stress. The tip remains undistorted.

If you achieve too high a degree of hardening, the blade will be so brittle that it will break under strain. That's the philosophy behind hardening it first to full-hard, then relieving it back to straw-yellow in the second heating.

On hand, surprisingly enough, is another screwdriver I made about 1960, grinding a short section of ¼-inch (.2502-inch is what it mikes) drill rod freehand on the grindstone that spun on the far-left end of the maudlinly-mourned Delta wood lathe. The same tool produced the handle out of a hunk of homegrown maple, with a reinforcing ferrule cut from a piece of 1¼-inch OD

This is the blade that was ground freehand, as discussed in the adjacent text, with a maple handle and aluminum tubing ferrule.

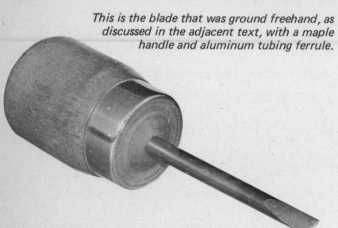

aluminum tubing and driven into place. I illustrate it here by way of showing what can be done without the helpful assistance of the B-Square Blade Maker set. At some point down the years, I managed to warp the working edge of that blade seriously out of alignment and it needs to be coaxed tenderly back to its original format and re-tempered, as cannily as may be possible in the current skills of its maker.

Squishy memory testifies that the maple handle of that aging screwdriver was center-drilled with a hole slightly smaller but close to ¼-inch, whereupon the concealed end of the blade had a few flats and grooves ground onto it, also freehand, and the concealed portion was seated into the undersized hole by pressure of the bench vise, with a small piece of scrap copper between the tip of the blade and the

A short section of aluminum hex-stock has been cut from the larger piece with a hacksaw to be made into the handle.

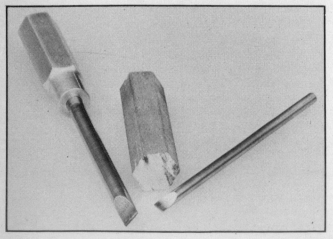

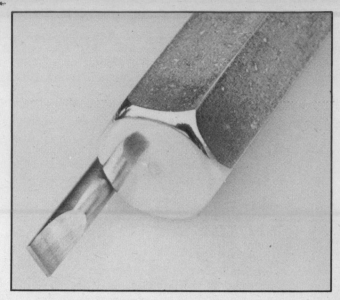

Secured by alternate flats in the three-jaw headstock chuck of the lathe, the butt end of the handle is faced off, the corners are rounded and polished before proceeding to finish the end of the handle that will hold the blade.

vise jaw to prevent premature burring of the edge. I can report that the edge may have gotten warped a little, but the blade has yet to slip detectably inside its handle.

The same Bob Young — not to be confused with Robert Young of *Father Knows Best* boob-tube fame — also laid off upon me a couple of lengths of hexagonal aluminum stock measuring .6876-inch between the opposite flats. One presumes that it was marketed as a nominal 11/16-inch item of merchandise (.6875-inch).

The Unimat lathe has transmuted the two supplied lengths of raw hex-stock into an impressive array of useful and invaluable artifacts, since it can grip such small forms quite helpfully with its three-jaw chuck. First, a workpiece is hacksawn from the hex stock, a trifle over 2¾ inches long, so as to permit final finishing to that length. It's chucked into the lathe and one end is faced off square and flat, followed by rounding the corners, smoothing and polishing. That will become the butt end of the handle, and you do it first to avoid the difficulties involved in doing it secondly.

At this point, the workpiece is removed, reversed and chucked from the other end. Any unevenness and toolmarks left from the hacksaw are faced away, and the hex stock is rounded for about 5/8-inch, turning it down to 5/8-inch diameter, rounding the corners and working down through progressively finer grits of WetOrDry paper to 600 grit, followed by a dab of Simichrome polish applied with a bit of rag as the workpiece spins in the lathe.

The next step is to put a drill bit of the proper size in the little tailpiece chuck of the lathe and drill the hole in the end of the handle to accept the shank of the blade. In this instance, a No. 7 bit of nominal .2010-inch diameter made a hole that fitted the shank to perfection. Yes, I know: I said the drill rod was .2026-inch, but a drill bit usually produces a hole that's just a squinch larger than its rated diameter. In this example, the shank fitted the handle so snugly that it was necessary to drive it into place by

Reversed in the lathe chuck, the flats have been turned down for a suitable distance, the corners rounded and a No. 7 bit in the tailstock chuck is boring the blade hole. Right, Loctite is used to secure the blade and handle.

beating on the working end of the blade with the invaluable mallet that has the polyurethane head.

A drop or so of Loctite Stud N' Bearing Mount sealant had been put into the hole before inserting the shank and, once seated, the area was given a moderate warming with the propane torch to hasten the solidification of the Loctite. Experience has shown that this approach results in a bonding that's as permanent as anyone is apt to need. I tried to remove a piece of ¼-20 threaded rod once, that had been attached this way, and the steel rod twisted apart while the Loctite held the seated portion in utter immovability.

The welding via Loctite completes the project. The working edge of the blade, be it noted, is .033-inch in finished thickness, and that seems to be just about right for a screwdriver of this particular blade diameter. The basic techniques can be used to produce similar tools to handle specialized applications. I've made up a few with short sections of brass rod in various diameters to serve as non-marring punches, and find them quite useful.

As is noted elsewhere, the hex-shanked blade inserts that come with the Brownell kit will convert the

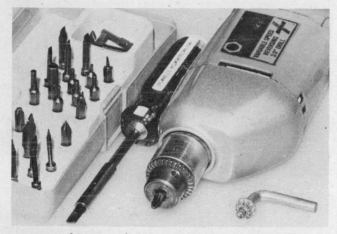

Above and below are views of the Brownell magnetic set of interchangeable screwdriver bits which, having shanks with six sides, can be held and used in the electric drill.

Three different sizes of cross-point or Phillips head bits as supplied in the Brownell kit illustrated at the left.

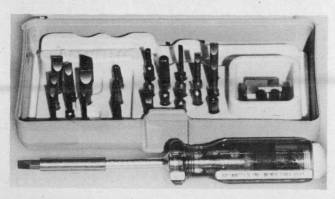

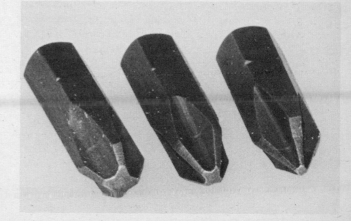

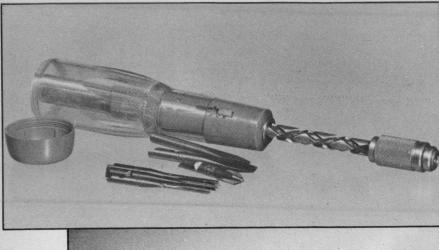

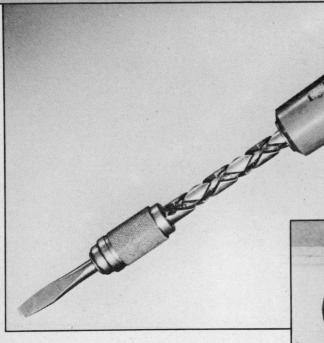

Often termed a "Yankee" screwdriver, this double-fluted design can be set to drive or remove screws by a simple push/pull movement. The hollow handle holds spare drill bits and screwdriver blades, as shown.

The versatile and efficient Easydriver kits are available in at least two sizes, of which this is the larger. Handle is reversible and fitted with a ratchet, with adapters to handle a wide assortment of available bits and accessories.

variable-speed/reversible 3/8-inch electric Black & Decker drill into a remarkably efficient power screwdriver that can save vast amounts of time and effort on operations that involve a lot of screwdriving or screw removal. For smaller screws, there is the little push/pull screwdriver with a supply of blades in its hollow handle, including a couple of small drill bits that enable it to be used for drilling the starting holes into which the screws will be driven; another useful tool that gets reached for frequently.

Another approach to screwdriving is the Easydriver, available in at least two sizes, of which the one shown here is the larger. It consists of a spherical handle carrying a one-way ratchet arrangement, with a square hole to accept the shanks of the blades furnished for it. The two hemispheres of the handle, in this size, are red and black. If you insert the blade in the black side, the ratchet will work to turn the screw out; counterclockwise, that is, and vice

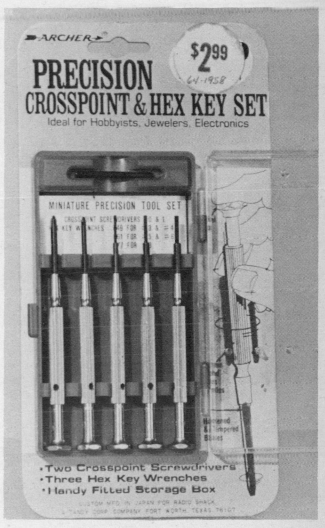

Radio Shack's extremely handy and capable kit of small screwdrivers, all with hollow-ground blade tips, in a neatly fitted carrying case. The price is higher now.

A set of cross-point and hex-key drivers from the same source enables the workshopper to cope effectively with all sorts of plaguing tiny fasteners in need of tightening.

versa. If you wish to etch that into your memory circuits, just think of "blackout," or "going into the red."

Several accessories are available for the Easydrivers, including a handle that fits over the sphere to provide added leverage, adapters to handle the various sizes of socket wrench hardware, and so on. One adapter accepts the little hex-sided blade inserts that are about ¼-inch across the flats — .2495, to be a bit more exact — such as come with the kits from Brownell's, as well as from the source of the Easydriver accessories. Thus, all can be used interchangeably and also with the electric drill.

The chain of Radio Shack electronics stores usually stock small screwdriver kits in plastic boxes. There are at least two versions: one with six screwdrivers for slot-head screws, ranging from 1/32 to 9/64-inch in diameter, having hollow-ground faces; the other has two cross-point (Phillips head) plus three hex key (Allen head) drivers. Between the

two kits, it's an inexpensive way to be able to cope with nearly all of the tiny screws that tend to come loose, such as in eyeglasses and the like.

It's customary among many manufacturers to include a few hex wrenches of the necessary sizes when packing their merchandise. As I'd unpack the given item, it used to be my custom to toss all newly arrived hex wrenches into a single catch-all drawer above the bench. They accumulated in profusion and I finally made up a small holding block to simplify finding the proper size for a given need. I've never heard exactly how many different sizes of hex wrenches there are, but I can report that the metric system has a progression of the things, all its own. Chapman Manufacturing Company, Route 17, Durham, Connecticut 06422, offers a midget ratchet kit — their No. 2307 — with a twenty-tooth ratchet handle and six interchangeable bits in the metric series. The dimensions across the flats are 1.5,

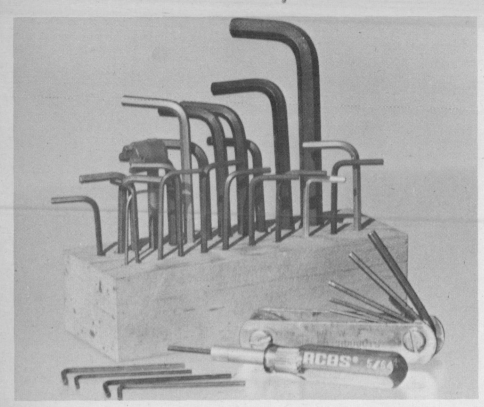

The bewildering profusion of L-shaped hex wrenches can be organized with a simple holding block, such as this one. Pocket hex wrenches with several bit sizes are available, as are the small hex drivers, as illustrated.

2, 2.5, 3, 4, and 5mm. An illustrated price brochure is free on request from Chapman, showing their several package kits and individual bits. The bits have hex shanks — also miking .2495-inch across the flats — and can be used in the three-jaw chuck of electric drills, although they aren't readily interchangeable with the Easydriver or Brownell bits. One of the Chapman kits, their No. 8320, comes with a nice little jeweler's screwdriver that accepts a pair of reversible-end bits to cover four sizes.

In an effort to provide a faint flicker of guiding light amid all the hex wrench chaos, I've gathered up all of the available inch and metric sizes and offer the following as evidence that there are *at least* this many sizes in use:

INCH SERIES	METRIC SERIES	
.049	1.5 mm	.0581-inch
.0615	2	.0728
.0782	2.5	.0983
.093	3	.1189
.1089	4	.1579
.1244	5	.1926
.1646	6	.2362
.155	8	.3129
.187		
.2182		
.3108		

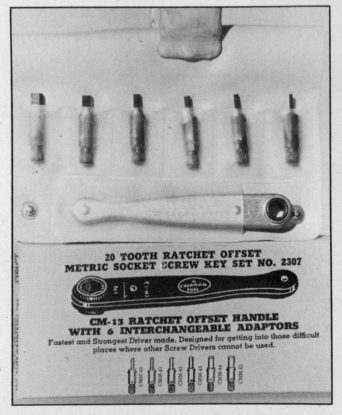

20 TOOTH RATCHET OFFSET
METRIC SOCKET SCREW KEY SET NO. 2307

CM-13 RATCHET OFFSET HANDLE
WITH 6 INTERCHANGEABLE ADAPTORS
Fastest and Strongest Driver made. Designed for getting into those difficult places where other Screw Drivers cannot be used.

Chapman's kit with the reversible ratchet handle and set of metric bits is supplied in a compact pocket pack. The bits are compatible with their other handles and kits.

I'll concede the distinct possibility that there may be other sizes, as well, of which I have no samples on hand. I've obtained the quoted dimensions through careful measurements with a fairly decent micrometer and I note

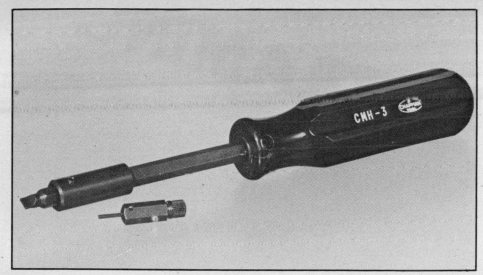

Chapman's handle, extension and one of their several bits go together to make up a handy screwdriver for nearly any needed requirement. The small hex-bit, shown at left and below, secures the bit to the extension and the latter to the handle, if that's needed.

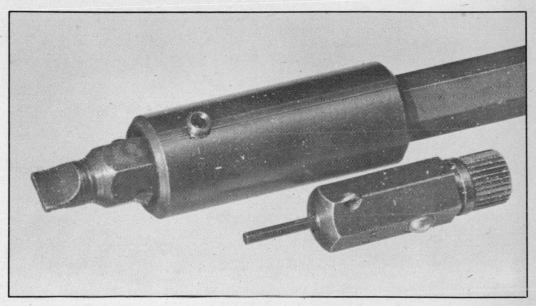

Chapman's No. 9600 kit provides a lot of different screwdrivers in the compartmented spaces of a remarkably compact and convenient carrying kit. Several other kit combinations are also offered.

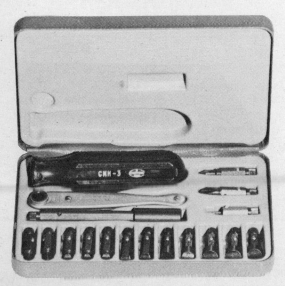

that nominal listings cover sizes such as .061 and .077-inch, so any minor variations probably can be reconciled to manufacturers' tolerances in production.

Earlier, we mentioned ways to cope with those coin-slotted screw heads that are encountered here and there. Well, you can use a penny, or a nickel, as needed — certainly among the more affordable of all screwdrivers! — held by hand or perhaps better secured in a small pair of toggle-lock (Vise-Grip) pliers. If you feel a heavy need for coping with such things, you could slot the end of a ¼-inch piece of drill rod, solder a steel washer of appropriate size into the slot, and fit a handle to it, as discussed here. I understand the U.S. Secret Service takes a dim view of people who solder or otherwise damage and deface the official coinage of this country. The steel would be stronger, in any event.

You can make hex-tip screwdrivers by cutting the shorter arm off one of the plentiful little wrenches and securing either portion in a tight-fitting hole in the end of a homemade handle, producing something that's usually more convenient to manipulate than those infernal little L-shaped wrenches. The important thing is not to let screwdrivers drive you screwy!

A long-lost oil painting recently surfaced, with frame of lumberyard moulding, cut to gappy corners. We'll be treating it to a new frame, hoping we can do better.

PICTURE FRAMING & MITERING

Chapter 13

Notes On Pursuing The Wily And Incredibly Evasive 45-Degree Angle

WITH NO MORE than a few limited exceptions, picture frames are four-sided affairs, with the corners meeting at right angles. I suppose you could make up a butt-glued picture frame, and it might seem a refreshing novelty, in the kindred vein of a limerick done in blank verse, but the stodgy and conventional way of doing such things is to have the corners meet in a neat forty-five degree mitered joint.

Executing a mitered right-angle joint so precise that you can contemplate it without wincing is rather more difficult than falling off the average log. That is among the first of the facts that you discover. The primordial bit of data is that professional picture-framers are hazardous and inimical to your check stub balance.

Quite a lot of years ago, a friend named Dick Eney was serving with the armed forces in Japan and he deemed it a kindly gesture to buy up and send us three handsome prints of the sort that the gifted people in that lovely land do so superbly. Suitably matted, they cover an area about fourteen by nineteen inches; an easy matter to verify, since they continue to add charisma to our front entry hall, down to the immediate moment.

After gloating over the colorful curling masterpieces/mistresspieces (I can't be certain) for a matter of some months, I determined to get them onto the walls, so I turned them over to a friend of that time who performed picture framing, along with his other activities. In a week or three, he presented them back to me, quite

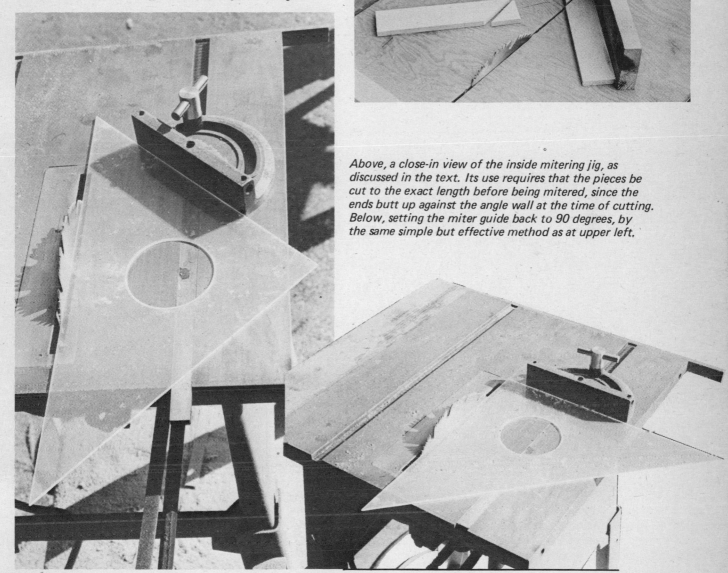

If your miter guide doesn't have stops at 45 and 90 degrees, here is an accurate, practical way to set it by loosening the adjustment and aligning it to the blade with the aid of a drafting triangle, using triangle's 45 angle.

Above, a close-in view of the inside mitering jig, as discussed in the text. Its use requires that the pieces be cut to the exact length before being mitered, since the ends butt up against the angle wall at the time of cutting. Below, setting the miter guide back to 90 degrees, by the same simple but effective method as at upper left.

nicely framed, along with a bill for $39, as dubious memory serves. As those were the days, fading out of memory's grasp, when such an amount would finance trips to the corner grocer for two or three weeks, the reimbursement left an impression upon the memory clearly recalled to the present. Since that distant day, I've framed all my own pictures, perhaps not quite so eptly, but ever so much more economically. I mean, really: The pictures were free, but the frames cost thirteen bucks apiece, in the days when a $13 bill was nothing at which to sneeze, nor blow your nose upon.

Somewhere around about that time — the early Sixties — I acquired table-sawing capabilities, probably via the first home-rigged modification of the old Delta wood lathe.

Given access to a table saw, cutting precise forty-five degree miters is as easy as pie, right? Not necessarily.

A cut comprising an included angle of forty-five degrees, zero minutes, and zero seconds — or acceptably close to it — can be executed on just about any well-preserved table saw, radial arm saw, or kindred device, but it's apt to prove handy if you've a good supply of scrap wood on hand for trial cuts and tests of the resulting adjustments.

The first thing you do is to make the indicated adjustment as closely as you can eyeball it, lock it down and make a trial cut on a couple of pieces of scrap. Align the mitered cuts on the scrap snugly and then use a gauge of a true ninety degrees — such as a drafting triangle, as discussed elsewhere — to check the squareness of the

resulting joint. This is done, please note, *before* you apply glue or commence to cut the stock you propose to use!

If the cut is just the tiniest, wee-est bit short or long of forty-five degrees, the resulting joint will be detectably off the mark. If you're tempted at this point to go with it and hope for the best, discipline your optimism a little. Errors in the preliminary angle cut are magnified by a factor of eight in getting around the entire periphery of a picture frame. If it's just a tiny tad over forty-five degrees, you have some gaps to live with at the inner corners, and vice — of course — versa.

So you have at least two choices. You can make test cuts on pieces of scrap until the two fitted pieces are congruent to your testing gauge within limits you feel inclined to live with.

Or, on the other hand, you can grit your teeth and, once/for always, build a mitering jig that will — it is to be wistfully hoped — spare you such arduous chores in the future.

One of my neighbors across the street is a fellow workshop fiend and he put me on the track of a nicely satisfactory solution to this particular dilemma. It's a mitering jig, handmade, that rides in the grooves of the saw bed on both the right and left of the blade. Up front is a carefully constructed pair of guiding braces positioned at a dead-on right angle to each other. In use, one side of the joint is held against one side of the guide in cutting and vice versa. The resulting miter, as friend Steve Herrett puts it so neatly, is a joint that's "good enough for who it's for."

Once such a jig is made up, and its accuracy verified, it can be set aside for use of the regular miter gauge at its customary ninety-degree setting or whatever, and brought back into use, eternally preset, when the need comes up for cutting accurate forty-five degree miters the next time.

In making picture frames, it is not enough that the angle cuts be made with fine precision. It is also necessary that the two horizontal members be *exactly* the same length and the two vertical members likewise. If this is not the case, then all your painstaking efforts are in vain.

With the need for keeping the opposite sides of the frame exactly equal in length, I made a modification in the mitering jig design. The one my neighbor made has the angle to the fore; mine has the angle at the rear, with the arms extending forward and outward.

In use, my first step is to cut the horizontal sections simultaneously, one above the other, with the outboard ends neatly lined up; doing the same for the vertical sections. Then, when cutting the miters, either end of the piece goes snugly against one side or the other of the inside of the angle. This seems to result in a set of frame sections that come just awfully close to matching in length and angle.

In cutting the frame sections, I alternate from left to right as I go around the cuts. If I cut a piece extending to the left and away, I make a small red mark on the back side to aid in getting them all together exactly as cut, with a blue mark — done in the red and blue Col-Erase pencils I keep for layout — for the cut made with the workpiece

5

6

1 A relief saw cut of about ¼" was made in the inner-rear corner of the frame sections to accept the painting, and the remaining edges were beveled at 45-degree angles.

2 After cutting, corner clamps were used to assemble two sets of frame sections, for greater ease of final assembly.

3 A close look at the joint in figure 2 shows a fairly neat fit.

4 The two types of corners for the Shopsmith Maxi-Clamp set are mirror images of each other, with the pair like the one at left here having a third hole in aluminum casting.

5 The cut pieces of scrap left from mitering the sections can be arranged in several ways for use. Refer to page 208 for yet another possible arrangement of the pieces.

6 The two sets of frame sections are being held in the Maxi-Clamp here. The frame is face-down and we've dropped the painting into the relief cuts to make sure it fits the size of the opening. Miraculously enough, it does!

Another view of the clamped-up frame as the glued corners are setting up. Principle of alternating the two types of aluminum corner castings can be seen in this photo.

extending to the right. Thus, each of the four pieces end up with a red mark at one end and a blue mark at the other, assuring that I won't get them mixed up.

As a by-product of the operation, you end up with eight little triangles of scrap, well worth keeping aside for future needs in bracing or reinforcement and the like. As illustrated, you can glue them together to make a novel octagonal ring, by way of using them up at once.

The painting being framed in the illustrations is one of some boat houses in Horicon, Wisconsin, that surfaced recently, after having been missing since our latest move, eight years ago. It's one that I did in 1949, before I drifted away from oil painting as the necessary time for such pleasant pursuits got scarcer and scarcer. It bore a frame of sorts, executed to my '49 level of skill at such things, with all the unsightly angular departures at the corners that I found so difficult to eradicate. Yes, I think I tried to cut it with a miter box, as I had no table saw in those days. Cutting nicely fitted miters is no snap with a table saw, being a matter of endless patient trials and readjustments to the miter gauge; seemingly always too much or too little. Trying to do it with a miter box, at least with one of the inexpensive wooden versions, is even more difficult.

On the other hand, if your initial happens to be G, there is this possible arrangement for the eight little right triangles left from the mitering operation. Efficient use of scrap pieces is a perpetual challenge, and merely hanging onto them in hopes a use will turn up will only get you buried in scrap!

In the process of getting the old 8" table saw re-aligned, another badly-needed improvement was made. The plastic miter guide knob had taken too many falls. It was replaced by a neat brass and steel knob quickly turned out on "Mister Atkins," the new Jet metal lathe from Corbin, christened in honor of my favorite guitar-picker.

I ripped and finished the four strips for the replacement frame from a length of redwood 2x4, a bit longer than the longest side of the frame needed to be. Frame strips must be longer than the given side of the picture, by a factor that varies with the width of the strip. If in doubt, make a lifesize layout of the frame on brown wrapping paper to obtain the dimensions by measuring. As a general rule, the length for a given frame section can be determined by taking the desired length of the inside opening and adding twice the width of the sections.

Bear in mind that you'll be wanting each frame section to be long enough to reach exactly to the outside corner. Another way to establish the approximate length is to lay the frame section next to the picture and place a straightedge across opposite corners, making a light pencil mark to show the line across the frame section.

The painting here is on canvas, mounted to a 1/8-inch steel wire frame — a readymade surface sold at that time under the name of StretchRpanel — so that the combined thicknesses of wire plus two layers of canvas at the edge is about ¼-inch, with overall dimensions of 16x12 inches. I planned to make a relief cut on the inner rear edge of the frame to bring the back of the panel flush with the back surface of the frame, which meant covering about the outer ¼-inch of the picture with the frame.

After the usual interlude of frowning and lip movement, I cut two of the strips to 18¾ inches and the other pair to 14¾. The strips are about 1-11/16 inches in width and 5/8-inch thick.

With the strips for the top/bottom and two sides cut to respectively uniform length, cutting the miters was a notably quick and simple operation: the great virtue of the mitering jig.

When building the jig, I foresaw the treacherous ease with which an unthinking thumb might end up at the rear of the angle brace during the cut, and took the canny precaution of installing a piece of one-inch pine, vertically, at that point to keep unwary digits away from the blade as the cut is completed. There is no ready way that I see to employ a guard at the front of the angle brace, so attentive watchfulness and caution are required to avoid trouble in holding the workpieces.

A purely subjective sidenote here: Just prior to making the frame, I had another go at trying to get the blade lined back up with the bed of the eight-inch saw. I'm not un-crossing my fingers yet, but I dare to hope I accomplished it — this being about the fifth such assault on the plaguing problem. The blade assembly, as noted elsewhere, is held to the bed by four screws that run through elongated holes. This time, I loosened the screws only slightly, using my

A joy for which there is no match
Is, when you itch, to up and scratch.
--Ogden Nash

As discussed, too much heat, used when dry-mounting a resin-coated photograph, can cause the emulsion layer to separate, check, and peel, in the distressing manner all too clearly evident above.
Below, a 1-3/8" hole in a piece of redwood scrap served as a frame for this photo of son Bill.

largest C-clamp to horse the blade assembly back and forth, meanwhile employing the vernier caliper to check the distance between the inner edge of the miter gauge groove and the front and back side surfaces of the saw blade. Through a lot of patient fiddling, and a few deleted expletives, I got it down to the point where the two were parallel within less than .002-inch, whereupon I snubbed the four holding screws down solidly with the socket wrench. A few test cuts gave gratifying evidence that it has returned to cutting with the impressive precision it displayed back in 1962, when new. I note this in hopes it may prove helpful, should you ever encounter the same vexing problem.

With the four frame sections cut and mitered, I made the relief cuts on the inner rear edges to accept the painting and cranked over the blade to a forty-five-degree angle to cut bevels on the three remaining edges. Such things are purely a matter of taste and preference. Further possibilities include cutting a few shallow kerfs (blade slots) uniformly in the front surface of all four pieces, or using a router with appropriate bit to modify the cross-section to your liking.

Redwood was chosen because its color seemed to complement the cool grays and muted chartreuse that predominate in the painting. The redwood also picks up and repeats the general hue of the center and right-hand

It's a good idea to miter a couple of pieces of scrap first, checking the accuracy of the angle with the drafting triangle. This one, cut on the inside mitering jig, appears to be acceptably close to the money.

Here, the two sets of frame sections rest on the mitering jig, ready to be mitered in the manner discussed.

boathouses. It's my contention that a frame should merge with the picture to form a comfortable and agreeable whole. At the same time, the frame should not distract from the picture.

Survival of more than three decades have left the underlying pigments undimmed. It was done entirely with a brand of paint called Permanent Pigments and I incline to feel that the name is warranted. The surface is, however, in dire need of careful cleaning and re-varnishing. No, you don't use floor varnish for such purposes — unless you want to turn everything ghastly amber. Copal resin, in a suitable vehicle, is more the indicated stuff. Do not, however, varnish over the built-up smudge and grime, or you'll never get rid of it.

Not all framing applications involve oil paintings on stretched canvas. You may wish to frame watercolors, line drawings, photographs or the like, done on various types of paper. In such cases, the first step is to get the fragile and curl-prone paper securely anchored to a more unyielding surface, such as heavy card stock, usually around 1/8-inch in thickness. As an adhesive medium, I'd recommend the

A side section is ready for its first cut. As it extends to the operator's left, it will be color-coded at the rear in red for ease in getting the pieces in correct relationship.

Speaking of making effective use of scraps, and discussed in detail on page 213, the novel frame for the pictures of Patti and Bob Carpenter was made from a piece of scrap that carried a loosened knot. It was split, edge-glued and treated to a wiped coat of tung oil, with the caption done as a "government project" on an IBM typesetter.

dry mounting tissue, made by Eastman and available through most photo stores. It is applied by means of moderate heat, using an electric flatiron at one of the lower settings — unless, of course, you've access to a mounting press. Put a piece of fairly heavy paper over the picture to protect it from direct contact with the flatiron.

I would urge you, in the strongest terms compatible with good taste, to avoid using rubber cement for mounting anything you wish to keep more than a year or so. With the passage of time — which always occurs — rubber cement gradually takes on a truly obscene shade of yellowish-brown, turning the picture and nearby surfaces the same nauseating color.

Some types of contact cement are reasonably satisfactory over the long haul, others less so. If they dry water-white and stay that color, give them a try, if you feel inclined, using a test subject of limited value before entrusting anything you cherish to that approach. Meanwhile, consider the Eastman dry mounting tissue for pictures/photos that you really care about.

Oil paintings, watercolors, or line drawings usually are

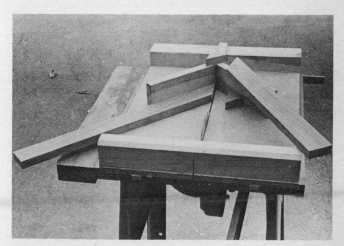

Here, the top or bottom piece has been cut to the right and coded with the blue pencil to show that it matches the side piece coded red. Parts were laid out for the photo, not left there while the actual cut was being made, need I say?

And — created for your viewing enjoyment — here is an example of the outside mitering jig, under construction in nearby photos. Unlike the inside version, both ends of the workpiece are free and you can cut to a pencil line. Note the vertical board serving as a blade guard at rear.

The miter guide on the 10" Rockwell saw has stops at 45 and 90 degrees, and they are impressively accurate.

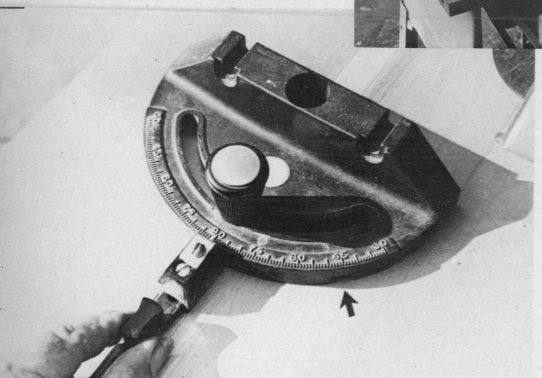

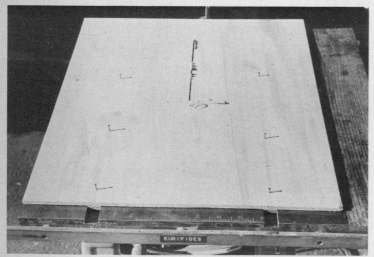

With the two guide rails temporarily secured by brads while the glue sets up, the blade has been lowered below the table surface and slowly raised to make a blind cut up through the ¼" piece of plywood, to which the jig will be aligned for final assembly. The brads come out, later.

displayed with nothing between the picture surface and the viewing eye, although this is by no means an inviolable decree. The subtle nuances of the surface texture are an integral part of the picture, particularly in the instance of oil paintings. That is not necessarily the case with photographs, where an unobtrusive protecting surface serves to preserve the picture, without diminishing the viewing enjoyment.

The usual protective layer for photographs is glass, available in glossy or non-reflecting versions. The latter is preferable, but it costs a worthwhile trifle more.

Another adhesive that's quite unacceptable for permanent mounting of photos and the like is the sticky wax used for laying out copy to be printed by photo-offset. It's fine for its intended purpose, since it allows the paper to be lifted and re-positioned, as desired. Photos attached with artist's wax show a strong and stubborn tendency to peel away from the mount, due to their curling with changes in humidity.

Within recent years, most makers of photographic printing papers have offered a resin-coated photo paper that is substantially waterproof. Such papers have many notable

With the saw blade well raised, a straightedge at the rear and a large 45-degree drafting triangle are used to lay out the lines for locating the right angle guide of the outside mitering jig that appears on the top of facing page.

advantages, but the emulsion of the print surface is extremely vulnerable to damage if excessive heat is applied when using the dry mounting tissue. I found that out the hard way, in the course of mounting a photo of one of the family cats dealing with a parasite problem behind her right ear, which seemed such a perfect illustration for the late Ogden Nash's immortal observation. Just a touch too much heat and the thin layer of emulsion shrinks and separates from the base paper, ruining the photo. I note this in hopes of sparing you the same problem.

Other novel framing approaches can be taken, particularly if the picture is rather small. The redwood-framed miniature of our son Bill was made by drilling a 1-3/8-inch hole in a piece of 3/8-inch wood cut 1¾ inches square, with the photo attached to the back of the frame by a small amount of General Electric silicone rubber in the translucent white color. That appears to be another promising adhesive for such purposes, since the frame has stood up well for three years without peeling or staining of the photo. Similar one-piece frames can be made larger, of course, and openings other than circular can be cut with a jigsaw, if desired.

Even the humble knothole can serve useful purposes, as illustrated by the double-framed photos of friends Patti and Bob Carpenter. This started as a knot, about 1-7/8 inches in diameter, in a piece of one-inch pine board. I had cut it off as scrap, noting that the loosened knot could be pushed out quite easily. A small light bulb materialized above my head and I divided the piece of scrap into two halves, glued the edges together and contrived to snap photos of the Carpenters to enlarge to appropriate size, adding the caption by means of an IBM typesetter to which I have occasional access. The end result is, I think, fairly close to unique, but you're welcome to use the idea as your own.

If you don't care to produce your own picture framing stock, there are many varieties of readymade versions available from stores handling art supplies, or picture frames. A further source worth checking out is the moulding sold at lumber yards. The latter tend to be considerably less costly, foot for foot, although they are unfinished wood. It is no great chore to stain and/or finish such frames, provided you take care to clean up any glue that oozes out of the mitered joints when gluing the corners together.

Chapter 14

WOODS

So the Deacon inquired of the village folk
Where he could find the strongest oak,
That couldn't be split nor bent nor broke, —
That was for spokes and floor and sills;
He sent for lancewood to make the thills;
The crossbars were ash, from the straightest trees,
The panels of white-wood, that cuts like cheese,
But lasts like iron for things like these;

— The Deacon's Masterpiece: Or The
Wonderful "One-Hoss Shay"
by Oliver Wendell Holmes, Sr.

A piece of birch board, from trees such as those on the facing page, shows the darker heartwood and lighter hue of the outer layer of sapwood, along with annular rings.

THE CHOICE of materials can make a lot of difference, as regards the splendor or mediocrity of a given project. The better woods enrich and enhance any artifact, by their vibrant or subtle colors, and by the indescribable beauty of their grain patterns. At the other end of the spectrum, in terms of ligneous pulchritude, we that wood of truly nauseous hue, widely used for constructing the humble shipping skid, and similar uses where no one gives a hang how it looks, which my friend Bill Stavdal delicately euphemizes as "obscenity-elm."

Many books have been produced on woods alone, so it's obvious that we can't be as comprehensive here as one might wish, within the scope of a single chapter. I've no idea what Holmes' "white-wood" may be termed today. I suspect it's basswood, a fast-growing, leaf-shedding (deciduous) tree fairly common in the Midwest. Its wood ranges in color from spectral white to the palest cream, uniform in grain and it certainly does come close to cutting like cheese, if we are thinking of the flintier cheeses, such as well aged Parmesan.

Basswood stands in flagrant contradiction to some discussions of woods with their arbitrary decree that hardwoods come from deciduous trees, while evergreens produce softwoods. The avocado tree tends to disqualify that, from the other end. It wears its leaves the year around, and I've seen some things made from its wood that were quite unlike softwoods, as exemplified by white pine or red cedar.

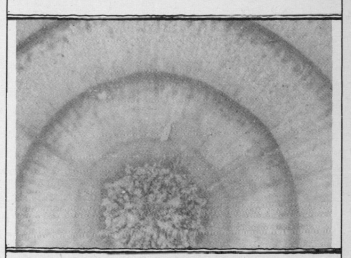

Speaking of annular rings, composed of earlywood and darker latewood, here's a good example, from the end of a board cut from the center of some species of pine.

There are a number of trees whose wood is superb, in one or several qualities, but they are not well known, nor popular, because they rarely or never achieve a useful amount of trunk diameter. In the Midwest, the red sumac is rated somewhere between a large weed and a small tree. Yet the trunkwood of the sumac, if you care to bother harvesting it, is a blindingly bright chrome yellow in color; not especially tough, but worthy of consideration for low-stress uses, such as inlays. In the West, the mesquite tree is rarely considered as a source for timber, chiefly because large pieces are seldom seen. The base wood is a rich, creamy yellow, with veins of deep reddish-black running through it. Desert parasites prey upon the mesquite tree, leaving unsightly holes that need skillful filling-in with brown-toned fiberglass in order to make anything useful and sightly from it.

Despite all the problems mentioned, I tend to regard mesquite a wonder-wood in at least one respect, other than

As ruefully noted, pines vary broadly in appearance and characteristics. Grain pattern of another example can be seen in this close-in photo of a mitered picture frame.

Tough, hard, and handsomely grained, here is a sample of oak's distinctive appearance; exact type is not known.

The shimmering beauty of tiger-striped Oregon myrtle comes through, even in a black-and-white photograph.

The elegant grain pattern of bocote, in dark- and darker-brown; an absolute delight to work, as noted here!

At about 3X magnification, this is Midwestern locust, known by several names. Tight-grained, hard and heavy, it's pleasant to work, and bright yellow.

Lauan, or Philippine mahogany, shows little or no visible growth rings and is a pleasant pinkish-tan in color.

Honduras or Central American mahogany is darker, harder, heavier and tougher than Philippine mahogany, or lauan, and this sample shows a slight growth patterning.

Tough, hard, close-grained and heavy, this is Osage orange, currently retailing at $3.90/pound; colorful, too!

its striking appearance. It seems virtually impervious to warpage from shifts in atmospheric humidity; one of the few woods of which that is true.

Quite a lot of the trees that produce useful and handsome lumber are of the sort that also produce nuts or fruits. Examples would include walnut, hickory, oak, cherry, and beech. It does not apply in all cases, by any means. Apple carries limited prestige in any of its many varieties that I've ever encountered, and the same applies for peach, as well as the several citrus varieties. The lemonwood used in archer's bows is thus termed for its color; it doesn't come from lemon trees.

Sometimes, when conditions are right, or fairly close to it, you can cut the timber, age it and go on to fashion useful items from it. When I was 15 or so, I had an interest in archery, and we cut down a hickory tree on the farm we rented at that time. In splitting up the trunk for the Winter's firewood, I managed to make off with about one-quarter of it, stashing it in the shop/toolshed for a year or so, at which time I made a longbow from the best part of the hickory stave. It was, indeed, a *long* longbow; a full six feet four inches from nock to nock, unstrung. I bought some cedar shafts from a sporting goods store in the nearest town, fitted them with tips, nocks and fletching, and had a lot of fun with that bow, until it gave way abruptly on its final draw, dabbing me a crafty one atop the head.

Despite facetious comments I may've made elsewhere in this book, my admiration and esteem for choice burl walnut is undiluted. It occurs in many sub-species, under assorted names such as English, Claro, Circassian and black, but I've never seen an ugly piece of walnut. Somewhere in the outlying family, there is a library table crafted from Kansas black walnut by my paternal grandfather, with the top, shelves, legs and decorative panels made of solid slabs of the gorgeous stuff, the top a full 1¼-inch thick, as memory serves. In these modern times, that much walnut could and probably would serve to make a hundred chipboard tables look for all the world like solid walnut.

Another of the more outstandingly elegant of native woods is Oregon tiger-stripe myrtle, illustrated nearby. I'm told that the distinctive patterning is due to a parasite that gets into the wood and leaves its darker track, though I'll not swear to that. The wood finishes up smooth and sensuous to the touch, with the background a rich yellow and the markings a nice burnt umber tone. Seldom available in large pieces, it finds its principal use in setting off small items with stunning beauty.

Here on the western seaboard, a lot of lumber seems to get sold under the lumped designation of redwood, showing the broadest degree of variation you could possibly imagine. Any time I visit a source of lumber, I make a firm effort to check out their display of so-called redwood, always treasure-hunting for unlikely items, and finding them, every now and again. As in most things, the considerable bulk of the display is sheer chaff, suited for uses such as building outdoor picnic tables. Redwood of almost any description is virtually invulnerable to the elements, to termites, and to almost everything else, short of a fireplace.

Once in a while, though, in so doing, you'll spot a treasure that no one else has glommed onto ahead of you. I

still have part of a six-foot length of 2x4, bought three or four years ago. It's incredibly feather-light, almost as light as soft balsa, nicely colored a soft nutmeg beige, with a handsome grain pattern and a texture that works up as smoothly as carving Ivory soap. I could fritter away fifteen minutes per shopping trip until eternity wears out, always in hopes of lucking onto another find of that magnitude. Part of the expended portion went into making the connecting crosspiece of the child's desk-chair described in another chapter. Most of the rest was cut into delicate parquetry to make up the floor of a doll house that a friend was building. I'm saving the rest for similar special needs.

Most of us have heard of bird's-eye maple, but have you encountered any bird's-eye pine? I have: twice, thus far. It turns up on rare occasions and I used up my first find of the stuff for the sidepieces of the seat on the desk-chair. Within recent times, I found one more slab of the scarce stuff, and when I cruise out the current offering of redwood in a wood store, I always check the pine stock, too, mindful of the outside chance. If you found a treasure every visit, it could bankrupture your checkstubs and glut your storage facilities. Hunting it is at least half the fun, if not more.

Our lead illustration for this chapter shows a handsome stand of birch, not far from the tiny hamlet of New Prospect, Wisconsin, retrieved from a negative I snapped sometime around 1952. In its prime, I'd nominate the birch tree as one of Mother Nature's more glamorous creations, with its radiant white bark and stark black knot marks. Once cut, cured and sawn into boards, birch remains eminently admirable. The lumber is hard, dense, tough, even-grained, attractive in appearance, and little in need of preservative or cosmetic finishes. It is the absolutely ideal material for bread slicing boards, chopping blocks, and similar uses, imparting no effects to the food that comes into contact with it, meanwhile remaining reasonably close to immortal in terms of standing up to long use.

The thing to remember about whole, solid, natural wood is that it was once part of the stem — or perhaps a branch — of a large living plant, termed a tree. In most parts of the world, there is sufficient seasonal variation in temperature and allied conditions to produce sharply perceptible growth-stages in the trunk, readily seen in crosssection, and known as annular rings.

The U.S. Department of Agriculture publishes several books and booklets of pertinent interest to those engaged in using and working with woods. One such book at hand is called *Wood handbook: Wood as an Engineering Material*. It's Forest Service Agricultural Handbook No. 72, revised August 1974, and marked as available from the Superintendent of Documents, U.S. Government Printing Office, Washington, D.C. 20402, at a price of $7.85. Anyone interested in obtaining an up-to-date copy should inquire first to determine the current cost, edition number, postage and handling, et al. The cited source offers a concise description of the wood-forming organism that I'd like to quote here, as follows:

"Between the bark and the wood is a layer of thin-walled living cells called the cambium, invisible without a microscope, in which most growth in thickness of bark and wood arises by cell division. No growth in either diameter or length takes place in wood already formed; new

Tulipwood: costly, colorful, comes in small pieces, with flaws and holes; works nicely.

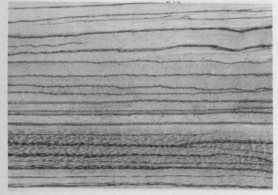

Zebrawood: light tan and dark brown, with striking grain pattern; fairly hard, tough.

The frozen flame of crotch-burl walnut, is spectacularly impressive to see.

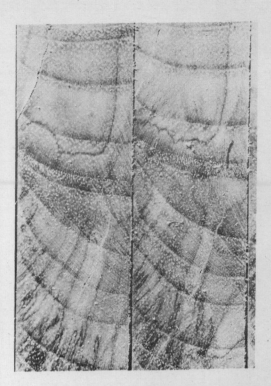

Above left, two thin slabs of Hawaiian koa, edge-glued together. Above right, end grain of Indian teak is arrestingly vivid.

The brown-and-gold glory of mesquite, in a custom rifle stock.

This African-carved figurine of ebony is about 8" high. Ebony is so flinty-hard I'd hate to try copying it!

growth is purely the addition of new cells, not the further development of old ones. New wood cells are formed on the inside and new bark cells on the outside of the cambium. As the diameter of the woody trunk increases, the bark is pushed outward, and the outer bark layers become stretched, cracked, and ridged in patterns often characteristic of a species. A bark cambium forms from living cells and this tissue separates the outer bark from the inner bark.

"With most species in temperate climates, there is sufficient difference between the wood formed early and that formed late in a growing season to produce well-marked annual growth rings. The age of a tree at the stump or the age of any crosssection of the trunk may be determined by counting these rings (...). If the growth of trees in diameter is interrupted by drought or defoliation by insects, more than one ring may be formed in the same season. In such an event, the inner rings usually do not have sharply defined boundaries and are termed false rings. Trees that have only very small crowns or that have accidentally lost most of their foliage may form only an incomplete growth layer, sometimes called a discontinuous ring, until the crown is restored."

The same source goes on to define earlywood and latewood as the lighter, larger portion of the annular ring and the smaller, darker boundary of it, respectively. They note, further to that: "In some tropical regions, growth may be practically continuous throughout the year, and no well-defined annual rings are formed."

Trees that grow in soil with an abundance of moisture and nutrients tend to be coarse in annular rings and unimpressive in physical characteristics. Wood from the same given species of tree that grew under more difficult and challenging circumstances tend to be harder, tougher, more innately desirable. With trees, as in many other situations, adversity tends to build character.

In many tree species, there is a distinctly visible difference between the inner heartwood and the outer sapwood of the trunk or branch. In most instances, the heartwood is darker in color, to a distinctive extent.

As has been noted, woods vary broadly in their several properties, even within a given precise species, due to factors such as the amount of available moisture and the nutrients present in the soil. The exact manner in which the wood was sawn into boards or planks likewise has a bearing upon the resulting properties of the lumber in such areas as its innate strength, its tendency to warp or resist warping, and so on. The visible grain pattern is, likewise, dependent upon the manner in which the log is sawn.

From the purely subjective viewpoint of the individual workshopper, woods tend to fall into distinct categories in terms of their workability and similar obvious properties. Some woods, even those that are quite hard by comparative standards, cut in a manner most delightful. Others seem to have been put on earth to try workshoppers' souls. An example of one apiece: On a recent foray to Gentry Woods, my nearby source for exotic raw material, I came away with small chunks of bocote and purple heart.

Bocote, pronounced about like Beau Cody, *(Cordia elaeagnoides)* — I wouldn't tackle pronouncing that Latin name with a ten-foot pole! — is a deep-brown wood, from Mexico, with fine, intricate grain patterns in darkest burnt umber hue. A piece less than two-thirds the size of this book cost $5.45: obviously not the ideal material for constructing a temporary dog house! When fed through the faithful table saw, with a planer blade installed, it slices with cheerful ease, to the exquisite precision that workshoppers dream about, with little hopes of encountering. The cut surface is silken-smooth to the touch, almost without detectable texture, more like milled metal than cut wood. It shows no slightest tendency to blade-burn: the painful bane of so many of the exotic hardwoods.

In stark contrast, there is the hunk of purple heart *(Peltogyne densiflora)* in my first and probably final encounter. I don't plan to buy any more of that. Even the stout-hearted 2½-hp motor of "Ole Norm," the big ten-inch Rockwell table saw almost gave up and quit in getting one slice off the stuff and the Fire-Tooth combination blade could be felt getting progressively duller with each dogged inch of gained kerf. Once a thin slab was haggled off, the belt sander took a long and tedious while to erase most of the toothmarks and copious blade-burn from the cut surface. When it finally was reduced to reasonable smoothness, the resulting color was more of an unpleasant brown. Meanwhile, just looking at it puts slivers in your fingers and, if you touch the stuff, be sure you've a pair of tweezers and a jeweler's loupe handy!

I also sampled some African padauk *(Pterocarpus soyauxi)* pronounced pah-DOOK, and was quite favorably impressed. The fresh cut is the most intense, fiery, flamboyant, scarlet imaginable. There is a moderate amount of blade-burn, but it sands off easily. Even the resulting sawdust is so gorgeous you're tempted to save it, soak it and make red ink out of it! Padauk finishes easily to a sensuously silky surface that is a delight in itself.

Likewise tried out was some rosadillo, pronounced rosa-DEE-yoh *(Sickingia salvadorensus),* a handsome, pinkish-tan wood, nicely textured, with attractive grain pattern that cuts with no more than moderate difficulty and a tendency to develop blade-burns that sand off fairly easily. I'm told that the nice color is apt to fade if exposed to strong light.

If you've an interest in full details on exotic woods, another excellent source of data is a book of specifications called *Fine Hardwoods,* available at about $5 per copy from American Walnut Association, 666 North Lake Shore Drive, Suite 1730, Chicago, Illinois 60611. Its charts cover such data as density in pounds per cubic foot, relative hardness, ability to resist shock, as well as descriptions of appearance and other characteristics.

Honduras mahogany *(Swietenia macrophylla),* is a handsome wood, pinkish-tan, with a good grain pattern, outstanding dimensional stability, and few if any growth rings. It is hard and tough, but works with reasonable ease. Its principal uses include fine furniture, veneers and for the wooden parts of precision instruments, such as view cameras. It's sometimes termed Central American mahogany.

Philippine mahogany, or lauan, is encountered in two forms: red lauan *Shorea negrosensis),* and white lauan *(Pentacme contorta).* Both see wide use as the decorative outer layer of veneer for plywoods, and are also available in solid form. Properties differ but little, apart from the color.

Left, magnified view of purple heart displays its unusually long grain pattern. As noted, I found it to be one of the most difficult of woods.

The 10″ Rockwell table saw, here with a Fire-Tooth combination blade installed. It has since been fitted with a 10″, 40-tooth tungsten carbide-tipped blade, said to be capable of cutting non-ferrous metals, such as brass, copper or aluminum, as well as just about any wood, even including purple heart. Note, please, that the blade guard is in place, where it should be if at all possible, to minimize danger.

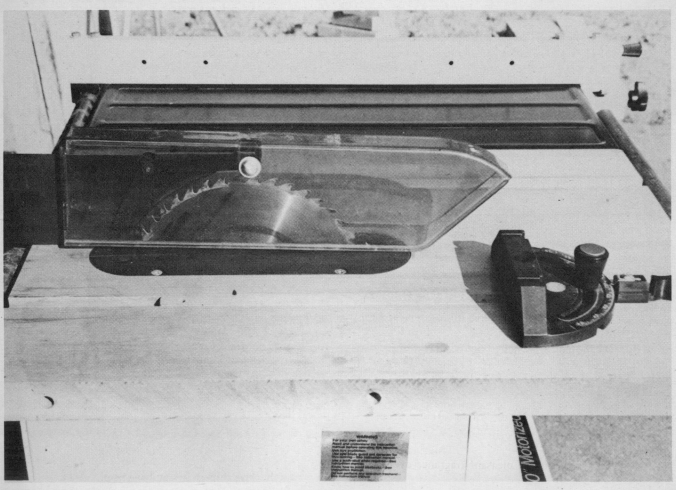

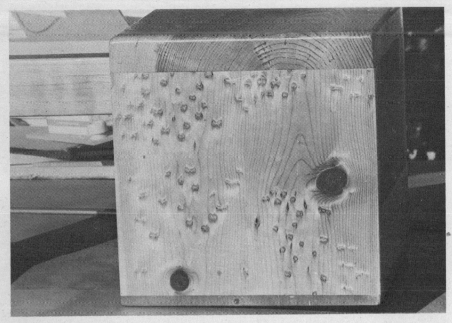

Bird's-eye pine — my private term for the stuff — is seldom seen, but well worth hunting. In color, this is a rich golden yellow, figured in vivid burnt sienna knots and markings.

Ebony occurs in several species and locales. Its density may run as high as 73 pounds per cubic foot. Water weighs 62.5 pcf, making ebony one of the few woods capable of sinking. Once the traditional wood for use in the black keys of pianos, the better grades of ebony are arrestingly expensive. Its color ranges from the darkest brown to nearly a perfect black.

I have three samples of teak, showing little resemblance to each other. One, termed Burmese teak, is a tawny brown with pronounced grain pattern that saws with moderate difficulty and sands with even more difficulty, since the removed dust is rather oily and sticky. The sample of Indian teak cuts more easily, sands nicely, and displays entrancing grain patterns that remind me of sectioned buffalo horn. A third sample, unidentified and received long ago, has uniformly colored heartwood of brownish red. The last is so hard that it seems to require working with hacksaws and metal files.

Rosewoods come from India, Africa, and South America — chiefly Brazil — and are among the hardest of all woods. A scale of relative wood hardness is based upon the weight required to embed a .440-inch steel ball in the surface to one-half of its diameter. For Indian rosewood *(Dalbergia latifolia),* the rating is an astounding 2630 pounds, as compared to 1010 for black walnut. As you might surmise, rosewood is a challenging material to work, although exceptionally attractive in final appearance, when handled properly. As noted elsewhere, the sanding dust from rosewood can prove irritating to the nasal passages, if inhaled. The same observation applies to several other woods and the dust from cocobolo is prone to irritate unprotected skin, in a manner similar to poison oak, ivy or sumac.

Cedar, like redwood, is noted for its durability, finding widespread use in roof shingles or siding for buildings. Chests of red cedar exude a pleasant fragrance over a long timespan, passing the aroma along to stored clothing and — some believe — discouraging the ravages of clothing moths, at the same time. The darker heartwood of the cedar is considerably more resistant to decay than its lighter sapwood.

Spruce occurs in several sub-species such as red, white and black Eastern; Engelmann; and Sitka. A fairly common term for the Sitka spruce *(Picea stichensis)* is "aircraft spruce," as it is a favored material in the aircraft industry, due to its strength/weight ratio and dependable durability under stresses. Other popular uses include the side rails of ladders, for which the various Eastern spruces also see some usage.

To designate a piece of wood as "pine" is hardly more specifically definitive than merely calling it wood and letting it go at that. One could almost believe that there are as many kinds of pine as there are individual pine trees. In appearance, pine can vary from the sublime to the revolting. Knotty pine is esteemed by some for its appearance in paneling, although the intrinsic value of knots is apt to seem dubious to the typical workshopper, particularly when they dry, shrink, and fall out. At its best, pine can display a clear, uniform structure, free of knots and with entrancing colors and grain patterns. At its worst, it's hardly fit for building garbage crates.

Much more could — and, probably, should — be said on the subject, but we've reached the end of the space available. It can be observed that anyone using the comment that, "Money doesn't grow on trees," obviously has not purchased lumber in recent times. The person who feels no desire for further knowledge of woods has, I think, little interest in the subject. The more I learn about woods, the more I wistfully wish I knew. It is a totally fascinating material and if the foregoing comments arouse your interest and lead you to explore the endless intricacies, I hope you'll find much enjoyment — as I have — and that you'll agree that the discussion served a useful purpose, painfully incomprehensive though it may have been.

GLUES, LUBES AND USEFUL COMPOUNDS

Notes On
Stickums, Slickums And Diverse Goodly Glops

Chapter 15

WE'VE SPOKEN of workbenches, tools, raw materials, as well as the personal skullsweat that goes into the creation of a truly satisfying and impressive piece of finished work. To the chapter at hand, we've neglected — or nearly neglected — those more or less fluid helpers that keep things all together, or in good shape.

Looking about the shop, I'm impressed by the profusion of bottles and cans of assorted compounds, practically all of which seem to be pretty indispensible at various moments of need.

I would have to pinpoint the major watershed — the Continental Divide — of my own workshoply career as occurring about the time in the early Fifties when a friend

persuaded me to try out some new glue that had recently appeared on the market. It was made by Borden's and sold under the brand name of Elmer's Glue. It came from the bottle as an opaque white fluid and cured into a reasonably transparent bond of surpassing toughness and tenacity. It proved to be just light-years ahead of anything else for the same purpose that had been on the market up to that time, and it absolutely revolutionized my outlook on putting pieces of wood together.

Wood glues, prior to the advent of Elmer's, had been feeble things, at best: much prone to let things come back apart at the most inconvenient and embarrassing moments. With that in mind, the canny workshopper tended to reinforce joints with nails, brads, screws, dowels and similar

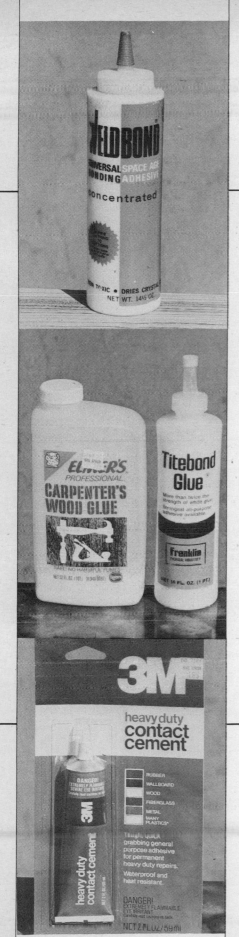

insurance. Even the dowels had to rely upon the dubious, pre-Elmer's glues that, among other handicaps, usually smelled dreadful.

We gradually learned, through experience, that Elmer's glue was not quite the utterly invincible adhesive we'd dared to hope it was. Under severe strain, particularly under sharp impact, it would come apart, usually carrying a fair portion of the glued material with it. The white Elmer's Glue, and its many chemically similar contemporaries, work best with moderately porous materials. They serve poorly for gluing metal to metal, glass to bakelite, and similar uses. If the material is too porous — such as the edge of particle board, for example — the joint strength is not apt to be up to your hopeful expectations.

Several other miracle adhesives have appeared in the years since Elmer made his taurine debut. The white glue is, I believe, termed a polyvinyl and the aliphatic resin glue, also offered by Borden's and several other makers, is usefully stronger and tougher than the polyvinyls. A problem in writing this book has been that it consumed time over a considerable number of calendar pages, during the course of which situations changed. As a result, the given status of the quo — as accurately reported in an earlier chapter — can shift and sometimes has shifted by the time another chapter is written. It may be pertinent to note that the several chapters were not necessarily written and produced in the exact order in which they appear here.

That's by way of footnoting a reference made elsewhere — earlier, I'm sure — to the gist that I buy Elmer's aliphatic resin glue, the straw-yellow stuff, in bulk bottles and decant it into Titebond bottles because the latter are less prone to blow over when sudden gusts of wind course across my driveway work area. I had mourned the fact that Titebond — that admirable stickum — was no longer available in the local area. It's no longer true, and I'm glad of that. My initial source for Titebond glue was a model airplane store

Four compounds that work well for getting rust and corrosion off of various surfaces. Unlike the 3M contact cement at upper right, Elmer's acrylic latex version is non-flammable.

in El Toro that huckstered the stuff at $3 the pint bottle. Shortly after stumbling onto Gentry Woods, I was delighted to discover that they stocked quart bottles of Titebond at a heartwarming tab of $4.25! The model airplane store, in the meantime, had gone out of business. I suspect a moral of some sort lurks in that observation.

I have used both brands of aliphatic resin glues, with such degrees of success and satisfaction as to almost inspire a feeling of guilt. The Borden's version goes by the brand name of Elmer's Professional Carpenter's Wood Glue, but that's okay, as most stores will sell the stuff to us amateurs without batting an eyelash. The Titebond label proclaims the contents to be the "Strongest all-purpose adhesive available." I remain, to the present moment, unconvinced that it is the ideal stickum for joining non-porous surfaces to either a porous surface or another non-porous one, thereby generating skeptical response to the "all-purpose" claims. I'll concede the possibility that it could be: It's just that I've not verified it empirically, thus far.

Both the white polyvinyls and the creamy aliphatic resins suffer from a handicap in that they are water-soluble, when dispensed and as hardened. For that reason, they appear less than ideal for applications such as building a boat, for just one example, although the solubility problem can be remedied to some extent by suitable paint or varnish to protect the joint from creeping moisture.

There is another adhesive that I've used extensively, with uniformly excellent results, and that is General Electric's silicone rubber, in its several various forms. Once the silicone rubber sets up, it is fully resistant to encountered moisture, and to just about anything else that's apt to come along. Further, it will join a non-porous surface to any other surface, porous or not, in a highly satisfactory manner. In curing, it remains rubbery, rather than drying to a brittle state. It does not change color and deteriorate, in the annoying manner of rubber cement. If you get the impression that I'd feel terribly bereaved if I suddenly had to make-do without GE silicone rubber, you'd be entirely correct. Dow-Corning markets a comparable silicone rubber.

In recent years, two further miracle adhesives have come upon the scene: epoxies and cyanoacrylates, both merchandised with impressive claims. Intrigued by the glowing promises of the makers, I've tried both types a few times, still without getting overly fanatical about the virtues of either. I know some people who have mastered the use of epoxies, employing them with great satisfaction. To the present moment, I've yet to achieve a satisfactory joint with any two-part epoxy, and much the same pessimistic observation applies to the cyanoacrylates, with one exception that we'll take up in a bit.

The epoxy glues are sold in the form of two solutions, that have to be dispensed in equal parts and mixed prior to use. It could be that I've yet to get the parts equal, or that I've not mixed them in the prescribed manner. The fact remains that every joint I've essayed to date, using epoxy, has come apart when subjected to a moderate test strain, even after it should've set up, according to the directions.

The cyanoacrylate glues are sold in tiny containers, holding perhaps 2cc of the given glop, and labeled with extravagant entrepreneural hoopla. They are the glues, which can weld unwary fingertips or eyelids together, necessitating a call to the local fire department to get you unstuck and operational again. Ostensibly, one square-inch of such a joint will lift a ton or so. To date, I've not had that kind of luck with the stuff, although I wistfully wish I had.

A chemical near-relative of the cyanoacrylates is the thread-sealants such as Loctite and, in that instance, I have seen the light and gotten fired with fanatic fervor, as mentioned several times earlier in the present work. Such compounds work only when in closely-fitted joints, away from air — anaerobically-curing adhesives is the correct term. A moderate amount of applied warmth hastens the seizing of the joint quite usefully, so that you can stick metal to metal in a matter of just a few seconds and, once it's done, you can abandon any hope for getting them apart again, should you ever wish to do so. Keep that observation firmly in the forefront of your mind as you employ the capable compounds!

Liquid Gold is my favorite furniture polish, sometimes used as a finish. Phenoseal is a seam sealant and dries to form a waterproof seal. Brownell's Rust Preventive No. 2 works well.

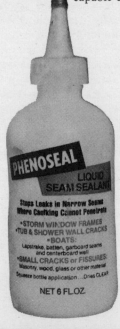

Chemically-secured joints differ in their resistance to strains and stresses, in accord with the nature of such things. Strains can occur in such forms as impact, torsional, shear, angular, or various combinations of two or more. Resistance to failure of the joint can and will vary, according to the nature of the stress, depending upon the given adhesive.

Back in 1976, when the fad for citizens band radio was at its brief peak, I used a dab of GE silicone rubber to attach a slide mount for a CB radio to the center of the dash of my Opel GT. It held well: Much-much-MUCH *too* well! Today, with CB slightly deader than King Tut's interest in Queen Tut, I'd love to remove that slide mount, which serves no current purpose, and is an eyesore besides. But the silicone rubber, cured to adamant tenacity by the blazing suns of several summers, might as well be steel weld, when it comes to getting it loose. I note this by way of advising that some of the available adhesives are so impressively capable that you'd be well advised to make absolutely certain you'll never want to get them apart again before joining things together with them.

It is not always the workshopper's goal to secure two surfaces in rigid relation to each other, muttering, "What glue hath joined together, let no strain put asunder!" Fairly often, you desire some amount of friction-free sliding about of the mating surfaces; in short, you need a lubricant, a lube: a slickum instead of a stickum. In the same or other situations, you may wish to protect a vulnerable surface against the ravages of corrosion, and I suppose we could playfully term such an effective compound a keepum.

The best, most extravagantly satisfactory slickum/keepum/kleenum I've encountered, up to the present moment, is a liquid sold under the brand name of Break Free. Its effective ingredient is Du Pont's Teflon, in microfine suspension, and gorblimey guvnor, it does everything they claim and a bit besides! I've grown prone to think of Break Free as liquid miracle, with ample justification. It's not quite the universal panacea, true, but, as some say about alcohol for treating the common cold, hardly anything else fails half so well.

Break Free is available in several sizes, both as a pressurized spray and in straight liquid form. I much prefer the latter, on a basis of economy, if not of convenience. Pressurized sprays tend to waste a lot of the good stuff.

As was noted of the GE silicone rubber, Break Free is so good as to be, on certain applications, almost *too* good. On one or two occasions, it has lubricated engaging parts so extravagantly effectively that they slip apart in an entirely new and not utterly happy relationship.

There is a fluid compound sold under the brand name of Liquid Wrench, designed to help free stubbornly-stuck parts from each other. It's good, it does what it claims to do, but Break Free does much the same, working with equally cheerful efficiency on matings of aluminum to itself and other metals, on titanium-stainless alloys and on other problem applications, with the same cheerful, bullet-proof *savoir faire*. If you can't find Break Free on sale in your area, a similar compound, called Triflon, is identical to sixteen decimals or so.

Getting back to adhesives, for a bit, we have contact cement, which is used to coat both surfaces that one wishes to join with inseparable tenacity. Contact cement is the indicated medium for attaching Formica to a given base material, for example. The earlier contact cements worked as claimed, but with several problems: The solvent was methyl ethyl ketone (MEK), an intensely flammable material, vaporwise, more than slightly discombooberating to inhale, unless nullified by extravagant ventilation, when used, and hard to clean up after use, unless you used some of the straight MEK, with its attending fire hazards and noxious fumes.

The good news is that an alternative contact cement has been available in recent years in an acrylic latex formulation that avoids the manifold problems of the MEK versions. Its smell is unobtrusive and pleasant, a bit like ripe bananas. It's non-flammable and non-toxic. Better yet, you can clean up brushes and spills with plain water. It goes on milk-white and dries to a clear, water-white film, indicating it's ready to be joined — requiring about twenty minutes to dry, depending upon temperature. It seems to hold with the

STOS is a good all-purpose grease. Capped and pressurized versions of Break Free, discussed in the text.

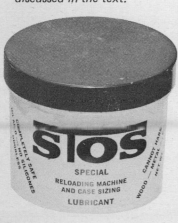

Elmer's acrylic latex contact cement, as discussed, is not only non-flammable, but it cleans up easily with water.

An example of the quick-setting cyanoacrylate glues as discussed here.

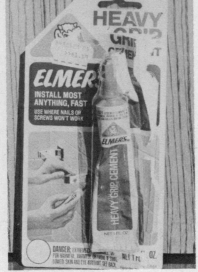

Another heavy-grip contact cement, also flammable and irritating.

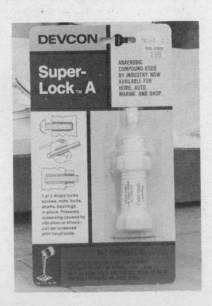

Devcon also makes an anaerobic-curing sealant called Super-Lock A, similar to the Loctite Stud N' Bearing Mount that I usually use with outstandingly good results. The label says that this can be loosened with hand tools.

same tenacity as the MEK type, possibly even a bit more. Although freeze/thaw stable, it works poorly, if at all, at temperatures below 65F/17C. Borden's markets it as Elmer's Professional Acrylic Latex Cabinetmaker's Contact Cement, and that's the only brand of the stuff I've encountered to date.

Phenoseal is termed a liquid seam sealer that works well for stopping leaks and general waterproofing applications. A couple of applications along the lower edge of the rear window of my elderly Buick seems to have corrected an annoying tendency for rain to leak into the trunk. I'll know for sure by the end of the rainy season, just starting. Meanwhile, I'm not uncrossing my fingers!

The right adhesive, properly used, can take care of many problems about the shop or house. There was, for example, a towel rack in the hall bathroom, precariously attached to the wallboard by tiny screws that kept coming loose. Finally, determined to cope with it, once and for all, I cut a 22x5-inch piece of ¾-inch redwood, beveled the edges neatly, gave a wipe of tung oil to the surfaces that would be exposed, leaving the back untreated, and smeared a few gobs of GE silicone rubber to the back and pressed it against the wall, using the bubble level to assure that it was perfectly horizontal. The silicone rubber had enough grip, even when fresh, to hold the board in position. I bought a new towel rack and installed it to the redwood panel with larger screws. The result was a towel rack considerably stronger than it needs to be, and pleasing to the eye as a welcome bonus.

There are various well-known household lubricants that have the objectional property of hardening to a gummy residue after some given amount of exposure to air and, for that reason, it is well to avoid them. Common motor oil, in about 30 weight, makes a decent lubricant for most uses, although it should be noted that it has relatively little capability for preventing corrosion.

Being situated not far from the edge of the world's largest birdbath, aka the Pacific Ocean, corrosion protection is an ongoing problem, with occasional western breezes bringing saltwater vapors across the area. Rust can and does turn up where unwanted, despite precautions. The best material I've found for removing rust is Naval Jelly, applied with 0000 grade steel wool and judicious amounts of elbow grease. It will remove the rust, quite easily and effectively, though it can't do anything about the pits left in the surface by really severe rusting. Avoid using Naval Jelly or similar compounds on metal surfaces with a black oxide finish, such as blued gunmetal, because the blue-black coating is actually a form of rust and the Naval Jelly will take it off, leaving the metal white. Small rust flecks can be removed from blued steel with fine steel wool and Break Free. Apply the BF to the area and let it stand for a day or so, if time permits, allowing it to soak in and loosen the rust particles, enabling them to be removed more easily by the steel wool.

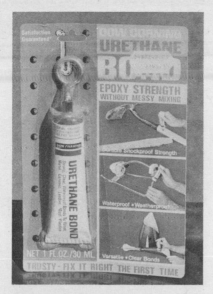

Dow-Corning urethane bond is said to offer epoxy strength, straight from the tube, with no need for mixing. My experience with it has been good, which is more than I can say for epoxies, as ruefully noted in the text.

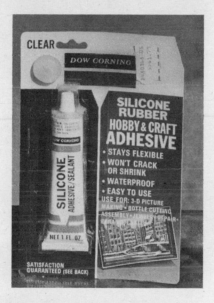

Charcoal lighting fluid, if used with appropriate care and precautions, mindful of its flammable properties, makes a useful solvent for cleaning up grease, oil and similar problem materials. Left, silicone rubbers, such as this one by Dow-Corning or from General Electric, make superbly strong and durable bonds, as discussed.

There are solutions for quick-bluing steel surfaces, but the finish they leave is vastly less resistant to wear than a hot-blued surface. The cold-blues contain copper sulfate, which deposits a thin wash of copper on the steel and then darkens the copper, by means of some other ingredient, so that your "blue" is nothing but the thinnest possible layer of stained copper. You can readily imagine how it stands up to wear, with that in mind.

Speaking of solvents, I'm still looking for one that will remove deposits of calcium carbonate — limestone — from surfaces such as glass shower doors and the like. I would welcome comments on that from any reader who knows of an effective, readily available product to handle such deposits.

Here's that "once-and-for-all" repair job on the towel rack. Not only has it proved to be considerably stronger than it needs to be, but I think it adds a pleasant touch

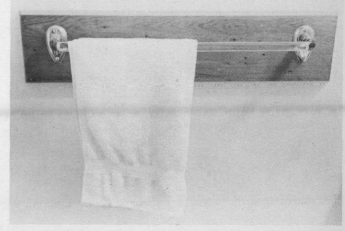

A CHILD'S DESK-CHAIR

Easy And Simple To Build, This Compact Piece Of Furniture Is Much Appreciated By Junior Citizens!

Above, Bobbie Lynn Grennell (now Langford) puts her enthusiastic seal of approval on one of the early desk-chairs. She got those two front teeth back, but not that Christmas!

Chapter 16

Here are right front and right rear oblique views of the more recent version, construction of which is discussed here. Scaled drawings appear on pages 230 and 231.

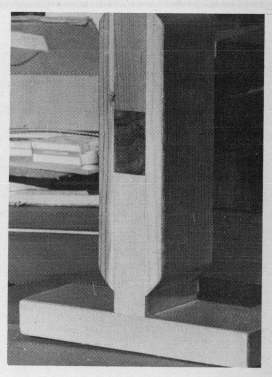

Right, details of the construction and assembly of the front column, with its stabilizing lower crosspiece and reinforcing boards on each side of the joint between the horizontal connector and the two column segments.

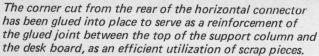

The corner cut from the rear of the horizontal connector has been glued into place to serve as a reinforcement of the glued joint between the top of the support column and the desk board, as an efficient utilization of scrap pieces.

THE FIRST-GENERATION version can be dated, tentatively, as having been built in late 1958, possibly 1959. About 1978, I turned up the nearby photo of daughter Bobbie Lynn hamming it up over her new desk-chair next to the Christmas tree of that year, whichever one it was. By 1978, I had another sub-sub-deb in need of a desk chair: a granddaughter Karen Lynn. Although I departed considerably from the original design, the photo was of much help in doping out how to construct the second version. At the moment, I need to produce another of the same, for Karen's sister, Katie May and, in accord with my usual philosophy in such matters, I expect that it will incorporate a few more modifications.

The first chairs — I built three, in all — used some Formica-covered plywood of ¾-inch thickness that had been on sale at a nearby lumberyard in the form of scrap pieces, about 20x24 inches in size: cutouts from kitchen sink tops, I believe. The remainder of those first chairs were assembled with ¾-inch plywood and solid boards in a straightforward, no-nonsense approach. That's to say they were more functional than elegant, but the customers didn't seem to mind in the slightest, and the desks saw a lot of use. The front uprights, as dubious memory serves, met the floor with only the raw edge of the board: no supporting horizontal base.

In working up the Mark II version, I saw the need of a bracing crosspiece at the bottom of the front column to lend added stability and the accompanying photos and drawings show how it ended up, more clearly than verbal description could accomplish.

The seat was built first, using a leftover piece of two-inch plank for the top, and ¾-inch boards for the other pieces. For some reason I no longer recall, I ran a ¾-inch dado cut on the bottom piece to accept the lower edges of the sides, adding an angled brace strip to reinforce the joint further. That necessitated cutting off the corners of the two pieces of board at the front and back, which serve to provide a handy storage space for crayons, paper and similar supplies. In building the next one, I plan to join the sides and bottom with a simple mitered joint, perhaps using the cut-off angle scraps as a similar corner brace, but cut ¾-inch short at each end to permit installing the retainer boards intact, for a simpler, neater appearance.

The joints between the sides and top of the seat, you'll note, carry reinforcing strips about 1½ inches square. Again, I'd change that, probably cutting them ¾-inch short at each end and covering the ends with upper lateral strips of the same width. Alternatively, I'd trim away those exposed corners of the brace strips with 45-degree cuts on

As noted, the end of the horizontal connector was beveled and the edges and corners were rounded with a power sander. The same treatment should have been given to the ends of the upper corner braces, partially visible here.

Here's a closer look at details of the joint between the bottom and side pieces of the seat assembly. Text carries comments on other approaches that would be simpler to build and more attractive in appearance, when finished.

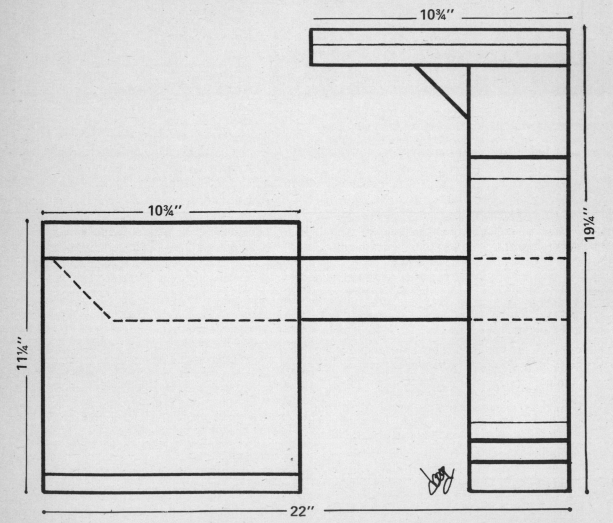

This is the right-hand view, drawn to a scale of three inches to one foot, as are the two views on the facing page. All three drawings are exactly one-quarter lifesize, so that any dimension not given can be measured and multiplied to determine the final size. Example: Width of the vertical column is 1″ here and 4″ on the original desk chair.

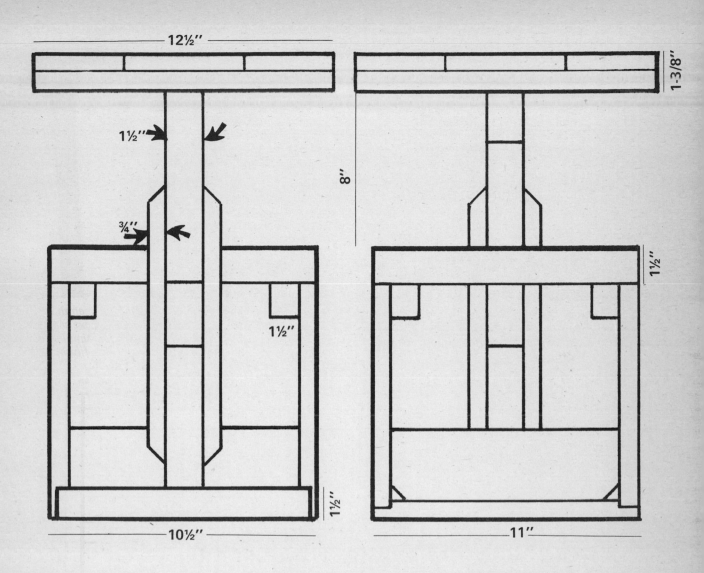

Front view at left and rear view at right provide further scaled details on parts and assembly. The desk surface is a cross-grain lamination of a nominal one-inch pine board, with its grain running right/left, topped by three pieces of redwood with grain running front/back. The redwood is slightly thinner than the ¾" actual thickness of the pine.

both exposed edges, so as to eliminate those unsightly and potentially hazardous sharp corners. Karen and Katie's way of going reminds one of tiny, adorable tornadoes — a trait they share with all the small Grennells I've ever known — and I took pains to round all the exposed edges and corners generously, so as to minimize the risk of injury if they fell against the artifact, or ran pell-mell into it.

The pieces of the seat were joined together with the usual aliphatic resin glue, and no nails, screws or metal fasteners were used in the entire desk. The connecting crosspiece was cut to a 45-degree angle at the rear and the cut-off piece was used as the angle brace for the joint between the upright and desk top. The crosspiece extends forward from the underside of the seat by about eleven inches and, once attached, it served to establish the distance from the floor to the top of the lower half of the support column. I just placed the seat on a flat surface, held a short piece of 2x4 vertically atop the piece that would be the front base, and drew a pencil line on the vertical piece,

using the lower edge of the crosspiece as a guide, cut it to the line, glued the base to the vertical member and the top of that to the lower edge of the crosspiece.

Following that, the upper portion of the support column was glued to the top of the crosspiece, the top to that and the angle brace was added after the glue of the previous joint had set up a bit. An oscillating sander was used to true-up the joints on both sides of the support column. Two pieces of ¾-inch board were beveled at the ends, as shown, and glued to the sides of the joints between the crosspiece and column.

The top measures 10¾ inches, front to back, and 12½ inches, side to side. It's laminated from two layers of crossed boards. The lower one is from a piece of nominal 1x12 pine board, cut to the quoted dimensions as one solid piece, with its grain running from side to side. The upper layer is made up of three pieces of 5/8-inch redwood, selected and arranged for a colorful and attractive striped effect with contrasting heartwood and sapwood. The grain

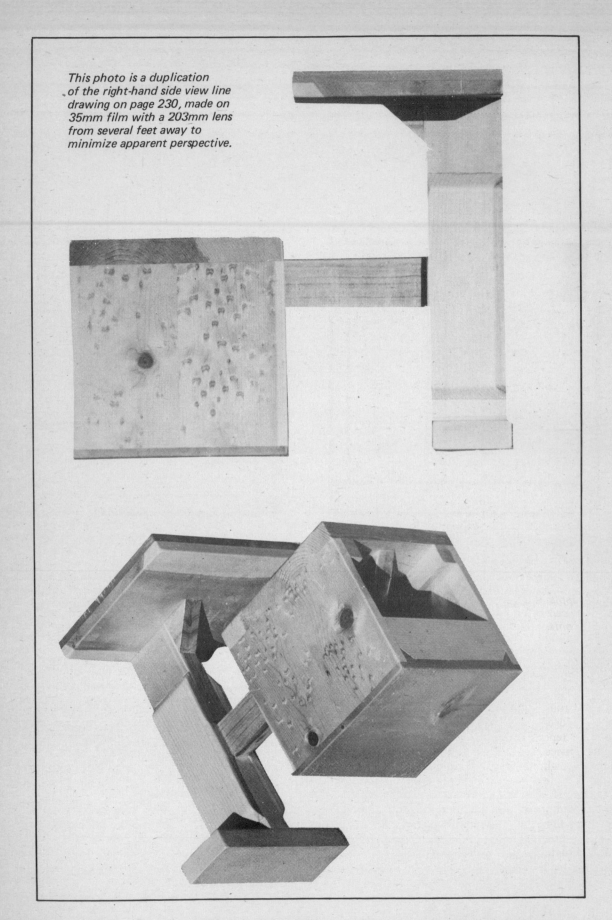

This photo is a duplication of the right-hand side view line drawing on page 230, made on 35mm film with a 203mm lens from several feet away to minimize apparent perspective.

Here's a left rear view, from below, showing further details of the different parts in their relationship to each other.

By way of supplementing the preceding drawings, here are photos of the rear view (left) and front view. Note that the rear view carries a reflection of the support column in the glossy finish of the top of the seat, introducing a potentially confusing image, which is a major reason for including the dimensional line drawings for added clarity.

of the top layer runs front to back, perpendicular to the lower layer, for added strength.

I'm happy to report that the Mark II desk-chair has weathered its service to date in a gratifying state of preservation, although the relatively soft redwood of the desk top shows a few small dings and divots. A well-beveled layer of Formica, attached with contact cement to the wood, would assure a smooth writing surface for a much longer time. As noted, it would be well to make certain that it presented no sharp edges or corners to unwary juvenile anatomy and, with that in mind, I would not consider covering the surrounding edges of the desk top with Formica, due to the difficulty of getting all the edges and corners properly rounded-off.

After completion of the basic assembly, as described, the oscillating sander was used, with a fairly coarse grade of

paper — about 80-grit garnet, I think — to round all of the exposed edges and corners — except for the corners of those two braces under the seat — followed by more of the same, with a 120-grit sheet of paper in the sander, and a final session with a sheet of the finest-grit sandpaper available, folded in thirds, and used by hand to finish all surfaces as smoothly as possible.

My technique for rounding an edge is to rotate the operating sander against the edge, over an angle of 90 degrees, back and forth, from one flat surface to the other, moving it up and down the entire length of the edge while doing so. This results in a nicely radiused curve, rather than a sharp edge or chamfered bevel.

Once sanded, the desk-chair was given two coats of spray-can Varathane varnish, with a thorough rubdown with 0000-grade steel wool after each coat had dried

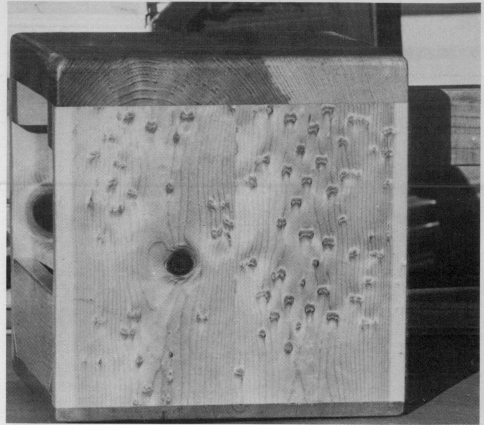

The side panels of what I like to call bird's-eye pine are made of two pieces, edge-glued together, as a striking example of letting wood provide its own decorative finish.

Looking down at the top surface of the desk, it's obvious that, while the redwood is gorgeous in its coloration, a harder surface might have stayed smoother in use.

Unlike the three prototypes, built in the latter Fifties, the latest version is a colorful affair, thanks to the natural color and grain of the woods used, and the protective durability of the Varathane spray varnish, even after a few years of intensive use by its owner and her younger sister, both of whom came equipped with turbochargers!

completely. Varathane is a polyurethane varnish of surpassing toughness and durability — similar to the finish they use for bowling alleys — and it served to complement the colors and grains of the various pieces of wood, quite nicely. The bird's-eye pine — as I prefer to term it — of the two seat sides looks exceptionally attractive beneath the varnish, and seem to shift and ripple with changes of viewing angle.

The three accompanying line drawings are drawn to exact scale from measurement of the Mark II desk-chair, at a scale of three inches to one foot — exactly one-quarter lifesize, that is — and I've asked our art department to make certain that they are neither reduced nor enlarged in final layout. The distance from top to bottom should come out precisely 4-7/8 inches between the outer edges of the two lines, if the drawings make it through production at the desired 100%. I note that so you can check the accompanying drawings with your own ruler. If the dimension stays 4-7/8 inches, you'll know that we made it and, with that verified, any dimension on the drawing can be multiplied by four to arrive at the actual measurement. The overall length, from front to back is 22 inches, the height 19¼ inches, and the top of the seat is 11 inches wide by 10¾ long.

I arrived at the quoted dimensions by means of a thoughtful session with Karen and a yardstick, deliberately scaling it a bit on the large side, to allow for growth during the next few years, and I'm gratified to report that the proportions seem to be right on the button for a child in the age brackets of 4 to 7 years. When/if I build another, I propose to scale-up the dimensions slightly, so that Karen can use it for a few additional years. There will, of course, be an implicit understanding that it's actually Katie's desk, but that Karen will be using it in exchange for all the time that Katie has spent and will be spending at Karen's desk-chair — if you follow the reasoning behind all that. To a small child, possession and territorial imperatives are quite important.

To the best of my knowledge, this is an entirely original design. I've never seen any other furniture like it, nor anything comparable that was available commercially as a readymade item. I can report that such desk-chairs are lavishly appreciated and intensively used by their small owners, to such extents as to richly repay the modest investment in material and shoptime that goes into the production of one. Starting from scratch is the hard and time-consuming part.

Feel free to build replicas for deserving small-fry of your own acquaintance, and modify the design, construction, bill of materials and finishing details to suit your personal taste. Forgive the redundancy, but I'd like to stress, one more time, the vital importance of rounding all the edges and corners, for the sake of conserving consumption of Band-Aids!

THE "EASYREADER" BOOK HOLDER
How To Make Addictively Convenient Accessories For The Incurable Printaholic

THE UBIQUITOUS paperback books, as I recall, made their first appearance in the early Forties; an offshoot of the great paper shortage of WWII. One of the earliest specimens that I encountered was the Avon edition of Raymond Thornton Chandler's *The Big Sleep,* in the first printing of October 1943, which turned up at the post exchange of the USAAF base at Tonopah, Nevada, some unrecorded time in early 1944, priced at twenty-five cents, with no sales tax added. The specimen in the accompanying photos is not that identical copy — it got mislaid along the hectic way — but, rather, a copy from Pocket Books' third printing of August 1950, with a cover illustration differing from the Avon edition of first encounter.

During the gathering number of years since 1944, the paperback book, usually abbreviated as pb, has carved for itself a large niche in the output of publishing houses and won itself an entrenched place in contemporary culture. There has been one obvious change in the pattern. At the start, the twenty-five-cent price tag was so universally accepted that most publishers didn't even bother to print a price on the covers. By the time the first three Travis McGee books hit the stands, in 1964, the tab had inched upward to forty cents a copy. The same three titles — Blue, Pink and Purple, as JDM aficionados term them — remain more or less in print and available, down to the present, at $2.25 a copy or so, perhaps more. I've not checked recently, since I *have* my copies, bought at the going price as each new title appeared.

But enough of all that. Do not let me get launched into a history of the humble pb thriller, lest we end up with a book eight inches thick. The pertinent point is that the

Chapter 17

popular pb, for all its compact size and comparative cost, is not the most convenient of all books to read, page by page. It is usually a two-handed project to hold the stubborn little volumes sufficiently wide-open to permit skimming the enthralling lines. Like many other pb addicts, I've long been prone to read while eating — by way of throwing two stones at one bird, as it were — and the challenge of weighting down a pb with nearby sugar jars and napkin dispensers to free at least one hand for using a fork was an obvious pain in the neck — particularly when officious restaurant personnel would work their way down the counter, rearranging things and losing your place when they grabbed your book ballast.

The various versions of pb reading racks illustrated here were dreamed up and built in a fairly successful effort to cope with that particular problem. The two sides of the holder are tapered from the underside, so that two fair-sized spring clips can clamp the sides of the pages to the holder on all but the thickest tomes. In extreme cases — such as works by James Michener — a third clip can be used to double up on the thickest side, as shown.

The bill of materials is modest enough, consisting of small pieces of two-inch plank for the base; a few inches of one-inch hardwood dowel for the upright and crosspiece; a few more scraps of 1½-inch strip (2x2, nominal); a short length of ¼-20 threaded steel rod; a ¼-inch washer and wing nut; and two small pieces of nominal one-inch board (¾-inch, as we've noted here, so many times) and, of course, the spring clips, usually purchased readymade, unless you can think of a way to produce them.

The first step consists of cutting the piece of ¾-inch board that serves as the holder. The one in current use, appearing in some of the photos, is 9¼ inches wide by 6½ inches the other way. It could well be seven inches high, since that's the height of a typical pb, but the unsupported upper half-inch poses no problem. A small strip,

Above, homemade disc of Masonite and sandpaper to convert a table saw into a disc sander. Below, this ¼ x 1" bushing was made from 1" dowel, sanded down slightly in OD, and used to assure perfect alignment of ¼" hole at end of 1" hole.

The block that goes over the horizontal arm is drilled 1'' for part of its length, ¼'' for the rest of its length, as on the previous page. The holes are a bit off center, as indicated. The thicker side is glued to the book-holding board to provide added clearance for the corners of the block that joins the horizontal and vertical dowels.

Here, the joining block is in the process of being beveled at the corners, rather than rounded in the manner of the other holder that appears here. Later photos show its final form, with all of the bevels cut on the various edges.

9x1-1/8x¾, is glued to the lower edge of the holding board to serve as a convenient ledge to keep the book in place as the pages are turned and clipped down again. That's an optional feature, but a handy one.

The tapered edges of the holding board are cut before attaching the lower ledge. Lacking a table saw for the operation, much the same effect could be secured by gluing a piece of 1/8-inch Masonite to a smaller piece of ¾-inch board, with the projecting edges of Masonite serving the same purpose. When cutting the board on a table saw, the saw blade is tilted about ten degrees from the vertical and left at that angle, raising or lowering it to make the two cuts to relieve clearance for the spring clips. If you wish, you can cut another tapered edge at the top, permitting the finished project to be used in the kitchen as a luxurious holder for recipe cards.

The base is 4x6x1½ inches, and a mark for drilling the one-inch hole for the upright was located by standing the piece of plank alternately on its left and rear edges and scribing a pencil mark against a scrap of ¾-inch wood. The hole was drilled on the drill press, using a one-inch Stanley Power Bore bit for a neat and splinter-free hole that extends about ½-inch below the surface.

I've built several such holders, so far, and note that they have a way of getting sweet-talked out of my possession when someone sees them, so that I have to build another. It's no serious matter, since I can usually think of a few more improvements to incorporate into the next one. As an example, you'll note that the one now in use sports a handmade "super wing nut" in place of the less elegant wing nuts from the store.

In early examples, the support column was made by mitering a six-inch and five-inch length of one-inch dowel at forty-five degrees and gluing them together at right angles to each other. The more recent approach has been to use a small section of nominal 2x2 as a means of getting around

As discussed, this Easyreader is being produced in a southpaw format, so the hole is in the far right corner of the base, viewed in normal use. Holes have been made in the joining block and in the end of the dowel to accept the length of threaded rod.

The ¼-20 rod has been turned into the 7/32" hole, using a Crescent wrench and the jam-tightened nuts. With the rod in place, nuts have been loosened and removed. A simple drilling guide, made up as discussed in the text, was used to center the 7/32" hole in the end of the dowel, appearing in the photo at lower left, page 240.

the corner. A shallow one-inch hole is drilled in its base and on the upper side to receive the shorter sections of one-inch dowel, and the top was rounded over, using a disc sander.

If you have a table saw, but no disc sander, it's a quick and simple project to remedy the lack of so useful a tool. I drilled a 5/8-inch hole in the center of a piece of 1/8-inch tempered Masonite, after laying out an eight-inch circle on it, then cut the circumference to fairly circular shape with a sabersaw, installed it in place of a table saw blade, trued up the edges with the saw running, and used spray disc adhesive to fasten a piece of garnet sandpaper to one side. It makes an excellent disc sander, readily adjustable for angles from forty-five to ninety degrees. When the sandpaper is worn out, you can peel it off — provided you used the right kind of adhesive — for replacement. If necessary, you can make up another disc and there's nothing to stop you from putting sandpaper on both sides of the Masonite disc, perhaps in two different grit grades of

your preference.

The horizontal piece of dowel, at the top of the support column, is about 3¾ inches long, of which ½-inch is glued into the one-inch hole of the same depth that was made in the upper end of the block from the side.

A two-inch length of ¼-20 threaded rod was cut from the larger piece with a hacksaw, and chucked into the drill press to round the ends with a flat file. Following that, a 7/32-inch hole was drilled in the outboard end of the horizontal dowel. Getting the hole nicely centered and parallel with the dowel is important. I made up a handy little drilling jig by putting a hole part of the way through a piece of scrap wood, using an Irwin Speed-Bor spade bit of one-inch diameter and then drilled a 7/32-inch hole the rest of the way through, centering it on the hole left by the point of the spade bit. Once used, it was thoughtfully set aside for use in building future book holders.

The 7/32-inch hole is drilled into the end of the dowel to a depth of ½-inch, or a trifle deeper. Our purpose here is to provide a tight fit to hold the end of the section of ¼-20 threaded rod and, once the hole is accurately drilled, we have to turn the threaded rod into it for half an inch or so. That could be a challenging hurdle, if we've forgotten the simple and effective technique given back in the chapter on drilling, tapping and threading. What we do, of course, is to put a pair of ¼-20 nuts on what will be the outer end of the threaded rod, jam-tighten them together securely, and use a wrench or perhaps a carpenter's drill brace to turn them into the dowel, the latter being held in the bench vise for the operation.

When installed in the outboard end of the support column, the threaded rod should be five inches above the upper surface of the base, and the exposed end will be in line with the right-hand edge of the base.

A sidenote, here: If you're building the holder for use by someone who is left-handed, by necessity or preference, it would be a thoughtful touch to reverse the construction as it appears here, putting the support column at the right-rear corner, so that the adjusting wing nut can be operated with the left hand. Southpaws tend to feel a bit underprivileged and put-upon as they grapple with the northpaw world, and they appreciate any such concession to their way of doing things.

The block that goes over the end of the threaded rod is another piece of 2x2, 1½ inches square in cross-section, by 3-3/8 inches long, with an off-center one-inch hole drilled to a depth of 2-1/8 inches, leaving 1¼ inches of solid wood at that end. With the one-inch hole drilled, use the central hole left by the drill point to locate the tip of a ¼-inch drill bit and run the ¼-inch hole on through. If you've done everything just right, there will be about ¼-inch of threaded rod protruding from the hole when you slip the block over the end of the horizontal dowel. If that is not the case, it's a simple matter to jam-tighten the two nuts back on the

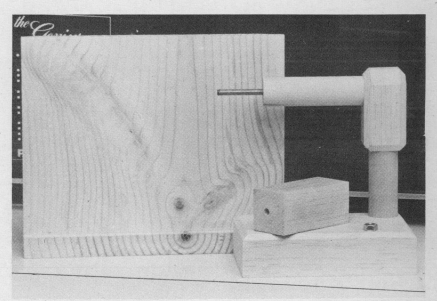

Edge beveling pattern on base and joining block can be seen here and on facing page. Ledge has been glued to lower edge of the holding board, with an effort made to match grain patterns of the two pieces. The block will be installed on the cross-piece and then glued to the board by the auto-locating approach that is described in the text on page 241.

Departing slightly from the text, most of the photos show the southpaw version under construction. At right is the northpaw type, from earlier model, showing the half-rounded top of the joining block, as noted.

exposed end of the rod and turn it in or out a bit, as needed.

We are now ready to glue the support assembly to the holding board and, again, there is a gratifyingly crafty way to make sure that the whole shebang goes together with heartwarming perfection, rather than ending up frustratingly slaunchwise. I've been trying to think of an appropriate term for such an approach, and I guess we could call it auto-location, meaning that you let the workpiece(s) serve as their own aligning guide(s).

What we do is hold the lower edge of the support board snugly against the upper surface of the base, with the block at the end of the support arm in contact with the rear surface of the board, outlining the area of contact with light pencil marks. Taking them apart, we apply thin, uniform coats of glue to the mating surfaces. In positioning the two pieces, make certain that the board protrudes beyond the base for the same distance at either end, for the

sake of symmetry upon completion.

After giving the two coats of glue a minute or so to commence air-drying, we put it all back together, the same way it was when we scribed the guide lines, assuring that the edge of the board and the top of the base are in snug contact. Then, it's just a matter of letting the glue work its useful magic for the appropriate while, depending upon the ambient temperature. With that attended to, install a washer and wing nut on the exposed end of the threaded rod and the basic assembly is completed. You may now apply a coat or two of the finish of your choice, preceded by staining to taste, if desired. Scrounge up a pair of spring clips, and you will have created a thoroughly handy device, available solely from helpfully guided workshoppers, since I know of no such item that can be bought in stores. Once you or the lucky recipient get habituated to using it, you'll probably wonder why no one makes these for money. I've often wondered about that, too...

Here is an oblique rear view of the southpaw model, almost entirely completed. The only further modification was to add a ¼" crosspiece through the aluminum knob of the clamping handle to provide a useful gain in leverage. As the board pivots downward, the lower edge of the ledge makes perfect contact with the top of the base, since they were in contact and centered at the time the horizontal block was glued to the back of the board by the auto-location method.

THE JIFFISNUF ASHTRAY

Chapter 18

An Easily Made And Handy Item, Engineered To Cope With By-Products Of A Dubious Habit

IF YOU'RE ONE of those militant anti-smokers who's about to write and read me off about the evils of smoking cigarettes, please donate the postage to the charity of your choice: I couldn't agree with you more. Having once given up smoking — for most of 1956 and all of 1957 — I have crystal-clear recollections of how nauseous other people's cigarettes smell to a non-smoker. Quite apart from the health hazards to smokers and their associates, the habit soaks up a truly horrifying number of dollars per year and, even worse, causes an impressive number of dollars' damage per annum through fires started — to use that familiar cliche of the newspapers — by careless smoking.

That, may it please the court, is my sole reason for adding this to the body of adjacent discussion. It is possible, and fairly easy, to construct an ashtray that will help usefully in minimizing the fire hazards posed by the unattended — and often forgotten — cigarette, meanwhile extinguishing it, when desired, tidily and positively, in an average interval of eight seconds, flat.

My personal term for such an ashtray is the *JiffiSnuf*. The term is not copyrighted, nor is the principle patented — not by me, at any rate. I dreamed up and built my first ashtray of this type at some unrecorded point during Harry S. Truman's full term; the 1948-52 interval, that would be. Since that time, the little snuffers fashioned in the likeness of Smokey the Bear have appeared. I don't know whether or not they are patented or copyrighted. They embody a tiny cavity — in the top of Smokey's hat, as I recall — but they lack the important second components of the JiffiSnuf, in that they do not include an integral holder that will control the partially consumed cigarette and put it out — nearly always — if it is deserted and forgotten, as happens all too often.

V-shaped clip of 1/8" brass rod and the base section of a fired .30/06 cartridge were soldered to the inside of the can. If the ashtray rests on a wet surface, protect the base with paint or a plastic cover of the same diameter.

All of which is to say that this chapter tells how to make a marvelously handy ashtray, for your own use or to bestow upon nicotine-addict friends, without intent of monetary gain. If, in reading this, your imagination is fired by visions of setting up vast factories and distribution networks for foisting the artifact upon a world that needs it but remains unaware of the fact, I suggest that you check out the pertinent legalities before investing heavily. For my own part, I think the world might benefit through broadened availability of JiffiSnuf ashtrays and, if in including this, it results in the avoidance of even one fire, or the saving of one person from injury or death, I'll consider it space fittingly expended; any conservation beyond that counts as pure gravy.

Most of the illustrated examples are starkly, painfully functional, although this need not be the case. I have made a few of the things, along the way, of sufficient grace and aesthetic charm as to gratify any eye not mortally offended by the presence of an ashtray, per se. A few years back, the local Ralphs supermarket — our favorite among the local chains — used to offer some elegant ashtrays of solid onyx, imported from Mexico, at a cost of a couple dollars. I would buy one to serve as the centerpiece or repository for used butts, mounting it on a suitable base of any handsome wood on hand at the time and embellishing the base with the holder and snuffer of the basic system. I note that to put your imagination into free-wheeling, so that you can go on to extrapolate to any extent for which you perceive a need.

The JiffiSnuf system comprises two basic and equally vital components: the holder, and the snuffer. My favored starting material for making the holder is brass welding rod, preferably of 1/8-inch diameter, although I've made a number from the next-smaller diameter, 3/32-inch.

There is no apparent reason why steel wire could not be used in place of brass, apart from that fact that it would rust, but the brass is easier to work. Aluminum could be used, as well, if you can get around the considerable difficulty of soldering the stuff. If you choose to go the really Spartan route, you can just cut a slender V-shaped notch in the edge of a tin can with a pair of tin snips and let it go at that.

As illustrated here, I made up a wire-bending jig that clamps into the bench vise, with a bending arm made by drilling a 1/8-inch hole through the end of a piece of ½-inch steel rod. It makes quick and easy work of the basic bending and you can accomplish the final forming by judicious use of the vise or a pair of Vise-Grips. The simplest and most economical holder is the basic slender V-shape, proportioned to accept butts from about 5/16 down to 3/16-inch in diameter, to cover the dimensional vagaries of the several brands.

Along the way, I've made S-shaped holders and even M-shaped ones, to get away from the two-tined-fork look of the V-shape or squashed-U-shape.

Apart from the formed-wire holder and the snuffer — to which we'll get, in just a bit — you also need a receptacle for extinguished butts. My favored receptacle is a tin can,

As noted here, non-filter cigarettes can and sometimes do burn their way partially or entirely through the holding clip, and could fall to the supporting surface, so watch it!

preferably one with a lacquered label, rather than a label printed on paper. The paper ones tend to fade, fray, and get terribly tacky in appearance, rather quickly. Once the label has been torn off, you have an unadorned tin can, radiating an objectional taint of Bohemianism — to my taste, at least.

The snuffing unit is comprised of a vertical cylinder, open at the top, closed at the bottom, of 7/16 to 5/8-inch in diameter and 7/8 to 1-1/8-inch in depth. If you make it smaller than 7/16-inch diameter, it will clog up too rapidly. If larger than 5/8-inch diameter, it won't work very well, if

Above, bending jig and a piece of ½" rod with a 1/8" hole in the end are used to form the wire clips, with the jig in a vise. Right, filter-tips, held as shown, burn down to the filter and extinguish themselves, if forgotten and left.

If tin cans and cartridges aren't your thing, other avenues are available. Holder was made of birch, brass wire and screws; needs to be fastened to a secure base. Snuffer was turned from aluminum rod, in teak and mahogany base.

at all. Shallower than 7/8-inch, it may not work and deeper than 1-1/8-inch, you may have to retrieve the extinguished butt with a pair of tweezers, or by inverting the entire assembly above a larger waste receptacle.

If you happen to have access to an adequate supply of retired cartridge cases, of suitable dimensions, they offer about the best of all possible raw materials for the snuffers. Most of the illustrated examples embody snuffers from such sources, for the good and simple reason that I have access to quantities of such things. The whole JiffiSnuf concept, in fact, was conceived as an efficient recycling of such things, when they had gone beyond the point of further use.

Lacking accessibility to spent cartridge cases of suitable size, you can substitute short sections of 5/8-inch outer diameter (OD) copper tubing, cut from the stock tubing with a disc of copper or brass soldered onto the lower end to serve as the air-sealing device. Other approaches are possible and practical, as we'll note in a bit.

The essential principle of the snuffer is dead-simple. To burn, tobacco or any other combustible substance requires oxygen, which comprises about one-fifth of this planet's atmosphere. If you put the burning end of the cigarette down into a small space, the burning portion quickly

consumes all of the available oxygen, whereupon the fire is extinguished: just that clear-cut and simple. With cavities of the general dimensions mentioned here, the burning cigarette will be fully extinguished in an average time of about eight seconds.

As the foregoing suggests, it is also possible to use wood for the snuffing cavity. The glowing coal at the end of the cigarette cannot set the wood afire for the same reason that it cannot continue to burn, in the first place. On hand is a lathe-turned ashtray of white oak that has withstood over two decades of use. Its integral central snuffing cavity remains in good shape, although it requires periodic scraping to remove the deposits of tars, resins and allied foul stuff.

Thus, if it sounds like a good idea, you can create a snuffing cavity by simply drilling a hole of about ½-inch diameter to a depth of about one inch in any reasonably suitable hardwood. Besides oak, I've used scraps of walnut, rosewood, and the like, with good results. No, I would not recommend balsa, for example.

The soldered tin can JiffiSnufs are easy, simple and economical to make, given the capability for soldering. I've tried using the cyanoacrylate miracle glues in place of solder, with thoroughly unsatisfactory results. After brief use, the glue fails and it all comes apart. Obviously, you don't want that to happen, perhaps allowing an unattended butt to fall free and start a fire.

The soldering procedure goes like this: Open the jaws of

The butt is dropped into the snuffer by gravity alone, not pushed in. It's extinguished by lack of oxygen in about eight seconds, and can then be dropped into the container.

the bench vise, about 1½ inches and lay the can on its side in the opening. Take a small tuft of fine steel wool and rub the inside of the can down to the bright tin at the spots where you plan to attach the snuffer and the holder. Apply a small dab of soldering paste flux to the cleaned area, lay the holder or snuffer on that, positioning it as desired, followed by a small section of wire solder on top of the holder, or against the side of the snuffer.

Light a propane hand torch and regulate its flame down to modest size. You don't need a vast amount of heat; just a bit of time and patience. Apply the inner cone of the torch flame — which is the hottest part — to the projecting portion of the holder or snuffer, taking care not to let the flame impinge upon the can. If you overheat the can, you'll scorch or char the label. Maintain heat on the exposed part until the bit of solder is seen to melt and flow down to join the part to the can. Withdraw the flame and allow the joint to cool until the solder is fully solidified. Clean away the residue of flux with a tuft of steel wool, and that's all there is to it.

Residing in Southern California, where brush and grass fires are a severe hazard during most of the year, you may be certain that my automobiles are equipped with JiffiSnufs. I never throw live butts or, for that matter, anything else from vehicles, moving or parked. It is a

misdemeanor that carries a stiff fine and/or jail sentence, and rightly so.

The problem of holding the ashtray securely in a moving car, meanwhile keeping it readily removable for emptying, turned out to have a remarkably simple solution, once I finally thought of it. The "tin" cans are made of steel, with the thinnest-possible coating of tin. I had purchased a quantity of small magnets, about ½x¼-inch, from Edmund Scientific Company. I used three of those, affixed to the Buick dash with dabs of GE silicone rubber, in a triangular pattern slightly smaller than the base diameter of the can, which is held quite securely by the three little magnet pills, but easily removable, when desired. A similar arrangement was used in the Opel GT.

There are at least two potential problems with the JiffiSnuf, of which you should be made aware. The more serious one is the fact that non-filter cigarettes can continue burning, on past the two sides of the holder, so that the burning butt can fall to the surface that supports the ashtray. They usually extinguish upon reaching the holder, but the possibility should be borne in mind and dealt with accordingly. For use with cigarettes in which the tobacco comes all the way to the near end, take pains to position the ashtray on a non-flammable surface. Filter-tip varieties, if clipped into the holder by the filter, can be relied upon to go out when the burning tobacco gets back to the front of the filter. Even so, caution is in order. This is not a foolproof system, nor is any other, due to the shortage of foolproof fools.

The other problem lies in educating the using public in proper techniques for extinguishing the butts. The lighted end should be dropped into the opening at the top of the snuffer, by gravity alone. There is a widespread tendency to squash the butt down into the cavity. In so doing, the lighted end breaks off and quickly clogs up the snuffing chamber, which must then be dug out clean with a small screwdriver or similar tool.

The basic design principle, as noted, can be employed at any desired level of elegance. Tin cans are convenient and nicely functional but they are...well...tin cans, after all. If the image offends, try making up a small box, of ¾-inch wood, plywood, or particle board, covering it with fitted sections of Formica, using contact cement or other appropriate adhesive. That's but one possibility of a great many.

If using spent cartridge cases, as shown here, it is quite important to make certain that they do not carry a live primer, which would be highly hazardous to your well-being and decorum if you tried to solder it to a can. The technique for flaring case mouths is to chuck the base into the drill press, start it up and insert a steel rod of about ¼-inch diameter into the open mouth, applying angular pressure to spin the flare in the case mouth. I usually use the shank of the drill press key for the purpose.

Repeating for emphasis! Use of a well-designed ashtray, such as the one illustrated and described, minimizes the fire hazard inherent in smoking. It does not eliminate the hazard entirely. Safe use of such ashtrays is the responsibility of the maker/user and neither the publisher nor author of this book assume any liability, express or implied, for damages alleged to have been caused through the use or misuse of such ashtrays.

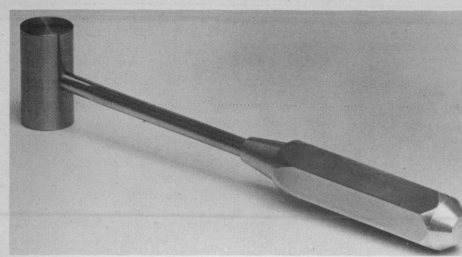

Chapter 19

EASILY MADE KITCHEN AIDS

Small hammers are handy around the kitchen. This has a ¾x1½" head, ¼" shaft and aluminum hex-stock handle.

Workshop Output Can Make Kitchen Chores Easier, And Here Are A Few Of The Many Possibilities

I N EXPLORING this particular field of endeavor, my motives are by no means as altruistic as you might assume. You see, I spend a considerable amount of time snorping about the kitchen, myself. I rarely follow recipes, preferring to innovate as I go along. That can and, on occasion, has led to some truly spectacular debacles. One recalls the time I decided to heat up a skilletful of canned pork and beans, stirring in and melting a quantity of crumbled-up Roquefort cheese. The odor alone made me dump it down the Disposall, untasted, and I worried for a time that they'd have to build a new sewage treatment plant.

Most of my unlikely explorations have been more successful, I'm relieved to report. As but one example, a judicious slosh of Grape-Nuts, added to pancake batter, produces memorably delicious flapjacks.

My mother used to bake the most sinfully delectable homemade bread I've ever tasted: calculated to make the gods atop Mt. Olympus choke on their ambrosia. Once, in later years, I coaxed her to bake up a batch and took careful notes of her methods, ingredients, quantities and general battle strategy. With the data thus craftily obtained, and a spot of trial-and-error, I was able to bake bread almost as good as hers. About 1959, I boiled all the lore into a few typewritten sheets entitled *Proceedings of the Irregular Street Bakers* (a brief pause, until the moans from devout Holmes buffs subside a little). Within the twelvemonth now a-dwindle, a nearby relative tried baking bread. The first run wasn't up to hopeful expectations. I got wind of the project, pulled a Xerox copy of the 1959 notes and passed it along. Virtue was its own reward, and much more. It got us a loaf out of the second batch,

absolutely up to par or a bit better than any loaf that ever came out of my mother's oven, or mine.

As a feeble effort to express my appreciation, I turned forth a bread slicing board, similar to the one made for our own use, long ago. The top slab is clear birch, with feet cut from dowels of the same lovely wood, countersunk a quarter-inch or so and glued in place with (guess what) aliphatic resin glue. That particular length of one-inch dowel was so close to the diameter of the hole from the Stanley Power Bore bit that, when I put a bit of glue at the bottom of the hole, distributing it with a fingertip, and pressed the leg into place with a protective piece of scrap and a C-clamp, the excess glue did not come oozing back up out of the hole. Instead, it was forced through the pores of the wood, emerging from the end-grain, as duly recorded in the nearby photo. I think it was the first time I've ever seen *that* happen and I sort of doubt if those legs will come loose in the near future.

In pressing the legs into place, the fit was so close that excess glue was forced out through the end-grain of the birch top (arrow), rather than oozing up around dowel.

With the 1″ birch dowel legs installed, the feet were ground on progressively finer grades of sandpaper, as here, and checked on the saw bed until they didn't teeter. Below, the all-birch slicing board was left unfinished.

As with most four-legged artifacts on a supposedly flat surface, our old, original bread slicing board is a teetery affair. Really, I suppose, the shrewd thing would be to make them with three legs, with the lone one centered at the end opposite which you're doing the slicing, readily reversible for use by southpaw or northpaw, alike. Until I started this paragraph, that'd never occurred to me.

I took pains to make certain that the latest board would rest to teeter-free perfection on any truly flat surface. Awarding it, I assured the recipient, "If it teeters, you can assume it's not on a really flat surface." What I did was to fasten progressively finer grades of sanding boards in the Workmate, grinding the ends of the legs down to exactly uniform length, until they showed no movement when checked against the bed of the table saw.

You can, of course, omit the legs entirely, cutting a board to appropriate size — slightly larger than the bottom of the anticipated loaves — positioning the board near the edge of the counter top to provide the needed knuckle clearance. In the same vein, a plain board of suitable size makes a useful hot-dish holder to protect the covering of the dining table. If you leave such boards unfinished, they'll stand up to use better than if varnished.

Speaking of table coverings: For many years, we've employed pieces of Naugahyde, suitably a bit larger than the top surface of the table. The first piece lasted for the better part of a decade and remains in use, even yet, as a protective tarp over the lawnmower. The second piece, in a smooth-surfaced metalflake pattern that the Naugahyde people term *Zodiac* — white, out of the several colors available — is currently in about its eighth year of fulltime duty, and it's bearing up right nobly, so far. It never needs laundering. A casual wipe with a damp cloth restores it to sparkling splendor. If it picks up a stain, a bit of scouring powder on the damp cloth erases that easily. Not strictly a workshop topic, true, but a solution so neat and handy I can't resist sharing it with you.

Through all of my recalled life to date, I've been a hopeless pineapple freak and fresh pineapples are my great delight. Preparing them has always seemed a chore so formidable as to be justified only by the delight of enjoying the finished work. As you'll've noted, in recent chapters, I finally got the new metal lathe installed and whirring contentedly upon demand. I am suffused with the radiant contentment of a flea who worked in the flea circus, saved and invested its money so cannily that, at length it was able to purchase a dog of its own.

One of the early artifacts knocked out on Mister Atkins — the new lathe, recall? — were a few of the pineapple cutters, illustrated nearby. Installing a metal-cutting blade on the table saw, some 1¼-inch OD aluminum tubing was cut into sections three or four inches long, chucked into the three-jaw chuck of the lathe to be trued-up on the top end, then reversed to be tapered, at about a seven-degree angle, from ID to OD at the working end.

Cutting 1¼" OD aluminum tubing to short lengths with a table saw blade that handles non-ferrous metals. Eye protection is vital, and the blade guard should be installed for safety's sake.

The compound feed of the lathe has been angled, per arrow, by seven degrees to taper one end of the piece of aluminum tubing.

Heretofore, in processing a fresh pineapple, I would cut off the ends, peel away the outer layers, quarter it vertically, and trim away the four resulting strips of tough, woody, inner core. With the cutter on hand, the technique has changed. Now, I peel it, as before, then slice it into lateral slabs, around 3/8 to ½-inch in thickness, and employ the coring tool to punch out the woody centers.

I can report that aluminum scalpels are not apt to revolutionize surgery within our lifespans. Nevertheless, employed downward on pineapple cores, against a birch supporting surface, the improvised core-cutters perform remarkably well, and seem to stand up to use better than you might expect. The resulting slices of pineapple have almost the elegance of those tinned up by the Messrs. Dole, et al., and taste notably fresher.

Lacking a metal lathe, it would be possible to craft up much the same useful device by means of hacksawing and a longer session of patient filing, holding the workpiece in a bench vise. Ideally, it should be produced from stainless steel tubing, commercially, and marketed through the usual channels. No one, to date, seems to have seen the manifest need and moved to fill the breach.

Once, long ago, in the hectic throes of setting up housekeeping, we needed a salt shaker. We had just finished off a metal-topped glass jar of ice cream topping, and I drilled a few holes through the top, field-tested it, and found it acceptable for routine use. It went on to become the family salt shaker of record for going-on four decades. Unlike a lot of commercially offered salt shakers, when you shook it, you got salt out of it.

The original manufacturer of the jar of ice cream topping probably never envisioned such a recycling of the furnished container, and thirty-odd years of exposure to sodium chloride's hygroscopic properties have had their effects upon the stamped steel top, though the jar itself remains cheerfully obdurate. Within recent times, I geared

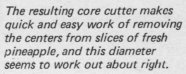

The resulting core cutter makes quick and easy work of removing the centers from slices of fresh pineapple, and this diameter seems to work out about right.

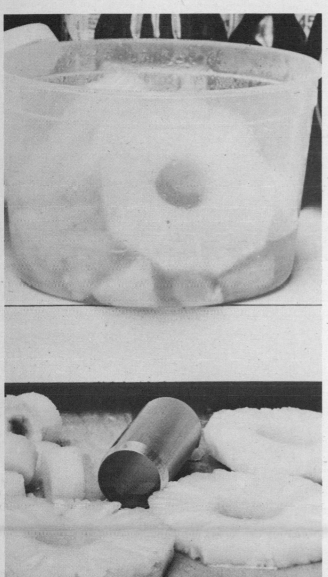

When cutting out the pineapple cores on the pull-out birch bread board, the edge of the aluminum cutter holds up surprisingly well, and can be resharpened, when and if needed.

Homemade salt shaker is going on forty years in use, and its top is showing signs of deterioration. A drill diameter of 1/16" works out about right and more holes can be drilled to speed delivery.

up and knocked out a replacement, using the container that came full of Smucker's red rapsberry jam. It looks to be good for another decade or three and, when it succumbs, another jar can be salvaged to produce a salt shaker that, gratifyingly enough, *shakes salt.*

Certainly, one of the most-used items in any kitchen is the knife, or collection of knives — humanity's oldest tool. A knife rack to organize the collection for ready use of accessibility, meanwhile protecting the vulnerable edges, is a useful thing to have and enjoy. The one illustrated nearby represents what I'd have to term the Mark 1/4 version, far from the level of elegant luxury I really have in mind and no, I really don't know how they rendered fractions in Roman numerals.

My simmering level of creative dissatisfaction with the current knife rack has very nearly achieved the critical mass that detonates to produce an endurable successor. Alas, it seems doubtful if its fitting placement is going to make it into the edition at hand, and I'm sincerely sorry about that. Likewise, still in the incubation phase is another marvel of luxurious convenience, ardently dreamed-of by galley slaves across the globe, that I think of as the Incredible Horizontal Onion Guillotine. With a spot of luck of the better sort, both may make it into the next edition, if that should eventuate in radiantly fortuitous glory. There has *got* to be an efficient way to slice an onion, and I mean to find it, some day, somehow, somewhere!

Another unlikely artifact that resulted from a perceived urgent need is the bread dough mixing paddle depicted here. Preliminarily, the baking ingredients are homogenized in a rotary mixer, such as the Mixmaster. When the dough starts to climb up the beaters at you, in that thin limbo between batter and actual dough, you need some manner of tool for taking over from the Mixmaster. Conventional wooden spoons, with their slender, graceful, delicate, *bustable* handles are deplorably unable to cope with the gaff. The bread paddle resulted, filling the manifest need, and with a bit to spare.

It was custom-contoured to my somewhat oversize

Many capped jars lend themselves well to use for making salt shakers, or similar condiment dispensers.

mitts, and the profile is more than slightly freeform, admittedly. Nevertheless, it was the ideal tool for getting the dry ingredients blended into the coagulating mass properly, through the stage when it got recalcitrant enough to need dealing with, *mano a mano.* Kneading bread dough is a notably fine way to vent off repressed hostilities, be it noted. It's but one of the many rewarding aspects I've missed sorely, since I gave up the practice, having run a cost accounting to learn that the gorgeous stuff was costing a frightening figure in terms of time away from the typewriter. I still say it was awfully close to worth it.

I'm not about to subvert the title at hand into a craftily cloaked Maverick Gourmet Digest — a work for which, as Dr. Watson was fond of observing, the world remains unprepared — so we'll omit the formulas for ground beef chow mein, Chicken Noodles Grennell, and kindred blandishments. As the fairly late Marie Antoinette responded, when advised that the poor had no books to burn, "Then let them burn coke."

I really *am* contrite about that. Forgive, please?

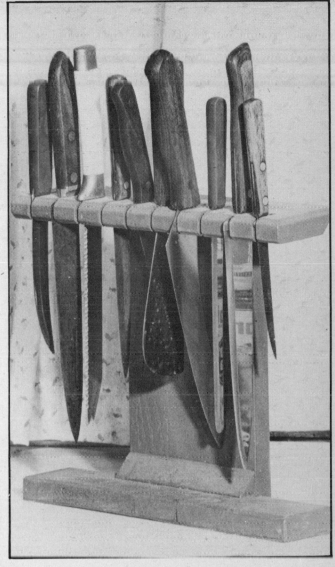

The knife rack at right was a casual production, at best, and it's more than ripe for re-engineering and replacement. The trouble with this one is that the knives are held quite precariously and they'll come cascading all over the countertop at a touch. Below, proportions of the bread dough mixing paddle, cut from ¾" birch and sanded to shape, can be judged from this 4-ounce canister of green tea.

CLOSING NOTES & PARTING SHOTS

In An Effort To Tie Up The More Obvious Loose Ends

Chapter 20

Here is a closer look at the separator between the cabinet and shelves, as discussed in the text. It is not fastened to either portion, but permits the top of the shelves to reach nearly to the ceiling, eliminating the problems of such construction, as noted.

AS WE REACH the point where five pages are all that's left, my personal reaction is an odd blend of "At last!" and "Good grief, *already?*" There are so many topics left to touch upon, so much still to say.

In the introduction, I expressed hope that we might have another try at building a custom-tailored chair but, as friend Becky Cartwright likes to phrase it, we never got a round tuit. Part of the formidable complexity lies in the fact that Becky traced my outlines on a few large sheets of paper, held together with white drafting tape, whereupon, we flopped the paper over and reversed roles, putting her outline on the other side of the paper. For such operations,

I should note, we taped a grease pencil to the end of a length of wooden dowel, observing all suitable proprieties.

The problem, as I was about to say, is that the tape holding the sheets came loose, the sheets of paper got shuffled, and I had neglected to key the sides of the sheets as to which was a portion of whom, or which portion was where on whomever. You perceive the obvious problem when I note that Becky and I are about a foot apart in overall altitude and, in the meantime, the Cartwrights have moved to Texas. That is an explanation, not an excuse.

Complexities notwithstanding, I still want to have at least one more shot at re-creating that long-lost and keenly mourned chair, and I mean to attack the project, Real Soon Now.

I hesitate to mention all the other topics that were considered for inclusion here, but didn't quite make it onto paper, for one reason or another. Painfully absent are such chapters as the ones on making lamps; staining, painting and finishing; toys and games for children of all ages; toolboxes; the construction and operation of a Spartan darkroom for which only a paltry fourteen square feet of floor space could be grudgingly spared; a properly lighted shaving/vanity mirror; veneering and laminating; sweating, soldering and light welding; construction and use of a skyhook routing support for contouring uneven assembly surfaces; and so forth, and so on.

As noted, I've qualms about mentioning the topics that are painfully conspicuous in their absence, fully mindful that it is apt to generate a reaction that some or all should have been covered in place of some of the discussions herein.

Ironically enough, the artifact that more or less led to the book at hand has not been mentioned, to this point. It is a sort of three-part display cabinet, with five open shelves in the upper portion, and a fitted door on the lower

A Spartan Darkroom...

Denise Hegert

segment. The door is covered with veneered strips of attractively figured redwood. There is a separating component between the shelves and cabinet that supports the top of the shelves up to within a fraction of an inch of the ceiling.

The separator consists of two sides and a piece at the rear, like a rectangle with the front side missing. Its value in the overall design can be appreciated when I note that son Chuck built a book case for a friend, measuring the height of the ceiling and proportioning the height of the book case to within an inch or less of the available space. When they

This is the corner storage/display cabinet that sort of provided initial stimulus for writing this book. The three-part approach seemed like such a neat solution to an otherwise vexing problem that I wanted to share it, together with a few other details, with other workshoppers.

got ready to install it, there was no way to rotate it into place, due to the immutable laws of geometry which decree that the diagonal of a rectangle is substantially greater than any of the sides. As in the caption of Peter Arno's immortal cartoon, it was a case of, "Well, back to the old drawing board."

With the supporting insert of the cabinet, diagonals presented no problem at all. The upper portion was raised, the support slid into position, and the superstructure was lowered and trued-up to taste. The assembly is held

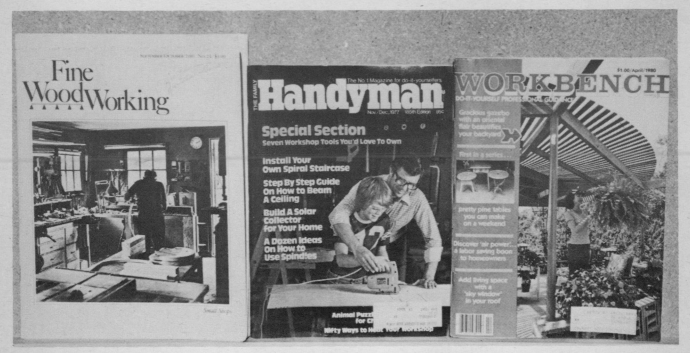

Here are three typical copies of the three workshoppers' magazines that you may not see displayed on your local newsstand. Addresses are given below, with current subscription prices which are subject to change, as noted. Such magazines supply many good ideas and are of useful aid in keeping you posted on new products as they are made available.

together by gravity — one of the more dependable natural forces — and, should it ever be necessary to re-locate the cabinet to some site with a differing amount of headroom, it would be a simple matter to trim down the support or build a higher one, as needed.

It was during the course of completing, installing and contemplating the cabinet that the small, glowing light bulb materialized above my head, eventually resulting in this book, as noted. Even so, there are several facets of the cabinet design that I'd modify, if I were to build another one. I think of that effect as creative disgruntlement, and find it a useful factor to harness.

It seems a disturbingly common attitude, among many people, to claim that they wish they could build things, but lack the natural aptitude for it. I respectfully submit that natural aptitude — assuming, for the sake of discussion, that such a thing actually exists — is far from the vital factor it's so often assumed to be.

As ruefully confessed, I cannot cut along a straight line with a handsaw, nor can I drive a nail with any gratifying degree of precision, and I present a truly dismaying spectacle when let loose with a screwdriver. I've never felt inclined to let such personal handicaps interfere with my constructive yens. Straight lines can be cut with the aid of a table saw, or a power hand saw and a guiding straightedge. Guide holes can be drilled perfectly perpendicular to the surface on a drill press or with the use of a drill guide, so that nails or screws have little choice but to go in straight, proper and Bristol-fashion.

In presenting the foregoing discussions, it's my sincere hope that many readers will have been shown that workshop activities are not really as complex, mystifying and formidable as they might appear upon first contemplation.

If your interest in such things has been aroused, there are many sources of further data that delve into such matters at vastly greater depth. There are, of course, the shop-oriented newsstand publications such as *Popular Mechanics, Mechanix Illustrated,* and *Popular Science.* Less often encountered are the more specialized periodicals, usually obtained via subscription. These include:

Fine Woodworking; $3/copy; published bi-monthly by The Taunton Press, Inc., Box 355, Newtown, Connecticut 06470 at $14 for one year (six issues); $26 for two years; higher to Canada and other countries; back issues remain available at $3/copy.

The Family Handyman; 95 cents/copy; published nine times a year by The Webb Company, 1999 Shepard Road, St. Paul, Minnesota 55116; $7.95 for one year (nine issues); $2/year extra to addresses outside the U.S.A.

Workbench; $1/copy; published bi-monthly by Modern Handcraft, Inc., 4251 Pennsylvania, Kansas City, Missouri 64111; $4 for one year (six issues) in the U.S.A. and its possessions; $5/year elsewhere; address for mail is Box 5967, same city and Zip Code.

It should be noted that the quoted prices are subject to change, as publishing and postal costs continue their swooping spirals.

In the section on power shop tools, it was noted that no response had been forthcoming from the firm currently making and marketing the Machinex 5 that replaces the Edelstaal Unimat lathe illustrated and discussed here. During the interim since that chapter was put down, a letter arrived from the company — American Edelstaal, Inc., One Atwood Avenue, Tenafly, New Jersey 07670 — explaining that the original request for a photo had gotten into the "answered" file by mistake. Certainly, I know how that could happen. They enclosed a copy of their current catalog, but no photos of the lathe were included. Here, at about the fifty-ninth second of the last minute, the photo turned up.

An interesting bit of information turned up, just a trifle too late for inclusion in the appropriate chapter. Steve Gentry, of The Gentry Woods, in Laguna Hills, California, informed me that there are over 70,000 known woods, of which about 10,000 varieties are in commercial use, somehow, somewhere. "We stock fifty kinds," he added.

Here is the photo of the Machinex 5 lathe, from American Edelstaal, as discussed above in the text. Catalog is $2 from the manufacturer at the address given, listing numerous accessories available for use with it.

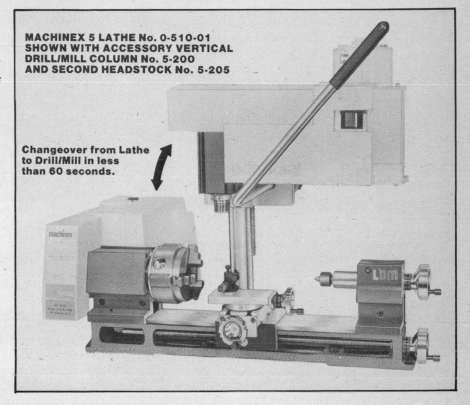

MACHINEX 5 LATHE No. 0-510-01
SHOWN WITH ACCESSORY VERTICAL
DRILL/MILL COLUMN No. 5-200
AND SECOND HEADSTOCK No. 5-205

Changeover from Lathe to Drill/Mill in less than 60 seconds.

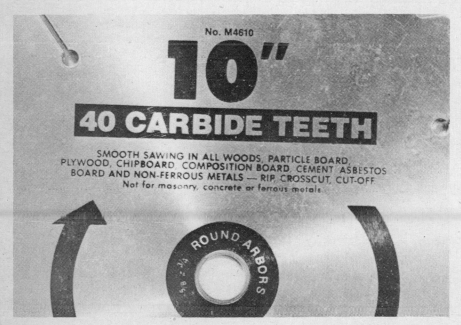

No. M4610

10"
40 CARBIDE TEETH

SMOOTH SAWING IN ALL WOODS, PARTICLE BOARD, PLYWOOD, CHIPBOARD, COMPOSITION BOARD, CEMENT ASBESTOS BOARD AND NON-FERROUS METALS — RIP, CROSSCUT, CUT-OFF
Not for masonry, concrete or ferrous metals

ROUND ARBORS

This is the second 10" carbide saw blade purchased in three days, but it has now lasted much longer than that and gives outstanding results on hard woods and non-ferrous metals when used with suitable care. Text discloses what to avoid in order to get maximum mileage from them.

The text below discusses this homemade holder for cutting circles out of aluminum sheet stock in a metal lathe. After the wooden disc had been bolted to the ¾" pine flange, it was trued-up in the lathe on its face and edge, using cutter.

As noted earlier, I blew about $33 for a ten-inch table saw blade with forty tungsten-carbide-tipped teeth. I can report it does an admirably capable job on woods up through and including the notably tough purple heart. It cuts a rather wide kerf, but leaves no blade-burns on the cut surface, even with those woods that seem especially prone to such discoloration problems.

It does cut aluminum and brass quite well, when used with proper care. Problems can crop up, however and, as a matter of fact, did just that. In cutting a short section of aluminum hex-stock, one inch across the flats, I held it with a flat against the front of the miter guide. I should have put the flat to the saw bed. In making the cut, about one-quarter through, the workpiece made a partial forward rotation, was grabbed by the whirring teeth and thrown about six feet, knocking ten of the carbide teeth off the brand-new blade in the process. Education can be an expensive thing, at times, and I pass these comments along in hopes of helping you avoid such a spooky experience. Never make the same mistake once, has long been one of my guiding precepts.

The big metal lathe is working out extremely well, a month after its launching ceremonies. My workshopper neighbor — whose wife claims it should be called a playshop, in his case — wanted to cut some circles from aluminum sheet stock to serve as the burners of a toy stove he was building. Between us, we schemed up and fashioned a holder from a piece of ¾-inch pipe and matching flange, with a wood holding board attached by bolts. The pieces of aluminum sheet were fastened to the board, with the stub of pipe in the three-jaw chuck of the lathe headstock and the cutter was cranked in to cut the circles free, with no distracting holes in their centers. It worked so well I thought it merited mention here so that you won't have to wait for the next edition, should it seem applicable to some challenging problem in your workshop.

And, with that, insofar as the first edition is concerned, we seem to have come to the

Here is the other side of the circle cutter shown above. It works quite well and produces a neat metal disc without a hole in the center. The thought-provoking scene at right was photographed on the outskirts of Plymouth, Wisconsin.